The Everlasting Stream

ALSO BY WALT HARRINGTON:

American Profiles

At the Heart of It

Crossings

Intimate Journalism

The Everlasting Stream

*A True Story of Rabbits,
Guns, Friendship, and Family*

Walt Harrington

ATLANTIC MONTHLY PRESS   *New York*

Some material in this book appeared earlier in *The Washington Post Magazine* in different form. Copyright © 1987, *The Washington Post*. Reprinted with permission.

Excerpt from "The Summons," by James Dickey, © 1962. Reprinted with permission.

Published simultaneously in Canada
Printed in the United States of America

FIRST EDITION

Library of Congress Cataloging-in-Publication Data
Harrington, Walt, 1950–
    The everlasting stream : a true story of rabbits, guns, friendship, and family / Walt Harrington. — 1st ed.
        p. cm.
    ISBN 0-87113-862-X
    1. Hunting—Anecdotes.   2. Harrington, Walt, 1950–
    I. Title.
    SK33 .H315 2002
    799.2—dc21   2002016411

Design by Laura Hammond Hough

Atlantic Monthly Press
841 Broadway
New York, NY 10003

02 03 04 05   10 9 8 7 6 5 4 3 2 1

To Alex, Bobby, Lewis, and Carl

"Life is ironic, that those who have a lot,

sometimes lack a lot, that those who have

little, sometimes possess some rich,

remarkable, puzzling things."

—ROBERT COLES

Alex Elliott

Bobby Elliott

Lewis Stockton

Carl Martin

The Everlasting Stream

First Morning:
Thanksgiving

"How long since you been shootin'?" Carl asked.

"More than twenty years," I answered. "Shot clay pigeons as a boy."

"But you never hit nothin' alive?" Alex asked, more to announce this to the other men than to get an answer he already knew.

"No, just walked the fencerows with my dad a few times," I said. "Then we moved to town and my hunting days were over."

"Well, you'll be seein' somethin' today," Bobby said confidently. "I'll put my dogs up against any dogs in Barren County. You'll kill rabbits today."

Oh, good, I thought, *can't wait.*

At six in the morning, not even dawn yet, I was up and traipsing along through the dark, the damp, and the cold, no stars in the foggy sky, on a farm near rural Glasgow, Kentucky, where I was a reluctant guest in borrowed orange jacket and canvas overalls, red shotgun shells lining my vest. I thought that I looked silly. But my father-in-law, Alex, had given me a new shotgun as a gift, and I was expected to shoot it. I lived in Washington, D.C., where most people I knew believed hunters were sick, violent men. That is a truly urban arrogance I had never held with conviction, having grown up in rural Illinois, where hunting came as naturally to men as commuting to work by then came to me. During my decades in the city, however, I had drifted toward the view that hunting was more or less archaic, a kind of cultural appendix. Without much thought, I had taken on the opinion that because hunting was no longer necessary to survive, men who persisted in doing it must be morally flawed. After all, they killed for fun, the brutes!

So I didn't want to be spending my Thanksgiving stomping through briars and corn stubble in a chilling drizzle. You see, I was a big-time Washington journalist—a staff writer for *The Washington Post*—and I preferred my vacations boating, being pampered at some resort, lolling around the beach on North Carolina's Outer Banks or the Delaware shore, driving the California coastline or hiking the national parks, taking in a show on Broadway or at the Kennedy Center for the Performing Arts, even knocking around bookstores. I'd rather have been back in the house watching an old Cary Grant movie than outside freezing my ass off, looking like some drugstore Rambo, listening to aging good old boys yak it up in a hick drawl I could barely decipher. But I didn't want to offend my new father-in-law, either, seem like an effete city boy who imagined he was too good to get down with the menfolk. I believed then that all this was complicated by my wife, her father, and his hunting buddies being black. I was white, and I figured it was going to be my worry to fit in. I visited Kentucky during hunting season only five days a year at Thanksgiving, and I could play-act my way through this minor social obligation. Obviously, my attitude was condescending as hell. As I wandered out to the hunting-dog kennels with the men that first morning, I stuck my cold hands into the pockets of my borrowed hunting jacket, where I found something soft, pulled it out, and discovered a tuft of old rabbit fur, which I quickly dropped, shaking my hand as I did, wondering what kind of germs I'd already acquired.

"Don't be afraid to shoot," Alex said. "'Cause old Carl, he'll just keep blastin'."

"Oh, boy!" said Bobby, who was Alex's brother and, it turned out, the keeper of the hunters' tales. He then gleefully told about the time Carl emptied his shotgun at a fluttering covey of quail and missed clean, at least so said Bobby and Alex. Then when one of the beagles nabbed a quail on the ground nearby, Carl fell to his knees and wrestled the dog for it, hollering that he knew damned well he'd hit one of those birds. As we loaded the dogs, which smelled about as sickening as wet dogs can smell, onto the trucks, their claws frantically scraping the metal tailgate as they yipped and nipped at one another while being stuffed into homemade wooden cages, Alex glanced at Bobby, smiled, then chuckled. Bobby nodded for his brother to do the honors.

"You find a lotta shot in that quail, Carl?" Alex asked.

Their friend Carl, a big man with a wide, wry smile and an unlit nub of cigar in the corner of his mouth, smirked and sighed, and said, "You heard 'bout the time out Roseville Road when Alex missed a rabbit comin' straight at 'im with three shots and then tried to hit the rabbit with his gun as he run past? Coulda broke his gun." It was Carl who laughed then, and his breath rose in the cold, brightening air as if he'd finally lit that cigar. The men's other lifelong hunting buddy, Lewis, who often began his sentences with excited Gatling gun bursts, would tell me much later, "Ol'-ol'-ol' Carl, he didn't find nothin' but teeth marks on that quail."

To say the least, these men were strange to me. They seemed like anthropological relics, throwbacks to a dim, unenlightened time when men were rough and benighted. I thought of them as country characters from central casting, quaint and amusing. In their late fifties then, about twenty years older than I, they were laboring men without college educations. Alex had retired from the air force as a master sergeant and master mechanic. Bobby had retired from the army and then taken a factory job in his hometown making truck axles. Carl had worked at the local Texaco for a decade out of high school and then spent the next thirty years working on a factory loading dock. Lewis hauled freight long distance. The men were all raised in or near Glasgow, a deep country town with only a few thousand residents when the men were born in the 1930s. It sits about halfway between Louisville and Nashville in south-central Kentucky, not far from the famous Mammoth Cave National Park. Glasgow is a town of about 13,000 people today. Its quaint courthouse square is still kicking, although strip growth on the edge of town has brought McDonald's, Taco Bell, KFC, and the rest. But outside Glasgow in surrounding Barren County—so named because the local Indians used to burn giant tracts of its land to create vast buffalo hunting meadowlands—farmers still harvest more tobacco and hay and raise more livestock than in any other Kentucky county. Carl and Lewis had spent their entire lives in Barren County, while Alex and Bobby had left for the military, traveled the world, and returned of their own free will. While my own male friends had come and gone, been serially abandoned as I moved around the country climbing the career ladder to land at *The Washington Post,* these men had remained friends for half a century. I knew only a little about them.

Alex was a lean, eccentric man who never hurried through anything and whose jeans always hung low on his skinny butt. His only vanity was a good toupee. A tinkerer, he kept an antique Model A Ford, an antique Coke machine, and an antique Seeburg jukebox in working order. That was okay. But the man also liked to eat baked groundhog and soused pig's feet. He liked to get a bottle of bootleg moonshine when he could. And Bobby, well, he'd actually been a bootlegger in dry Barren County when he was young. With his profits he had hired a chauffeur to drive him around town—at age fifteen, Bobby wasn't yet old enough to drive. He had grown up to be a short, round, bald man who never told a story the same way twice, although he told many stories more than twice. He read Louisville's *Courier-Journal* and watched CNN, and he liked to show off his knowledge, something his friends joked about incessantly. Lewis was the coat-holder of the crew, the kind of man who liked to get other men arguing and then kindly offer to hold their coats while they fought. Lewis, the men said, would walk a mile to say something sarcastic about somebody. Carl, who turned out to be the best hunter of the bunch, was a soft-spoken bear of a man, thick all over—face, neck, chest, stomach, legs, arms, even his fingers. Not fat, but thick, like a bear. He was universally popular in Glasgow, a genuinely nice man.

Carl and Lewis smoked cheap cigars, and all of the men enjoyed a hard shot of whiskey, ate red meat, and laughed and laughed at one another's foibles, flaws, and failings. All of them spoke in a lyrical, undulating drawl with skipped syllables and slurred words and without any respect for commas and periods. In their dialect, ellipses had become part of conversational usage, with one man often finishing another man's sentence before it was done. When they all talked at once, which was often, it reminded me of an unfortunate time I had stood on a Cairo street corner listening to two Egyptian taxi drivers argue about who had run into whom.

That first morning, I climbed into Carl's pickup truck and we drove maybe five minutes, pulled off the narrow macadam road, and juddered along a gravel drive to an old unpainted barn in which yellow stalks of tobacco hung drying. We parked and, as the men went about releasing the dogs and getting their shotguns from the beds of their trucks, I surveyed the landscape, which was beautiful. In one direction— I had then no idea which—the clouds were billowing, as if flexing for a muscular storm. In another, a small pond sat as dark and smooth as a smoked-glass tabletop. In another, a tall forest rose high into a translucent gray sky. In still another direction, a field of weeds rolled away in compound inclinations. We each clicked three shells into our guns and, in what had become a rainy mist that looked to be falling upward with the gentle wind, spread out abreast and walked through the rolling field. We walked a long time before the dogs scared up a cottontail rabbit where the weeds met a patch of young trees. The rabbit raced along the edge of the wood at what seemed to me an awfully fast speed. I fired and missed. Bobby didn't miss.

"I think you winged 'im," Bobby said in an attempt at politeness.

Not a chance. We hunted for a couple more hours and the men each shot two or three rabbits. I missed and missed and missed, and I didn't care. I was cold, wet, and tired. Getting back in the house and away from these men was my only ambition. But late that morning, back near the dog kennels behind Bobby's house as we were thankfully getting ready to call it a morning, a rabbit jumped up and ran away from me in an open field. I fired three errant shots before the rabbit reached the cover of a four-foot-high pile of cedar logs. Instantly, the dogs were atop the pile, howling mad, frantic, digging into it from all sides with their paws and snouts, creating a frenzy that rubbed off on me in the way that a bellowing crowd at a Washington Redskins game would rub off on me. Carl put his shotgun aside, climbed atop the pile of logs, and began tossing them away like so many twigs. "I can see 'im! I can see 'im!" he shouted, as he drew the .22-caliber pistol holstered on his belt and aimed into the pile. "Should I shoot 'im? Or let Walt shoot 'im?" That was a true test of Carl's country manners.

It was an odd moment for me. I had thought hunters were brutes. Yet there I was, reloading my gun, striding toward the cedar logs, feeling, quite frankly, on fire, feeling an intriguing brew of exhilaration and guilt. It had begun to rain harder. I didn't care. I took up a spot at a corner of the woodpile and, for a moment, through the wild howling of the dogs, thought about how that rabbit was so little, about his heart pounding, the four men with firepower, Carl burning to blast him, me ready to do the same. For a flash, it all felt wrong. Then the rabbit made a break. He leapt from the woodpile my way, but Old Red, the best of the men's dogs then, grabbed him in his teeth on the fly, which was so stunning an athletic feat that an image of it has remained clear to me ever since. The other dogs were on the rabbit with Old Red that quick, and I couldn't risk a shot. Suddenly, another rabbit broke unexpectedly from the woodpile. I whirled, lowered my gun, and fired. At thirty yards, he dropped. Instantaneously, the dogs, in a bellowing blur, were racing toward the dead rabbit. The abandoned rabbit stumbled, dazed from the dogs' attack. I pumped a new shell into my shotgun's chamber, fired, and killed that rabbit, too.

"I got him!" I shouted, surprising myself at the purity of my exuberance.

At that moment, my life changed, although I didn't know it yet. It would be another year before I understood that I should have been using not a full-bore choke in my shotgun barrel that day but rather a modified choke that creates a wider pellet pattern to give me a better chance of hitting my prey. It would be several years before I learned to abandon the lighter Number 7.5 pellet shotgun shells for Number 6 shells with more killing power. It would be at least five years before I could do what Alex, Bobby, Lewis, and Carl could do routinely—let a rabbit they've flushed get out twenty-five yards before pointing their shotstrings just in front of the bounding animal so that the pellets hit its head and foreparts at the shot pattern's edge, leaving the rabbit's meaty hindquarters undamaged for eating. Most important, it would be nearly a decade before I would realize the honor of entree the men had offered me that day, and I would begin to record their story, which by then had become my story. I sometimes wonder how my life would be different today if that rabbit hadn't scampered into that pile of cedar logs, if Carl hadn't resisted his temptation to shoot his pistol, if I hadn't met Alex, Bobby, Lewis, and Carl.

But all that was ahead of me. On the first morning, there was much merriment for a while, talk of my good shots. I tried to stay cool, act as if I'd done this before, but my adrenaline was pumping. By local tradition, I had earned two slugs of whiskey. When we were back at the barn and our guns unloaded, I knocked back the hits of bourbon, a hot knot exploding in my chest with each shot. Naturally, I had no idea how to clean a rabbit. So I watched the men for a few minutes and, no longer worrying about the germs I might acquire, began for the first time the maneuvers I would carry out again and again in the coming years. I submerged the first of my dead rabbits in a bucket of icy water so its fur would not come off in my hands, twisted off its head, and peeled off its skin. The cold water and the wind that had picked up by then made my hands numb. When I sliced open the rabbit's belly to sweep out its heart and lungs and bowels, I remembered that this rabbit had been alive only minutes earlier. Its innards warmed my freezing hands.

I gagged at the stench and turned my head to clear my nostrils so I wouldn't vomit. Nobody noticed; at least, nobody said anything. I moved through the cutting and gutting in the way that I would move for the first time through a set of complicated computer instructions or the steps of a new dance routine: the discrete actions just didn't make a whole. The rabbit's skinned carcass felt slick and satiny in my left hand. In my right hand, its mass of gleaming sacs and snaking tubes felt like the spaghetti you blindly bury your hands in at the Halloween fright house. The men all talked at me at once, enjoying the chance to be mother superiors to a novitiate. They poked bloody fingers toward my rabbit, telling me to do this or not do that with this or that organ. I quickly forgot the specifics. When I finished, the back of my right hand, the gutting hand, was bloody to my fist knuckles and the palm was bloody to my wrist. It was gruesome. I got through it by mimicking the resignation I feel while taking an invasive doctor's exam.

The men's dutiful praise for my shooting wore off quickly, and the story of my kills began to sound like Alex, Bobby, Lewis, and Carl talking about one another—how ridiculous I looked all tensed up before I shot, how I was running mindlessly in place without even knowing it.

"And by the way," Alex asked, "how many shells you fire to get those two rabbits?"

"Hmm," I said, counting the empty shell pockets in my vest. "Seven, eight, ah, nine."

"You'll get better," Bobby said in another effort at politeness.

"Not with that blind eye," Alex said.

Everyone laughed and the polite moment passed.

Back at my father-in-law's house, I soaked my rabbit carcasses in salted water and vinegar to draw out the coagulated blood, sliced out shot pellets trapped under the skin, cut off and discarded shattered bones. When the rabbits were finally done, ready for the freezer, they were clean and neat as chickens from the Safeway. I took my rabbits and a few more from Alex's freezer back home with me to Washington, D.C. The next weekend I threw a rabbit feast, cooked them up in wine sauce, marjoram, oregano, and snipped parsley, lit candles, and sat down at the table with some of my truly urban friends. Then, when they were enjoying their meal, I told them the story of where the meat on their plates had come from. They grimaced and groaned.

"I can't believe you killed those little bunnies," said a woman I had never liked much.

"But I did," I told her. "And I think I'm going to kill some more."

Twelve Years Later:
Thanksgiving

I awake from the dream and look at the clock: 4:35 A.M., almost an hour before Alex will poke his head in the bedroom at five-thirty and, as he always does, say in a gruff whisper, "Hey, time to get up." I never have this dream when I am at home the rest of the year, but at the farm during hunting season it comes to me again and again. I call it a dream only because it occurs in my sleep. It's really a memory: I am in a wood of towering trees with a tall, thick canopy of branches but no underbrush to block my sight. I am walking up the stony side of a mountain that drops maybe fifty feet in a hundred and fifty feet of run to a gully that rises in about the same topographical configuration on the other side. The gully ranges half the length of a football field.

I am alone. Alex, Bobby, Lewis, and Carl are behind me somewhere, still walking the field that comes before the woods. It's cloudy, mid-morning, and warm enough that I have unbuttoned my jacket. It's cold enough that the steel of my shotgun makes my hands tingle. Most of the leaves are off the trees and those that remain have turned crisp enough that when the wind blows gently they make a muffled, clattering sound, like seeds rolling inside a long gourd. The fallen leaves have been down long enough that they are no longer the individual hands of hickory, oak, walnut, black gum, persimmon, and beech. They've become a bland, brown carpet tamped down by gravity and microbes and turned dark and glossy from last night's rain.

I am not hunting just now. I am listening to the trees, hiking up the hill, my shotgun held at my side. A dog's chop carries from the field behind me. Then two more chops, a yowl, and the yowls of the other dogs. I stop and turn and look down the gully to my right. A long way off, the rabbit comes bounding along the basin like head-waters leading a flood. Rarely do you see a rabbit so clearly from so far away. I station my feet something like a batter at home plate, heft my shotgun, point it behind the rabbit, and slowly swivel my torso and gun along the rabbit's path until my barrel rides just in front of the animal and matches its speed. I now know that thirty-five yards translates into a tenth of a second between pulled trigger and hit prey, which translates into leading the rabbit by two outstretched body lengths. So much time—two, three, four seconds—to shoot. I have this thought: What if I were at war and that rabbit were an enemy, a man? Would I fire? I fire, and the rabbit tumbles like a stumbling acrobat and stops, dead. I lower my gun and start down the hill.

Remember, this is a dream only because it occurs in my sleep. It's really a memory of a day and a moment and a glancing thought that happened years ago on a small mountain in a rural hollow named Lawson Bottom. Whenever I have dreamed that memory during the many Thanksgiving vacations I now have hunted in Kentucky, I've wondered why I did. It contains no Daliesque symbols. It's a documentary dream. A cigar is a cigar. But you don't need a shingle hanging in Vienna to know it has to do with pondering whether hunting, like war, qualifies as justifiable murder. I've never been back to that exact place on the mountain. I've tried to find it a couple of times but never have. Still in bed this morning, half awake, I am thinking about this when Alex cracks the door and pokes in his head, the hallway light blazing behind him.

"Hey," he says in a gruff whisper, "time to get up."

My story is about: Alex, Bobby, Lewis, and Carl; my father, my son, and myself; rabbits, dogs, and shotguns; flora and fauna; blood and death; guilt and responsibility; ambition, achievement, and satisfaction; affection of the old rugged male as opposed to the modern sensitive male; friends as family; conversation as ceremony and affirmation not therapy and revelation; pristine moments; and, most of all, memory—the memory of it all told and retold, sharpened like a good knife blade, until the minutiae of living becomes the meaning of life. I know that's a lot to lay on four good old boys, but I think they can carry the weight. Over the years I've become convinced that Alex, Bobby, Lewis, and Carl have discovered the secrets to living life well. I don't want to sentimentalize them, do the greeting-card rendition of life's meaning, argue that simple people living simple lives have it all over us upwardly mobile Yuppie types and that we should abandon Hugo Boss, café latte, and self-help books for country life. I just want to tell you what I've seen and heard and felt while hunting with these men year after year.

The men are men in the old-fashioned way. In their late sixties and early seventies now, they show their affection for one another in piercing humor that demands a thick skin and a belief that a man doesn't have to say "I love you" or "You are my friend" to love you or to be your friend. I am of the sensitive, diaper-changing, "I-love-you-son" generation of men, but being with Alex, Bobby, Lewis, and Carl has reminded me that my own father raised me to know men in the old-fashioned way and, at least in part, to raise my son to know men that way, too.

There's so much talk these days about the New Manhood. Freed from being the sole paycheck, men no longer carry the pride or burden of being the family hunter who goes off to stalk the world every day to put meat on the table. Women, too, have become hunters in the marketplace. Men baby-sit, wash laundry, mix formula. Men who are middle-aged and younger have been expected to do for their sons what their fathers didn't do for them—hug them and kiss them, show feelings. All this is good. But I still remember clearly what my father told me as a boy: "It's not what a man says but what he does that counts." My dad believed that words and promises, displays of emotion, declarations of love were suspect. He worked every day to feed and clothe me. He protected me. He taught me right from wrong. He made me tough in mind and spirit. And he did it without ever saying "I love you." My time with Alex, Bobby, Lewis, and Carl has reminded me that the old brand of male love and friendship is still deeply appealing to me. I confess: I miss it. I want my son to know, despite the expressive friendship fashion of the day, that real friendships among men are forged in the shared experiences of a lifetime and require few words as proof of intimacy. After years of learning to show my sensitivity, learning to tell my son it's okay to cry, I have, with the help of these country men, remembered that simple truth.

Alex, Bobby, Lewis, and Carl would do anything for one another. They'd loan money. I think they'd even lie. But they'd never offer a kind word. Behind one another's backs, they agree that Carl can hunt like a son-of-a-bitch, Bobby knows a lot about a bunch of stuff, Lewis has a sharp wit, and Alex can fix anything. But face to face, Carl is hoggish about shooting rabbits, Bobby is a know-it-all, Lewis is a troublemaker, and Alex is a perfectionist who will drive men crazy if they're working together to fix a fence, repair a truck, put up a flag pole.

Lewis: "You shoulda seen Alex and Bobby puttin' up that flag pole."

Bobby: "Your father-in-law doesn't know when enough is enough."

Carl: "If we did everything like Alex, we'd never get anything done."

Alex: "They never *fix* nothin'. They just move the problem around."

Me: "You guys should go into therapy together."

Blank stares all around.

Then, a chuckle from Carl: "That'd help them three, all right."

Bobby: "They'd lock Alex up."

Alex: "Maybe they'd learn how to put a straight pole in the ground."

The idea that these men had anything to teach me didn't come to me for many Thanksgiving vacations. Year after year, without much reflection, I returned for my obligatory hunting ritual. Up at 5:30 A.M., putting on bloodstained pants, jacket, and bright orange hat, slipping shells into my vest, walking out into frigid morning air so clean it smelled like nothing at all, loading the stinking dogs onto the trucks, piling in and heading out in a caravan to Lawson Bottom, the old Collins place, the land behind B.C. Witt's farm, the Square, Bobby's home place, Nate Smith's dairy farm, just as the sun was popping and the deer were abandoning the harvested fields for the protection of the forest. The men taught me to kill rabbits pretty well. But that turned out to be the least of their hunting knowledge and the least of what I would learn from my years of hunting with the men.

Alex, Bobby, Lewis, and Carl know the individual voices of their dogs—Earl and Red, Bullet, Spud, Shorty, and Rowdy. They know when Earl's bass yowl is a call to the chase or a howl of frustration for having lost the scent. They know that rabbits will find a warm, comfortable hole in the ground when it gets cold enough to hunt in long underwear and that, when the temperature rises, rabbits will be out looking for food. They know every variation on what a rabbit might do while on the run from dogs—sprint way ahead to outrun the pack, or race to the edge of his habitat and then circle back behind the dogs, or hunker down in a harvested field and wait for the dogs to barrel past, or scurry into a skunk hole or a hollow log or briars so thick even the dogs can't penetrate them. Or a hundred other rabbit tricks. The men know this place and its change and constancy in a way that is close to perfect. How many of us can say that about any place in our lives?

As boys they hunted the fields we still hunt today. They know every patch of honeysuckle, stand of sumac, thicket of briars, and island of broom sedge. And they know it's all home to rabbits—rabbits whose own forefathers have been hunted for hundreds of rabbit generations by these men and their fathers and uncles, grandfathers and great-grandfathers going back to before the Civil War. Out in the field sometimes, as I listen to the men tell their hunters' tales, I imagine rabbits sitting in the groundhog holes they occupy in the cold months, telling heroic stories to their young about the century and a half of evading these men and their ancestors, as if animal and man relied on each other for purpose and resolve.

All through our hunts, through the dogs' musical yowling, the sun is rising, pillars of mist are hanging over a nearby pond, droplets of water are dripping like clock strokes from leafless branches, brush is crackling under boots, and briars are *zipping* across canvas coats. Spiderwebs spun and dropped from high in the trees the night before are sparkling like fine Christmas tinsel draped from tree to tree. If I move one step to my right, I lose the light's angle and the wall of glimmering webs disappears. A thorn pricks my left ear. I touch the spot and find blood. My gun is cold in my hands, so cold my palms ache. But I don't wear gloves. They make it harder to feel the flick of the safety and the pull of the trigger. During these moments, I am as close to unself-consciously alive as when my children were born, when I am making love, or when I am praying. In behavior so many believe is inhumane, I have come to sense pure humanity.

Not in several lifetimes would I ever have imagined teaching my son to hunt before I met Alex, Bobby, Lewis, and Carl. A decade later, however, by the time Matt was nearly fourteen, I had trained him on a BB gun, then a .22 rifle, then a .410 shotgun. He was already a graduate of a state-sponsored gun safety course. On a sunny Saturday a month before the Thanksgiving trip that year, I took him to Marty's hunting and fishing near my home outside Washington and told him he was ready to hunt with the men. As a boy, he had always watched for us to return from the field and joined us to clean the morning's kill. Matt looked and listened as we passed around the bottle of bourbon and the men told stories about that day's hunt and hunts years or decades, even a half century, past. I never hid any of this from him. Matt once went inside to my wife and in tears said all the men were

talking at once, and he couldn't understand anything they were saying, except the cuss words. He heard some rough language. And shots
of whiskey aren't my idea of good parenting. Even so, I decided it
was best for him to see, as Dan Jenkins writes, "Life its ownself."

I bought Matt hunting boots, pants, cap, and a Mossberg
12-gauge shotgun. I took him skeet shooting for the next few weeks,
and when he came out that morning in whistle-clean hunting clothes,
cradling that Mossberg in the crook of his left arm, he was already a
dead-on shot—a far better shot than I. Just after dawn that day, we
pulled into Burkesville, Kentucky, a town of two thousand people
tucked into wooded mountains and crop fields an hour southeast of
Glasgow. The family of Alex and Bobby had settled nearby in Lawson
Bottom at least a hundred and thirty years earlier. It was forty-one
degrees that morning, and the sky was so bright a gray that a man
had to squint to look at it. We stopped, as we always did, at the C&J
Restaurant, where they served "Home Style Cookin' Breakfast Lunch
and Dinner Open 4 A.M. to 8 P.M." Before we went in, I suggested
quietly to Matt that he not eat the men's usual fare of fried eggs, ham,
bacon, grits, biscuits, and gravy because digesting all that food would
sap energy from his muscles, something I had learned in that hunting safety class I took with him. Matt laughed.

"Dad," he said, "the breakfast is part of the ritual."

I relented. We ate everything.

I worked in Washington, D.C., for fifteen years. It's a city that
has arrived where the rest of America wants to go. It had the highest
average household income in the country, the highest proportion of
male and female professional workers, the highest percentage of people
with college degrees. Yet it's a city where people don't have friends—
they have associates. It's a city of frenzy, with working husbands and
wives racing to day care before the dollar-a-minute late charge kicks
in at 6 P.M. It's a city that honors work and achievement over all else,
where people live for future ambitions without relishing present
accomplishments. It's a city where people seem incapable of living

in the moment. It is a city without memory. And Washington is America's future.

The men I hunt rabbits with live in a place and a fashion that we should all be afraid to see lost. They are exactly the kind of men who a century from now urban folks will romanticize as they lament their extinction. I won't pretend that I or most people can ever really recapture these men's world. The change has gone too far and much of it is for the better. The men are a vestige. But after years of hunting with the men, I took away some lessons. When I honestly thought about it, I realized that I didn't remember evening galas at the White House, appearances on national television, or the praise of my journalistic colleagues with the pleasure I remembered that morning when the wall of spiderwebs sparkled before me like fine Christmas tinsel. In Washington, I was growing tired of the traffic jams, the commuting, the day care, the whole deal. Mostly, I was growing tired of the way so many people saw life, the way I saw myself seeing life—as a blur of ambition and achievement with so little relishing of life, so much racing through its tangible moments.

In the beginning, I couldn't imagine being satisfied living in the narrow world of Alex, Bobby, Lewis, and Carl. Eventually, I came to see that their world is like a poem: it is a narrow world made wide. I arrived at that insight slowly over the years by experiencing the indelible moments in fields and forests in fitful interplay with the unfolding chapters of my decidedly modern life. My time with Alex, Bobby, Lewis, and Carl—these anthropological relics—eventually spurred me to reconsider my life. Honestly, that still amazes me. The very year of my first Thanksgiving hunt, I had finally arrived into a career I'd worked like a plow horse to achieve. The legendary *Washington Post* editor Ben Bradlee—a man I had revered since my years in college during the Watergate scandals—had just announced that an article I'd written about then Vice President George Bush was one of the best political profiles he'd ever read. I had just been promised the first of pay raises that would eventually more than double my salary. I was about to travel to Africa with Jesse Jackson for a profile of that enigmatic man. I was flying high. Yet unknown to me, my life was already moving insistently on to its next stage before its last stage was even done.

In Glasgow, a dozen years later, at six in the morning on Thanksgiving day, not even dawn yet, wearing my bloodstained pants and orange cap, shotgun shells lining my vest, 12-gauge in my hand, I walk out into the morning air. I no longer believe that I look silly. Alex, always late, is still in the house searching for the shotgun shells he has misplaced. Bobby hasn't yet come out of his house next door, and Lewis and Carl haven't arrived in their pickups. I sit at the picnic table and pull on my boots, lace them up. It's going to be a warm day. Already, it is forty-three degrees, no wind. I'm always a little tired the first morning hunting. The drive from Washington to Glasgow the day before has always been a killer, thirteen hours no matter which of several routes you take. Unless bad weather changed my mind, I'd head west out of Washington, then southwest to about halfway down into Virginia, then across West Virginia and Kentucky to Elizabethtown, and, finally, south to Glasgow. My choice was purely aesthetic. In West Virginia, the Interstate, for a couple hours, turned into a weaving two-lane past places named Cedar Grove and Gauley Bridge and Belle, past the Hawk's Nest State Park vista that always gave me a touch of vertigo, past rock outcrops where young lovers probably long divorced once recorded their eternal devotion in red spray paint, past eroding single-cabin motels from the 1930s, and past at least several yard sales at which hardscrabble people seemed to be selling every item of housewares, furniture, and clothing that they owned. The route was always a kind of decompression, a reminder of the bubble in which I lived.

This morning, Matt, nearly seventeen now, strolls out of Alex's house dressed in his hunting clothes, his boots laced, carrying his gun hiked up on his shoulder. He sits at the picnic table with me. In the three years he has hunted with the men, Matt has grown almost a foot, lost his cherubic cheeks, and replaced his boyish effervescence with a studied nonchalance.

"Pretty night," he says, nodding at the sky.

Every year at Thanksgiving the stars above us are in the same places in the sky. I didn't know that until I had sat out here enough times to begin to wonder what I was seeing and went out and got a star guide. Every year, I look nearly straight up and see the North Star, which, contrary to common belief, is not the brightest star in the sky. This morning, the moon hasn't yet risen, leaving the stars alone to claim the sky through broken clouds and patchy mist.

"Where's the North Star?" I ask Matt, figuring he won't know.

"At the end of the Little Dipper's handle," he says, pointing overhead.

"How'd you know that?"

"Everybody knows that."

"Yeah, well, where's Orion?"

Matt scans the sky. I know I've stumped him.

"There," he says, pointing to the south-southwest at about ten o'clock.

Indeed, it is Orion the Hunter. Three stars in a row make up his belt. Just above it lies the red star Betelgeuse, a corruption of the Arabic that means "armpit of the great one." At Orion's left foot is Rigel, at his back is Saiph, at his shoulder is Bellatrix. And there is Orion's club, forever poised to strike Taurus the Bull in his bull's eye, the star Aldebaran.

"Those stars with Taurus," Matt says, "those are his hunting dogs."

"They are?"

"Yeah, Canis Minor is the little dog, Canis Major the big dog."

"How'd you know that?"

"Don't know, just know. Greek mythology."

These mornings have all blurred together over the years but always the sounds of morning unfold with the fresh light. From a neighboring farm to the north will come the neighing of a horse. That will set off one of the four donkeys Bobby keeps mixed in with his cattle to scare away coyotes that he fears will attack his calves. To the northwest, the donkey will *hee-haw, hee-haw, hee-haw* for maybe fifteen seconds. That will inspire a cow in the field to the west, which will set off the hunting dogs out at the kennels to the south. On the prettiest mornings, the sunrise lays a pink blanket atop the far tree line to the east and the dark sky turns a pale ghost-blue. Then pink segues into purple, the morning mist disappears, and the birds in Alex's grape arbor crank up like a collection of discordant chimes. In the fresh light one morning, a flock of birds flew over in a whirling V formation and, like minnows in a school, dove and swirled in synchronized unison.

"Look at those birds," I said to Matt. "Is that amazing?"

"Yeah. Hey, Dad, can I drink a beer with the guys when we get back in today?"

"No," I said, suddenly remembering that Matt wasn't yet reading between the lines of our hunts, that his boy's memories hadn't yet come back around to him as a man.

"How 'bout a shot of whiskey?"

"No."

The men are running late this morning, and it's a while before Carl and Lewis pull up the long drive between the houses of Alex and Bobby, who comes out his door as the men park at the front edge of the nine-acre wood behind Bobby's house. We meet at the trucks and nod hello, the fallen leaves *whooshing* with each of our steps. Behind the replica of an old-timey country store and gas station Alex is building to house his '34 Model A and the beat-up '66 Mustang he bought recently, the hunting dogs are going crazy, jumping against their kennel fence, yipping, and wagging their tails. They know what's up. The men have aged well. Carl, who for years has sported a tuft of beard just below his lower lip, has two days of white beard that is bright against his dark skin. He holds his unlit cigar between the middle and index fingers of his right hand, the back of which really is the size of a thick pork chop. He keeps his elbow cocked and his hand up to his chest as if he's about to put the unlit stub in his mouth. Sometimes he does and gnaws on it. Sometimes he takes a lighter out of his pocket, leans his head to meet his cigar, and lights the thing, blows a puff of smoke. Usually a single button holds his straining jacket shut above his stomach. This morning, Carl tucks his cigar in the left corner of his mouth, leans against his truck, and twiddles his huge thumbs.

Carl and Bobby have retired from the factory jobs they had when I first began hunting with them, but they hustle around now raising fifty head of cattle and cutting and baling two hundred giant rolls of hay on Bobby's fifty acres and on sixty acres the men own together fourteen miles away near Coral Hill. Lewis, who bought his own eighteen-wheel rig a few years ago, still hauls freight. Alex, retired since he returned to live permanently in Glasgow nearly twenty years ago, stays buried beneath an endless list of pursuits—building his gas station replica, restoring his Mustang, crafting a flintlock rifle, whittling a good slingshot from a redbud branch and searching out a collection of nicely rounded stones to shoot at crows and starlings, which he always misses. All the men still work on their own cars and trucks, cut their own lawns, paint their own houses. They rarely sit still.

"I hear you got a deer," I say to Bobby, who has a habit of crossing his arms at his chest and then reaching up with his left hand, touching the bill of his cap, and adjusting it ever so slightly. He does this so often the brim is smudged. He's short and straight-backed with a good watermelon belly and a jaunty way of cocking his head rightward. He has more stories than Aesop, a great smile, and a contagious, wheezing laugh that makes those stories all the better.

"Yeah, I done got down outa my stand and was startin' outa the woods. I was just about to the edge of the wood when me and the deer seen each other. He took off."

"So you got him on the run?"

"Hmm-hmm."

"Did Alex, Lewis, and Carl believe that?"

"From where I hit him, I expect they did. Shot him through across the back."

Nobody disputes Bobby's claim. It must actually be true. Bobby asks if he has told me about the time he and Carl stopped at the C&J to eat when they were deer hunting in Burkesville.

I shake my head no.

"The waitress was saying, 'You guys been comin' over here almost twenty years and your crew is gettin' lighter and lighter.'" Everybody laughs at that, but it's dark laughter. The men's hunting friend Charles had a car accident years ago and has been in a wheelchair ever since. R.C. died of cancer a few years ago. Ed Lee has gotten too feeble to hunt. Lewis has had a mild heart attack. Bobby has had heart surgery and gone blind in his right eye. Carl, who keeps getting wider and wider, knows he should get off fried bacon, sausage, chicken, rabbit, and every other fried thing, but he won't. He and Bobby have a touch of arthritis. When the weather gets bad these days, the men don't say the hell with it and hunt anyway, as they used to. They know they are counting their remaining hunting seasons one at a time. But at least the C&J Restaurant expired before the crew. The place was bulldozed into a parking lot last year.

"Too bad," Carl said when he heard about it. "Good ham."

"You see the price of tobacco?" Bobby asks, showing off his *Courier-Journal* knowledge. "Up to an average dollar-ninety-six a pound." From there, Bobby's off on how the price of cigarettes has jumped with the $250 billion state settlement with the tobacco industry and the so-called program to reduce juvenile smoking, which he says won't work. "Doin' what they ain't supposed to do is what juveniles do," Bobby says. Nobody speaks for a respectful moment. The dogs Lewis and Carl have brought in the cages on their truck beds and the couple more Bobby has fetched from his kennels and packed in with them aren't so respectful, and they start yapping.

"I got a dog that'll make a rabbit," says Lewis, who stops talking but keeps moving his mouth as if he still is. It's those false teeth, the men always say. Lewis is a small, wiry man who stands squarely on both feet, his hands tucked deep and bulging in the pockets of his unbuttoned hunting jacket, which tugs open to reveal splotches of dried blood that stain its lining. Lewis's most distinctive mannerism is the way he sputters out the first word of his sentences in staccato repetition when he gets excited, then glances at the ground, kicks his foot in the dirt, and twists a tight forty degrees on the balls of his feet, all of which he does now when speaking of his dog.

"He-he-he, he'll start huntin' right off," Lewis says in one of his quick bursts, which is about to launch the kind of disjointed, laconic back-and-forth that once disconcerted me as a newcomer. I felt lost inside one of those endless Frederick Wiseman films in which the meaning of mundane talk is disturbingly unclear to an outsider because it is so deeply and unconsciously assumed by its characters. All detail and dialogue, no context. Yet, over time—years, really—it has turned out to be the men's everyday talk that has most revealed the affection and lilt and sweet indulgence of their friendship and that has made me wonder at what I and men like me have lost in our lifetimes.

"Lewis's dogs can't ride with my dogs," Carl says. "My dogs beat his dogs up."

"I got city dogs," Lewis says. "He got country dogs. They ain't civilized."

Bobby interrupts to snap impatiently, "Where's Alex?"

"I bet he got up 'bout four o'clock to start cookin' for breakfast at six," Lewis says.

The men fall silent.

"Truck turned over out West last night," Bobby says. "One-hundred-mile-an-hour wind."

Another respectful pause for the day's news.

"Walt," Lewis says with a distinct hint of sarcasm, "most a these city huntin' partners ain't no good, but you all right." The men look at me and start to chuckle.

"What's he after?" I ask warily, knowing that something's coming my way.

Carl shrugs. "Don't know."

Lewis walks over and taps the hood of my Ford Taurus.

Without missing a beat, Carl picks up his lines. "You know what Ford stands for?"

"What's it stand for?" Lewis asks, as if he hadn't started the conversation.

"Fix Or Repair Daily," Carl says.

Everybody laughs. In fact, they laugh for at least a minute, really hard.

"Matt," Bobby finally says, "I see you got a whole box a shells. I'm gonna borrow some."

"I got another box inside you can have," Matt says, as he heads toward the house.

"Nah, I only need a few," Bobby says, meaning that he rarely misses a rabbit.

Over his shoulder, Matt hollers, "My ass!"

The men like that response and they all laugh. They then talk about chicken hawks, red-tailed hawks, Carl's old .22 rifle, and coyotes that supposedly carried off two of Bobby's beagle pups. During the half hour of waiting for Alex, the sky has turned blue except for a congregation of long, layered cloud plateaus that are beginning to stack up on the eastern horizon. It must be fifty degrees, and humid. That'll make it harder for the dogs today and harder for us. During the hunting seasons I've gone from thirty-six years old to forty-eight, I can feel the difference. I've never been in danger of being mistaken for a robust woodsman. The beard I've worn for thirty years is more Wolf Blitzer than Jeremiah Johnson. I'm just taller than short, a touch bottle-shouldered, and wider of beam than a man likes to be. I'm always worried about taking off those extra twenty pounds, although after so many years I doubt they qualify as extra anymore. These days, I breathe harder going up hills and tramp briars more gingerly. Imagine my stamina in twenty years when I am these men's ages.

"Where's your grandfather?" I ask Matt when he returns with Bobby's shells.

"He's in the garage," Matt says.

Just then, Alex hollers from the garage. "You got my shells? Can't find my shells."

"You won't need none," Carl bellows, implying that Alex can't shoot worth a damn. "Come on, get yourself a stick." Finally, Alex shambles out, his feet lightly brushing the ground with each stride, boots untied, coat unbuttoned, hat askew. He arrives to curses all around. Alex smiles and bobs his head a touch. He enjoys the notoriety that comes with always being the last man to the party. Alex is the handsome one of the bunch. He has kept his trim, athletic build, and when he dresses up for church or funerals he wears a suit gracefully, not uncomfortably like the other men. Cleaned up, Alex could pass for a preacher, if it weren't for his language.

"Carl said you were up at four and still not ready," says Lewis, conveniently forgetting that it was he, not Carl, who said Alex had gotten up at four.

Alex ignores the gibe. "Lewis ain't got any dogs worth a shit."

Bobby reaches up, touches the brim of his cap, adjusts it ever so slightly. "I'll tell ya what," he says to Matt. "Your *granddaddy . . .*" and Bobby's voice trails off in exasperation as the crew of hunters, with dogs still yapping, climbs into the trucks and rolls out.

Old Collins Place

The blackberry briars are ripping me apart. They slice right through my cotton overalls and my long underwear, which I don't really need on so warm a day. When I get home, I'll find a score of red scratches on the front of my thighs, which always take the brunt of it when legs yank through fighting foliage. The backs of my exposed hands, which face forward as I carry my gun high to protect my face, are crisscrossed with lean gashes along which droplets of blood are oozing. The cuts hurt like pinpricks for an instant but then begin to itch like crazy. Nothing to do but ignore it. Through this Brer Rabbit briar patch is the only way to get to my favorite hunting spot, which I finally reach when I come to a tractor path that separates the blackberry briars from a wood at the far northwest of the old Collins place—no longer owned by the Collins family but by Billy Elmore, a friend of Alex's. The sunny edge of a forest is always a dense wall of seedling trees that will keep marching out into the field until no field is left. In forest climates, fields are unnatural. They are man's paltry creations, and they require him to return and battle the forest with plow or Bush Hog every year or two. After that, bring a bulldozer.

I push through the guard gate of young saplings into the wood. To say that a forest is like a cathedral is pretty worn, I know, but people say it again and again because it is so apt. Instantly, the temperature drops a good ten degrees, and the air feels like a hand grasping loam, heavy with cool moisture. I've been sweating out in the sunlit briars, but in the dim wood I feel suddenly chilled. I button my open jacket and head down the slope, which begins almost immediately. The ground here is hard and slippery, and I step sideways down the hill, gouging the edges of my heels into the red dirt as I go. I've learned to do this after falling in past years. A hundred feet overhead, the leafless trees are a latticework of natural architecture. Nature seems to abhor right angles, and I can see the sky only in asymmetrical patches. The ground is mostly clear of undergrowth, but I must step around dead-hinged branches and fallen limbs. The going gets easier when I come to a highway of groundhog paths connecting a village of holes with naked corncobs spread around them like animal lawn ornaments. The paths lead circuitously to my destination—the bottom of an earthen bowl with a wall of rectangular limestones laid by men into the hillside from which pours a natural spring. The water catches in a basin about the size of a child's wading pool. It seems to sit motionless until, as if from a pitcher, it pours over a rocky lip and runs into a little stream, bubbling and gurgling and clinking like ice in a glass as it skitters off over shiny rocks into a branch that twists down the hill and through the wood.

So much of life is in the way we see. We don't see a desert at seventy miles an hour from an Interstate the same way we see it at, say, thirty from a two-lane. We don't see the Great Plains from a car on a two-lane the same way we see them from a bicycle. We don't see the Appalachians from a bike the same way we see them when we hike the trails. And we don't see the mountains in the same way when we hike as when we stop and stay in one spot for an hour or a day or a year. Or, in the case of Alex, Bobby, Lewis, and Carl, nearly three-quarters of a century.

My father was a milkman by occupation and a fine amateur landscape painter by avocation. He once told me that there were two ways to see the world he painted. One was to stand back, squint, and see the landscape in a beautiful blur of colors. The other was to get down on your hands and knees and examine the flowers one petal at a time. He often told me, "Everything's beautiful if you look at it right." When I began hunting, what I saw was all impressionistic wash: the expanse of field; the dome of sky; the swaying crush of branches; the assault of autumn grays, tans, yellows, browns, and reds. When I saw anything resembling the petals of a flower, it was because a snake or quail or coyote had surprised me into looking at it clearly. Even when I shot at a rabbit, my motions and my vision, hearing, and touch, my thoughts were indistinct to me, blurry. My senses couldn't separate the film before me into frames. Then, a decade ago, Carl took me to the earthen bowl.

"I got somethin' to show ya," he said.

In the early years, I was a glutton for stomping out rabbits, and I had been in the briars playing beagle hound while Carl was posted ahead of me outside the thicket waiting to pick off what I scared out. I wised up pretty fast and quit that job after a couple years. Anyway, that day maybe Carl thought I deserved some reward for my dog's work. I like to think it was something more, that for some reason Carl thought I might appreciate this place that he appreciated. I'll be honest, Carl and the other men aren't exactly free with their thoughts and emotions. What I've learned from them I've learned mostly by watching and eavesdropping. I like to think that Carl taking me to the earthen bowl that day was meant as an unspoken gift.

"Watch your step goin' down," he said.

I wish I could remember everything else about those moments years ago. But I can't because I saw the place differently then—a wash of trees, hills, rocks. I was just glad I didn't fall on my butt. I saw those huge animal burrows and worried that an angry groundhog might charge out and attack my leg as I passed. Rabies, you know. Carl told me to watch out for the poison ivy vines that grow thick as a woman's wrist on the trees and, suddenly, poison ivy was everywhere. Finally, at the bowl's trough, Carl put his gun to his side and nodded to the wall of rectangular limestones and the chalice of clear water cupped before it. He told me that somebody in the last two hundred years had laid those stones as the back wall of a springhouse that had once stood over the pool. The springhouse kept meat, milk, and butter cool even in the summer, and the spring gave forth pure drinking water year-round. Carl said that as a boy he had walked half a mile every day to a spring over which his daddy had laid two wooden planks. Carl would dip two buckets of water and lug them back home.

"Where was that?" I asked.

"Just past Temple Hill."

"I'd like to see that spring."

"If it's still there. Ain't been back in forty years."

Every time I come into the old Collins wood, I see something for the first time. The edge saplings, which a decade ago looked all the same to me, are actually a collection of ash, elm, dogwood, and hickory. In a hard winter, if you look closely, you'll see that some of their trunks have been girdled near the ground by rabbits eating the soft, nutritious bark. Deeper in the wood are beech and maple and poplar trees. There's even an old cherry tree the harvesters must have missed when they combed the countryside for furniture wood. Green-brier bushes are chomped off chest high where the deer have munched them. And some of the poison ivy blanketing the place is actually harmless Virginia creeper, although I'm still not sure which is which and avoid them both. Along the stream, damp rocks are coated in a seeming infinity of selaginella mosses. In the winter, the mouth of the springwater pool registers fifty-one degrees. In the summer, it also registers fifty-one degrees, giving it a refrigerator's consistency.

I've never shot a rabbit in the earthen bowl. Not that I wouldn't. Just never happened that way. Behind me now, the dogs begin barking as a pack, and I know they're hunting the blackberry briars with the synchronicity of that flock of birds I mentioned earlier this morning. This grabs my attention away from the spring. The dogs barrel into the wood, their guttural chorus echoing inside the cathedral. I hear individual dog voices but, unlike the men, I can't tell Earl from Rowdy, Bullet, Red, Shorty, Spud, or the pups that haven't yet earned names. Then comes a piercing, elongated yowl—ten feet away, a rabbit is up. With the indivisible motion of an ocean wave the dogs are after him. One burrows through a fallen branch, another leaps it, another skirts it. But they all fly off in a single leap. The rabbit is gone too quickly for me to shoot.

"Your way!" I holler.

No shots. For twenty minutes, the dogs are taken on a chase through the briars, the wood, the briars, the wood. This is one wily rabbit. I always think that we should let a rabbit that runs this well get away. I will think that, but then the dogs will make their howling way back toward me and my excitement will rise. I'll remind myself of the chicken factory I once visited with its thousands of shock-white chickens stuffed many to a cage and of a slaughterhouse I used to walk past on the way to work early in the mornings as truckloads of wailing pigs were being delivered like so many boxes of produce. Then I'll grip my gun more firmly, lift to the balls of my feet, and without a second more of guilty reflection I'll want to shoot and kill that little rabbit that is no longer than a big man's forearm, no heavier than a good-sized brown-sack lunch. The dogs have moved away from me again, and I find a tree trunk with no questionable vines and two welcoming branches and lean my back and shoulders into them as if they were the arms of an easy chair. Little blackbirds are *tick-ticking* in foliage nearby. A single dog is sniffing near the prattling birds. They sound like crackling radio static. I'm listening to the birds and the distant dogs when two shots fire. Then more shots. The dog voices rise a few octaves and the dog near me rockets suddenly toward the music. I lean deeper into the arms of the tree.

Take my word for it. If you had known me a long time ago, you wouldn't believe I was in this wood right now, happily listening to *tick-ticking* blackbirds, studying the selaginella mosses, trying to tell Rowdy's voice from Earl's from Shorty's. I still can't quite believe it myself—me in the woods! I had good friends from the 1960s—Nina and Joe—who did the Back to the Land thing, abandoned their suburban roots and bought land outside John Day, Oregon. They installed a hydroelectric power plant on a river that cut through their property. They built a stunning, rough-hewn house with their own hands and made a good life. Joe was a land management guy who told ranchers how many cattle could live on how many acres of grass. He knew birds and bears and plants. And he was a hunter. When he and I were living near each other in Columbia, Missouri, when I was in graduate school in sociology, Joe lived in a rented house in the woods way outside town. He and Nina had dogs and a horse named Vega, after the star. I lived in a musty basement apartment with a gold shag rug and a roommate with a giant light organ that translated musical notes into a rainbow of pulsing colors. I loved to play Led Zeppelin. Once in a while, Nina and Joe came into town to use the light organ. They played James Taylor. I bought Joe boxes of .22 rifle shells. In return, he hunted squirrels, cleaned them, and gave me half his kill, which was enough to keep my freezer filled for a year. On my two-hundred-dollar-a-month grad student stipend, Joe's marksmanship was a boon. I had a dozen squirrel recipes. But never did I have the urge to go out with Joe and shoot my own meals. A few times, I hiked into Joe's woods with a blanket, a girlfriend, and a bottle of wine, but my attention was never on the squirrels.

I had grown up in the sticks—a place people in town called Skunk Hollow—and I was hurrying to leave it all behind. I was what people called ambitious. One spring Sunday when Nina and Joe were having an all-day bash at their place, I got up at six and worked until noon on a thirty-page sociology term paper titled "A Discussion of the Potential Complex Organizations Offer for the Study of Rumor Communication." I went out for dinner at two, had a good time, drank a glass of wine. By four, I was back contemplating the rumormongers. I don't like to hold a grudge or to name names, but I'm still a little miffed that Professor J. Kenneth Benson gave me only a B on that paper. I think I deserved an A. Maybe if he'd known I had skipped the party.

In my defense, I wasn't always such a drudge. I had spent way more time drinking beer and chasing women in college than study-ing. Still I studied plenty and did well, and I knew why. I was a working-class kid, and I saw my stark choices. I could excel in college and, as my mother and father had told me ad infinitum, "make something of yourself," or I could do what my father did for a living and what I did to earn college money in the summers: I could work as a milk-man. Or at the Ford factory. Or deliver Coca-Cola. Or swing a ham-mer at nails. Or drive long-distance trucks. Or join the Marines. Thanks, but no thanks. I was pretty weird about it. I once had a col-lege girlfriend who wanted to start having sex. She wasn't taking birth control pills so I said no. Condoms prevented pregnancy only ninety percent of the time, I told her, and I wasn't taking any chances that I might have to drop out of college to support a wife and child. My ambition could even supercede my ethical beliefs. When my affluent college friends skipped their midterms one semester to attend an anti–Vietnam War rally in Washington, D.C., I stayed behind on cam-pus to take the tests. I did end up once sloughing off my grad school duties in the spring of 1973—to watch the U.S. Senate Watergate hearings on President Richard M. Nixon.

I was hooked. I told my favorite sociology professor, Peter Hall, that I was leaving grad school in sociology for journalism. He said, "You want to get to *The Washington Post*." I really didn't know what he was talking about. But he knew me better than I knew myself then. My entire generation of aspiring journalists wanted to be Bob Wood-ward and/or Carl Bernstein, whose reporting for *The Washington Post* had helped oust Nixon from the White House.

I got even more ambitious. To finish up my master's degrees in sociology and journalism in time for a plum internship I wanted, I worked all semester long from eight in the morning to midnight, seven days a week. I was stringent about getting my eight hours of sleep, so that I could keep working without getting sick. Except for an occasional Friday or Saturday night, I cut out almost all social life. I got the internship. When I took my first journalism job in Springfield, Illinois, I couldn't believe how easy it was. I'd start work at eight and always be home by eight, leaving me four hours a day—more free time than I'd had in years—to spend with a new woman I'd met, named Keran. Sometimes I'd take off a whole Saturday or Sunday, and we'd just goof around together. But almost always I worked some of every weekend day.

I once told Keran that she was "hitching her wagon to a rising star." She laughed uproariously. I drove a '65 Ford Falcon with a giant hole in the floor on the driver's side, a heater that blew only cold air, and a baby-blue door I'd salvaged from the junkyard and installed on the dark blue car. I wore $49.99 double-knit Robert Hall suits and Thom McAn shoes. I earned $165 a week. Keran hugged me and said, "I love you because of your sense of humor." At my next job, my editor once asked me when I was going to marry this nice girl named Keran. I'm embarrassed to tell you what I said: "I don't think I'll ever get married. It would interfere with my career."

I took three new jobs in three years—moving from Springfield to Harrisburg, Pennsylvania, to Allentown, Pennsylvania. Keran, who worked in the insurance industry and had no trouble finding good jobs that paid more than my paltry journalism salaries, moved along with me. We finally got married. Before we did, I warned Keran that as a journalist I'd probably never earn more than about $20,000 a year. Could she live with that? She smiled and said of course she could. She would work, too. In those days, it was nothing for me to put in sixteen-hour days. Another reporter might be smarter, write better, but he was never going to outwork me. By laboring twice as many hours on a story, I could double its depth and quality. I had a plan. If my stories stood out as better than most everybody else's, my work would someday be valued enough that I'd get perk assignments and plenty of time to do them. I believed that good journalism could save the world, that it was no accident Superman had worked at the *Daily Planet.* But my idealism was also entwined with my ego: I liked the reputation good work brought me. I liked the attention. I liked the respect. After a few months at my job in Allentown, a newsroom union steward took me aside and said people were talking about how there was no way I was doing all those stories in a regular workweek. The wags were right—and I wasn't submitting overtime. My little paper never would have paid it. I was working for free.

"You better be turning in overtime, or we'll file against you," the union man said.

"Fuck off," I said.

I never heard from him again. Three years later, I was at *The Washington Post.*

Bob Woodward had hired me.

At the *Post,* everybody worked like a maniac. I got my first inkling of life in the fast lane on the day I interviewed. After running a gauntlet of editor interrogations all day, I was ushered into the glass-walled office of the great Benjamin C. Bradlee himself. Sitting behind a cluttered desk in one of his trademark two-tone shirts, he motioned for me to sit in the single chair in front of his desk. He asked me only one question: "Do you write for the fun of it?" I was surprised at the simplicity of it. I said yes, which must have been the right answer. "Well," Bradlee said in his beautifully gruff voice, "they want to hire you. And if they want to hire you, they can hire you. But it's a long way from Allentown, Pennsylvania, to *The Washington Post.* And if you fuck up, it's their ass. And if it's their ass, it's your ass." He stood from his chair, reached across his desk to shake my hand, and smiled a magnificent smile. "Welcome to *The Washington Post.*"

As a lowly editor on the Metropolitan staff, I worked weekends. I worked holidays. The first Christmas in Washington, Keran was seven months pregnant, and I worked Christmas day. She stayed in the city with me. For the first time in her life, she didn't get back home to spend Christmas with her parents. She cried on Christmas morning. When Matt was born, I took a week off and then went back to implementing my master plan. Instead of spending my vacations taking trips, I worked doing articles for the *Post's* Sunday magazine. I stayed at the office writing until midnight. I worked on my days off. Tough duty. But in a couple years I was gone from the Metro desk and writing for the magazine. I used my old strategy and expanded the depth and quality of my stories by working fifty, sixty, seventy hours a week. Only Keran knew how long and hard I worked. I didn't tell my editor. I wanted it to seem as if I wasn't breaking a sweat.

I didn't ignore Keran and Matt. At the magazine, my work hours were my own—as long as the stories kept coming. I didn't get to the office until about 10 A.M., so I had several hours each morning with Matt. During the days, I could break off and go to a pediatric doctor's appointment or a neighborhood kid's birthday party. When Matt got older and Keran was back at work, I knocked off at 2 P.M. twice a week during Little League baseball season, picked up Matt at day care, and coached his ball teams through afternoon practices. When my daughter, Kyle, got older, I coached her ball teams, too. On a regular workday, I could usually be home by seven to eat dinner and play with Matt and Kyle until they went to bed. Then I'd get back to work until midnight or one or two, whatever. It took six years, but, finally, the summer before Alex gave me a shotgun, I wrote that profile of George Bush. Ben Bradlee praised me. *Time* magazine wooed me. Naturally, as a man who had missed a springtime feast to study the power of rumor communication in complex organizations, I let word of *Time's* courting leak out, and the *Post* suddenly decided to pay me what I always thought I was worth. In the next few years, I would be granted months to do long magazine articles on Jesse Jackson, Jerry Falwell, Jack Anderson, Lynda Bird Johnson Robb, even the legendary Watergate reporter Carl Bernstein, who no longer worked at the *Post.* Finally—perk assignments and plenty of time to do them.

At age thirty-six, I thought I had arrived where I had always wanted to arrive.

In the wood at the old Collins place, the dogs have gone quiet again. I trudge back up the hillside and step out of the forest, where I find Matt standing in the bright sunshine.

"You get a rabbit?" I ask.

"Yeah," Matt says proudly, as Bobby and Carl amble up.

So far this morning, Matt, Bobby, and Lewis have shot seven rabbits between them. It isn't unusual for me to be without game, but Carl, well, he's a different story. A man who kills no rabbits in a hunt is said to be "on the egg." When a man shoots his first rabbit, he will say, "I'm off the egg." I've been on the egg plenty of times. And I've been off the egg with a single kill many times. But Carl is almost never on the egg, almost always the day's high man. So when he's lagging behind, his friends start teasing, and he begins, as the men say, "huntin' hard."

"Two rabbits still back over yonder," Carl says and heads off.

As Bobby has said before, "Old Carl's gonna start stompin'."

We spread out. I go back into the wood. I love hunting the wood. You can see the mathematics of the dogs' search, see them overrun the rabbit's scent, then circle tight, turn, and backtrack. As I have done for years in the old Collins wood, I put my right foot up on a stump, lean into the downside of the hill, and rest my elbow on my knee. A shot fires. Way out of my range, across the stream on the far bank, I see a rabbit taking long bounds in a straight, horizontal path as a single dog races without howling or barking or yipping maybe fifteen feet behind. It's a disconcerting sight, like watching a basketball game on TV with the sound off, unnatural, even disorienting. Carl will later tell me the dog must have been a no-name pup that didn't yet know he was supposed to announce his quarry loudly to attract the other dogs to the chase. Out of the corner of my eye, I see the flash of a rabbit's white tail go into vine-laden brush. No dogs are nearby so I step in myself, lifting my thighs high and dropping my feet straight down, mashing the brush, and hoping to scare out the rabbit. No luck. Matt and Carl come into the wood.

"So you figured out how to hunt," I say to Matt. "You hang close to Carl."

"Ain't workin' too good today," Carl says with a disheartened laugh.

"I'm not worried," Matt says. "I'm off the egg."

I look at Carl. "Let's spread out and get a rabbit."

We hunt our way back toward the trucks, through the brush at my feet, the blackberry briars, another wood, a field of corn stubble that allows us to see a rabbit down but not across the rows, and come to a low-cut field that abuts a cedar forest. The old Collins place is a rabbit haven. From a distance, the briar field looks like a wild gnarl of foliage. But when I take my father's advice and get down on my hands and knees as if to examine the flowers one petal at a time, a wooded plain with intersecting animal highways and byways is revealed beneath the jumble, and it's clear why a rabbit would connive to be thrown into a briar patch. In the summer, the field is a rabbit smorgasbord—a table spread with not only blackberry but timothy and honeysuckle, sumac and lamb's-quarters, goldenrod, foxtail, and poke. With my chin to the ground, I can even see where sharp rabbit teeth have cut the goldenrod at a forty-five-degree angle. With forest on three sides and plenty of groundhog holes and brush piles in the wood, the old Collins place must approach the land's maximum carrying capacity of one buck rabbit to every five acres and one doe to every two acres—seventy rabbits on a hundred acres.

The day has really heated up. Although a ten-mile-an-hour wind has begun blowing from the southwest, it's still hot, sixty degrees or so. Everybody's coat is open. The dogs' tongues are hanging slack. Carl has killed two rabbits, which has taken the edge off. I still haven't taken a shot. I used to shoot more when I first started. I shot at rabbits out of range. I shot too quickly when rabbits leaped up from almost beneath my feet, not giving them time to get out far enough for a good shot. Ten years ago, I shot a rabbit on rocky ground that I should have noticed, and a pellet ricocheted sideways and hit Alex in the leg. He has never let me forget it.

"Man shot his own father-in-law," Alex has said maybe fifty times since then.

"Walt, where the rabbits at?" Lewis asks as we stand with Alex in the low-cut field about thirty feet apart outside the cedar forest, where the dogs are making shovels of their snouts and breathing in hard, muscular bursts, like machines pumping.

"Lewis," I say, "I always know the answer to that question, don't I?"

"Well, you the man with all the education," says Lewis, who has tucked the butt of his gun under his left armpit, pointed its barrel toward the ground, and looped his forearm under the gun's stock to hold it in place. I've seen Lewis in this exact stance before but with his pocketknife open in his left hand, as he forgets about hunting and peels and slices a pear he has salvaged off the old Collins place pear tree. Careful to point his knife's blade tip away from his face, he will pop entire slivers of pear into his mouth while his gun barrel bobs gently with each arc of hand to mouth. I'm wondering if he is about to reach into his jacket pocket and pull out a pear when a rabbit breaks from the wood. Exactly where the forest's edge meets the cut field, he turns at a right angle and runs to my left along the tall foliage. Alex shoots and misses. I raise my gun and follow the rabbit. This isn't like shooting the rabbit in my dream. He is closer to me so my shotgun's spread will be tighter when it arrives, which means I must be more accurate. And because the rabbit could leap back into the thick edge of the wood at any instant, I must hurry. I fire, fire, fire before the rabbit falls. When I get to him, he's still alive, something that happens maybe once out of every ten rabbits you shoot. I use the butt of my gun like a deadfall, club the dying rabbit in the head, and then hold him up for the dogs to see that he's dead. "Good boys,"

I say, as they dance on their hind legs nipping at the corpse. I know I'm about to take some grief.

"That rabbit must have had really thick skin," Lewis says.

"Must have," I say. "He didn't fall even when I kept shootin' him."

"Yeah," Lewis says, bringing the coup de grâce, "then you had to knock 'im out."

"That rabbit slowed down every time I shot," I say.

"He slowed down, all right," Alex says. "When you hit 'im with your gun."

We walk back toward the trucks parked by the farm's storage sheds and outbuildings, the late morning sun casting our shadows tight behind us. At the sheds, we occasionally run into Billy Elmore, Alex's friend and the owner of the old Collins place these days. I'm a little surprised whenever I see Billy, because he's a white man. I'm always reminded then that Alex, Bobby, Lewis, and Carl *aren't* white men, which is something I've become oblivious to over the years. The men's lives are pretty much segregated. They have plenty of white acquaintances but their best friends are black. Of the dozen hunting partners who've gone out with us over the years, none except me has been white. I suppose it may be hard for white people to believe, but despite my early worries that it would be hard for me to fit in with Alex and his friends, race mattered not a whit that I can tell. Keran told me it wouldn't. "These guys are more who they are because they're country than because they're black," she said. "Don't worry about it." I didn't and soon forgot about it. Once in a while, the men and I would run into white hunters or we'd stop and talk with white folks who lived near the places we hunted, and I couldn't understand what the country white people were saying any better than I could understand what my friends were saying. The white folks talked about the same litany of matters the men discussed constantly—the weather, farm animals, trucks, wholesale tobacco prices, the availability of game. The men sometimes joked about how white guys can't play basketball. Sometimes they talked about how blacks couldn't get decent jobs in the old days or how in the fifties blacks only got to swim in military pools on the day before the water was changed. The stories were always told with darkly ironic humor that made white folks look pretty ridiculous. Mostly race just didn't come up.

Back at the trucks, we empty our guns, lay them in the truck beds, take off our jackets. Carl hollers, "Yo! Yo! Yo!" in basso profundo and fires his pistol to call the dogs. I pull out four cigars I've brought— Arturo Fuente Curly Head Deluxe Maduros. They aren't expensive, two bucks, but they're fancy to Carl and Lewis. The men usually bite the heads off unclipped cigars. So I snip one head and hand it to Carl, snip another and hand it to Lewis.

"Thank you," Carl says.

"I got a brother," Lewis says. "You got one for my brother?"

"Hell I do," I say, snipping one for myself.

"I need a kill cigar," Matt says, meaning as a reward for killing a rabbit.

"Don't tell your mom," I say, snipping and handing him my last cigar.

"Everybody got a rabbit but me," Alex says, probably figuring it's better to bring this up himself before somebody else gets around to it.

"Matthew," Bobby says, "what's the deal on cleanin' rabbits?"

"Low man cleans," Matt says.

"I don't have *low*," Alex says. "I don't have *any*."

The men laugh.

"You guys wanta retire to Bobby's barn?" I ask. "I brought Wild Turkey."

"Let's go," Bobby says. "We ain't got all day."

Bobby's Barn

A freshly killed cottontail rabbit lying on its side in the palm of a man's hand droops like a frown, the tips of the rabbit's toes reaching almost straight for the ground, its head cast back, ears perked up as if listening, teeth clenched, the fur beneath its neck and belly a lustrous white, eyes black and blank, its vibrant brown-gray coat specked with creamy stalks of fur visible only from closer than arm's length, its cottony tail resembling a puff of real cotton. Sometimes the rabbit is mangled from the shotgun blast and blood has dried in dark mottles on its fur, or its head is gone, or its rear legs are shattered and dangling in boney tatters. More often the rabbit looks as if it is simply sleeping in your hand. You can't even see where the bits of shot pierced the rabbit's skin and severed its heart's aortic arch or shattered its left atrium, killing it instantly.

No matter how many rabbits I clean, I must flick a switch in my mind, turn off the part of me that has had pet dogs and cats since I was a boy, played with Matt's hamsters, slept with the tabby kitten curled next to my chest. If killing an animal with a gun is a loud announcement of moral choice, cleaning what I kill is always a silent reflection on the consequences of my staying alive. I eat meat. I like meat. I never give its source a moment's thought. A steak on the table is so antiseptically distant from the farm cow with her moist, gazing eyes and her amiable amble.

I flick the switch.

"You notice that bottle hasn't been opened," I say as I hand Carl the Wild Turkey. I say that because Alex has a habit of filling empty Wild Turkey bottles with Early Times or Ten High or, once, something called Edgewater bourbon, and passing the cheap whiskey around, hoping the guys say how good it tastes. He will never reveal the bait-and-switch to them, but he'll tell me later and laugh and laugh about how the men can't tell expensive liquor from cheap. Drinking with the men from a shared bottle of whiskey is an act of ceremony always undertaken with some pomp and circumstance. A few jokes about who will hog the bottle. A joke about how I will take the smallest sips, a friendly questioning of my masculinity. A man must learn to tip the bottle high for the theatrics while regulating the pinch of his lips to get the right dose. It took me a couple years to figure out that, although the men made much of their whiskey ritual, they never drank much whiskey. This morning, Carl's giant right hand envelops the cork. Everybody stops and watches in the way a family pauses in unison around the table to watch the first slice cut from a holiday turkey. With his left hand, Carl twists the bottle, and the cork audibly pops out in his palm. He chomps off a bite, smacks his lips, and passes the bottle to Matt to pass to me. Unexpectedly, Matt steals a quick slug—then lets out a long breath and a rough cough. The men laugh. I don't say anything, but I look at him with brows raised and mouth pinched.

"I earned it," Matt says. "I got a rabbit."

"One rabbit, one sip," Carl says.

"You're lucky that's smooth whiskey," I say, sipping, quivering, and passing it to Lewis.

He takes a swig. "That there's the real stuff."

"Old Lewis ain't never brought nothin' to drink, has he?" Alex asks.

"I stopped in Tennessee the other day to buy some wine," Lewis says.

"But they was closed, right?" Bobby says.

"Lewis, you got your teeth in?" Alex asks. "You're suckin' on that bottle."

The men can banter while they clean rabbits. I can't. I must concentrate. A water spigot at the cattle fence behind Bobby's red barn is open and gushing. It has created a muddy puddle from which water splashes like exploding fireworks to about calf high. We are spread in a half circle around the spigot and the puddle, and we're standing back a foot or so trying not to get splattered, leaning over at our waists and reaching into the spewing water to wet the rabbits' fur so it doesn't come off in our hands when we peel away the skins. Carl has the remains of the Fuente unlit in the corner of his mouth. Matt is the only one still wearing his jacket.

"Why don't you take off your coat?" I say. "You must be hot."

"I'm fine."

Right away, I think: *Why did I say that? He's not a child; don't treat him like one.*

"Okay," I say.

Matt was four years old that first morning I'd reluctantly gone hunting with the men. Alex got up early and cooked breakfast—scrambled eggs, grits, bacon, toast, and fried bull gonads. I'd never eaten bull gonads. Alex wanted to treat me to the country delicacy and, I suppose, see if he could make me squirm. They were good, tasted a little like mushy chicken livers. I was eating at the kitchen table when Matt walked sleepily out of the dark hallway into the light. At that age, he was still wearing pajamas with feet. I don't remember the color but it was almost always little-boy blue. The genetic soup of my pale Irish-English skin and Keran's glowing creamy coffee complexion had combined to give Matt beautiful light cocoa skin and dark, wispy, curly hair. His head was still a touch too big for his slim, angular body, and the shaggy hair that Keran wouldn't let me get cut made him seem all the more top-heavy as he tripped along, rubbing his eyes. He climbed onto my lap, put his head on my chest, and dozed. I finished eating and carried him back to bed. It went on like this for years, Matt always waking up on his own and coming into the kitchen. When he got a little older, he'd follow us out the door into the garage and watch us collect our coats and hats, fill our shell pockets, and hoist our shotguns onto our shoulders. I'd say something like, "Take care of your mother" or "Why don't you walk your little sister out to see the cows later."

Matt eventually took to saying, "Shoot me a rabbit, Dad."

That always made me feel good.

A son at four years old is a nice age for a father. It's all glory. A friend, six-feet-five inches tall, once told me that when his son was four, the boy believed he had the tallest dad in the world. My friend was deeply saddened when his boy met a man who was taller. When Matt was that age, I was once driving with him to the hardware store. Out of the blue, he asked, "Sons can grow up to be their daddies, right, Dad?" This was no small struggling for insight, and I was careful in my response. No, I said, sons can't grow up to be their daddies. They can grow up to do the same work or to be like their daddies in some ways, but they can't *be* their daddies. They must be themselves. Matt would hear nothing of these subtleties. He insisted that his friend Justin would grow up to be his daddy and that he would grow up to be me.

"Sons *can* grow up to be their daddies!" he said defiantly. "They can!"

I didn't argue. It made me feel good.

My memory of those early years of our hunting mornings always ends when Alex and I walked out the door into the dark and Matt went back inside. I knew from Keran that Matt climbed back into bed for a couple of hours then got up and went with Kyle to see the cows or played with his He-Man dolls or watched cartoons on TV. When we returned four or five or six hours later, Matt always popped out the door just as we were climbing out of the trucks. He came with us to the barn and watched us skin and gut the rabbits and listened to us jack our jaws.

"Which rabbit is mine?" Matt once asked.

I hesitated trying to decide if he was serious or joking. I couldn't tell. I reached into the pile of dead rabbits, pulled one out, and said, "This one's yours." By the way he smiled, I realized he had made a joke and I had fallen for it. The men would tease Matt a little. They'd hold out a bloody rabbit in his direction and ask if he wanted to finish cleaning it. Matt would half frown, half smile, knowing they were kidding, and shake his head a distasteful no. They'd ask if he was enjoying his days off from school or if he'd gotten better at basketball this season. Mostly, Matt would hang back outside the circle and stay quiet. He has always had intense dark eyes, though, and I could see him taking in the scene. I sometimes worried that watching animals get sliced to pieces, their innards tossed blithely into bloody buckets, might make a boy emotionally callous. I sometimes reminded him that beef and chicken and pork all start out alive. I mentioned that Alex, Bobby, Lewis, and Carl don't curse in polite company. I pointed out that taking a couple of slugs from a whiskey bottle was something I did only after hunting.

Really, I rolled the dice. I knew that most affluent city people would shield their sons from such rough men and gritty settings. But after my first few years of hunting I decided that the forests, fields, wind, rain, moon, stars, leaves, weeds, guns, killing, blood, cursing, drinking—and, naturally, the men themselves—would be good for Matt. I don't remember my early years of hunting chapter and verse. I can't tell you exactly what Alex, Bobby, Lewis, and Carl said and did that made me want Matt to join us. But I can tell you why. I was a journalist obsessed with my journalism. I spent the largest piece of my life writing down people's words, jotting notes on their gestures and facial expressions, noting the brands of their shirts and shoes. I had become a professional observer. I had a journalist friend who was a decade or so older than I. He had taken a year off, packed his family into a van, and driven the length of South America.

"That would make a great story," I said when he told me about his year on the road.

"That's not what the trip was about," he said.

I had no idea what he meant, figured he'd gotten lazy in middle age. I think he sensed my critical judgment but he smiled and said nothing. I'd like to apologize to him now. Hunting in Kentucky was becoming my trip through South America. Walking the fields and woods, listening to the language of the dogs, the quipping of the men, joking with them myself, made me forget I was an observer. Only when I would get back home again would I have the distance to marvel at how all-engulfing was my time hunting and hanging with the men. It was as if I had entered an alternate world. When Matt was maybe eight years old, he and I were walking out to the kennels one evening to feed the day's garbage to the dogs. The sun was setting and its glow on the autumn colors gave the whole scene an amber cast. It was chilly, and I remember that Matt was wearing a bright blue and gold stocking cap. The men and I had hunted that morning, and Matt, as ever, had joined us afterward while we cleaned the rabbits and settled in for chatter and a drink or two. Matt and I walked along quietly. He seemed thoughtful.

"Dad," he finally said, "Grandpa and the guys don't always like each other, do they?"

"No, not always," I answered.

"But they're still friends, aren't they?"

"Yeah, they're still friends."

Matt smiled. "Kinda like you and mom."

It was my turn to smile. "Kinda like you and me."

If not at that moment, then pretty soon after, I decided I wanted Matt to hunt with us someday. He had sensed what I couldn't put my finger on: these men loved one another. They were rough and foul-mouthed. Nobody had advanced degrees. They weren't movers and shakers. Yet I consciously decided they had what Matt needed, maybe what every affluent, suburban boy needs. I decided I wanted

him to join us in the hunts and watch life, death, nature, and friendship among men unlike himself play out before his eyes. I wanted
him to know something beyond clowns and ponies at his birthday
parties; every animated movie ever made; *Goodnight Moon* and *Where
the Wild Things Are;* the quiet chair; my Ford Taurus, everybody else's
Chevy Suburban; Disneyland; sleep-away summer camp; trick-or-
treating for UNICEF; cooking meals once a month at the homeless
shelter; lessons in swimming, piano, and Suzuki violin. I wanted Matt
to have a dose of experience that would cast doubt on the world he
assumed and reveal humanity in a different guise. When we got back
to Washington, I bought Matt a BB gun and taught him to shoot.
Someday, I told him, he'd hunt with the men. I rolled the dice, and
we have ended up this afternoon in the alternate world behind Bobby's
barn.

I look at Matt cleaning his rabbit this morning, and
I think of a time last year when Matt asked, "Dad, can you get this
bladder? I'm worried about popping it."

"I'm as likely to pop it as you are," I told him. "Go ahead and
cut it out."

Matt looked at the carcass in his hand as if it were a puzzle,
turned it to see the bloated yellow sac from several angles, then moved
in with his grandfather's knife.

"I got it," he said, as the sac fell into the gut bucket.

"Matt's a gut man now!" Alex declared.

"Should I cut the tail off, too?" Matt asked.

"Yeah," I said, "but don't cut your finger."

Shouldn't have said that, I thought. *He knows not to cut his finger.*

"Don't worry," Matt said. "This knife isn't very sharp."

Alex feigned anger. "You could bring your own knife."

That is still a good idea, and I decide this morning to buy Matt
his own hunting knife. In the early years I always borrowed one of
the men's knives to clean my rabbits. Carl and Bobby have had a whole

49

collection of hunting knives over the years, most of which they've lost. Alex has a knife with a bear-head handle that he has used for thirty-nine years. He bought it after he shot and killed a black bear while hunting in Washington state. I finally bought my own knife, a nice knife with a three-inch blade that folds into a handsome stag-horn handle. I take it out of my pants pocket, use my thumbnail to flip it open, then stab the blade's tip into the soft top of a fence post for safe keeping while I use both hands to finish soaking my rabbit beneath the spigot.

There is really no pleasant way to describe skinning and gutting an animal, even now after I have memorized and considered the discrete steps from beginning to end. It isn't that I've become inured to the gruesome act. If I let myself think about the green excrement caked under the curves of my fingernails, the bacteria rabbits carry in their intestines, the parasites that live in their skin and organs, I will still feel a queasiness rising. But I don't think about it that way anymore. I think about gutting the same way I think about cleaning up a sick child's vomit or diarrhea: I do it without squeamishness because it has to be done. I remember a time when Matt was sick as an infant, and I was holding him close to my face, trying to soothe him with words when he vomited into my mouth and I swallowed before I could carefully put him down and get to a sink. I didn't even gag. It was part of life. Killing and eating an animal is part of life. Over the years, I've talked myself into believing that intellectually. Still, every time I go to clean a rabbit, I balk for an instant, and I wonder: *Is it weakness in me that I still feel guilt? Or is it my conscience telling me that hunting is wrong?*

Then I flick the switch.

I stand back from the faucet, take the rabbit's head in my right hand, hold its body firmly at its chest in my left hand, and twist as if I were opening a stubborn jar of pickles. There's a crunching sound as the rabbit's neck snaps. I yank the head away to break the skin at the neck and then discard the severed head in the gut bucket. I grab the ends of the rabbit's front and back legs and stretch the stiffening carcass to loosen it. I take it by the front legs, hold it before me, and shake. The rabbit's innards drop toward the rear of its abdomen, nearer to the ground.

I pick loose a circle of fur and skin at the last joints on the rabbit's front legs. Using finger and thumb, I pull the skin on each leg down to the rabbit's chest. I grab the loose skin in my right fist, lift my left hand, and, with a few gentle tugs, pull the rabbit's skin down to its tail. This makes a sucking sound something like pulling adhesive tape off your arm. When I do this, the rabbit's carcass is level with my eyes and a foot from my face. As if the skin were a winter parka, I slip the fur garment down over the rabbit's rear legs. Then I pluck off its cottony tail, which is dirtied with feces that sticks to my fingers even after I shake my hand a few times. Carl can take his knife, put its blade at the last joint on each of a rabbit's legs, and, with his thumb on the other side of the joint, snap the bone and cut the skin in one flick of his wrist. I'm not strong enough to do that. I retrieve my knife from the fence post, lay my rabbit on a loose board, press with my weight to break through the joints, and toss each rabbit's foot into the gut bucket.

The naked carcass isn't very bloody. Rabbits have few blood vessels between skin and body and so don't bleed much when the skin is removed. Without the strong scent of hot blood there is no nauseating smell. The carcass is glossy crimson where its meat is un-damaged and dark red, almost black, where gunshot wounds have made blood pour into tissue. At times, I have thought a skinned car-cass looks as fragile as a newly hatched bird. At other times I've thought it resembles nothing so much as a classical statue of a naked athlete, all muscle and sinew. I hold the carcass in my left hand with the rabbit's belly turned upward and its back legs hanging toward the ground, poke just the tip of my knife into the soft skin at the rabbit's rectum, and run the blade upward to the top of the rabbit's chest, exposing its organs and releasing an awesome stench. It took me years not to gag every time I sliced open a rabbit's belly.

A rabbit, like all mammals, is built pretty much like a human under the hood—the heart with outgoing arteries still bright red from oxygenated blood and ingoing veins dark with blood that was returning for a fill-up; lungs now collapsed like deflated pale balloons; stomach with gleaming gray leathery surface and filled with digesting greens; silky salmon pancreas; yards of serpentine small intestine; glands that only an hour ago secreted fear and flight into my rabbit when the dogs howled; and the damp, gauzy membrane that connects the uterus to the bladder and encases the red, pinprick-sized lobules that would have become eggs in the spring.

I shift my knife to my left hand, slip all the fingers of my right hand down behind the rabbit's heart, and sweep the wet organs, slurping as they go, out and into the bucket. Bits of organ stay behind and must be picked off the carcass like pieces of lint. The urine sac must be cut out carefully from behind. I break the boney pelvic bridge where a rabbit's back legs are fused into a single, powerful jumping machine, and remove the last bits of feces with my fingertips. During the Depression, when wild rabbits were called Hoover hogs and sold commonly as food, a rabbit's tail bone was always left so people could be sure they weren't getting a cat. I lay my rabbit on the loose board and cut off its tail. In the kitchen later, I'll slit the skin where blood has coagulated so soaking can disperse the viscous puddles. I'll search for pieces of shot buried in the meat by rubbing my fingers over the surface to feel for the tiny lumps and cut them out. I'll pick off countless bits of fur that will have still clung to the carcass. But I'm done for now. I lean over to the spigot, flush the inside of the carcass, rub it clean with my thumbs, put it in a plastic bag, wipe my hands on my pants, walk over to the tailgate of Carl's truck, and take a long sip of Wild Turkey. The water is off, the rabbit carcasses are bagged and lying on the tailgates, and the men have moved away from the puddle and spread themselves around Carl's truck.

It's story time . . .

The men, to borrow an old country colloquialism, have got more stories than Carter's got pills. Bobby usually starts. He's the uncontested storyteller. I've seen visitors from out of town try to best Bobby. It all starts simple enough. The visitor tells a funny story. The men laugh, then wait. Bobby tells a funny story, maybe about the dumb guy, the pipe, and the cross-eyed mule; or the dead man named Bubba with two rectums; or the woman who the morning after gives fifty dollars to a guy wearing size-14 shoes; or the man who goes into a bar carrying a big club and leading an alligator on a leash. Then the visitor will tell another story. Then Bobby. Then the visitor. Pretty soon, it's clear what's going on, and Lewis, it's always Lewis, will be saying after each of the visitor's tales something like, "Oh, Bobby! That was a good one. Bobby's gettin' ready, he's gettin' ready!" Lewis will have his hands in his pockets, excited. Everybody will be looking at Bobby and he will be looking away, a vague smile on his face. "I tell ya what," he'll say. "There was this joker . . ." At dueling stories, I've never seen Bobby lose. If he did, none of us would realize it anyway, certainly not Lewis, who will always declare Bobby the victor.

"Ol' Bobby was cookin'!" Lewis will say proudly and then kick the dirt.

The wind is whipping up now, getting ready to move to the northwest. Before the afternoon is over, it will be gusting at more than thirty miles an hour. Lewis, Carl, and Matt, still wearing his jacket, lean against the side of Carl's truck bed in the bright sun. Bobby, facing the men, stands in the shadow of the barn behind him. Alex and I are looking off to the south at the cow pond a couple hundred feet away where Matt and Kyle used to catch catfish a foot long every summer. As usual, Bobby starts. He tells a story about a man who always defecated in his friend's barn and covered it up with cow manure. So one day the barn's owner sneaked into the barn behind his friend, slipped a shovel under his butt, and carried the stuff away.

When the man turned to cover up his leavings, he looked everywhere and couldn't find anything. It's a story I suppose only country men would find droll, and they do. Alex laughs so hard he cries.

"Alex," Carl says after the flurry, "go down home and get my quart a whiskey."

"Carl," Alex says, "your cousin called last night and said you were wrong."

"Alex bet a quart a whiskey," Carl says.

Everybody settles in to hear for the umpteenth time the story of how Alex once claimed Carl's cousin's address in Indianapolis used to be 2004 North Harding Street. Carl insisted the address was 2000 North Harding. They bet the whiskey. "I've come up with three witnesses," Carl says. "One was a mailman, Jackie Woods, who ain't no kin to me. I forgot about Bernice, her, too. That's four people who know the address, and he's still holdin' back my quart."

Alex smirks and shakes his head, as if to say, "Ah, he's lyin'."

Stories, stories, a lifetime of stories—stories remembered and re-remembered with an energy and freshness that make them forever new. I listened to the men's stories for years before I began to glean their real meanings. At first, there was a you-had-to-be-there-to-appreciate-them quality to the men's tales. Then I realized that was the point—Alex, Bobby, Lewis, and Carl *are* there to appreciate their stories, which have become the secular liturgy of their lives.

The time Lewis's dog walked up and whizzed on Bobby's leg in the Oak Grove Cemetery. The time Carl and Bobby told Gerald, Carl's city brother-in-law who comes to hunt with the men, that he needed to take his new shotgun to a gunsmith and have it "zeroed in" (which is not something a shotgun needs). The time a white man asked Carl to kiss his new baby girl so she wouldn't be prejudiced against blacks when she grew up. "He needs to go back and check to see if it worked," Bobby says. "She's about eighteen now." The time the men sent their long-dead friend F.B., who wasn't known for his brains, to buy oysters, and he came back and said the store owner had told him that he'd have oysters "in the month that starts with R."

"When's that?" I asked the first time I heard the story.

"A long time," Bobby answered dryly.

The time they had to hunt down and shoot a pack of wild dogs killing calves on Bobby's property. The time a hog jumped out of Carl's truck at forty miles an hour, and Carl was too embarrassed to tell the vet, and the vet said, "Well, the hog's problem has to do with his brain but I don't think it's catching." The infinite number of stories about long-deceased hunting dogs—Old Red, Leroy, Lead Foot, Head, Bingo, Queenie, Jack, Joe, Bo, Sue, Whitey, Trouble, and Gal.

"Gal or Gail," I asked when Bobby first mentioned the dog.

"Gal," Bobby said. "In Kentucky, Gal is pronounced *Gail.*"

"How's it pronounced if her name *is* Gail?" I asked.

A long pause. "It'd be the same."

The time their friend Charles lost his dog, Red, and they searched for two days before they found him in the trunk of Charles's car trunk, safe and happy to get out. The time Lewis and Carl were going to a potluck Fourth of July picnic at Barren River Lake and Carl didn't have a dish. He pulled over, took his .22 rifle out of his truck bed, walked into a field, and shot a groundhog for the feast. The time a man from near Carl's boyhood home told his wife he was going to the spring for water, hung his bucket on a fence post, and never went home, disappeared.

"When was that?" I asked Carl.

"In the fall," Carl said, pausing to set me up. "About eighty years ago."

Through the laughter, I look over at Matt, who has climbed onto the edge of Carl's truck bed. He has finally taken off his jacket. He's laughing and shaking his head. It's a long way from Suzuki violin. I rolled the dice. I hope it was for the better.

This afternoon, the time has come for us to head home for Thanksgiving dinners. The Wild Turkey is only half gone, and I make sure I get my hands on it before it grows legs. The men seem reluctant to call it a day, stretching and looking around at the barn and pond and Guinea hens that are now nipping the ground around us. A gray moon, a waxing crescent—God's thumbnail, as my daughter calls it—has finally risen and is pasted against the blue sky. Next to Carl's truck, Carl is now teasing Matt about something, and he's laughing. The men believe Matt has become a good shot but that he has a lot to learn about hunting protocol.

"You gotta learn like Carl and Bobby," Alex once told Matt. "Your first shot today, you didn't *miss.* You were turnin' the rabbit so you could get a better shot."

"Yeah," Matt said, "the first shot I took was to turn him. That's why I kicked up the dirt next to him. The next shot I nailed him."

"You're learning," I said.

"Learning what?" Matt asked.

"Excuses."

"No, really," he said. "I planned that turn. Honest."

Lawson Bottom

The drive to Lawson Bottom, out Burkesville Road and several other two-lanes for fifty miles, is always beautiful. Farmhouses and barns, fences curving around gentle hillsides, sheds enveloped in so much foliage only their roofs are visible, harvested fields of corn and tobacco, hulking rolls of hay, forests and foothills, a deer in the distance. This morning, just after dawn, fog rises from the ground in tall, billowy columns until the southwestern breeze disperses it to light wisps and reveals a high and clear and clean sky. The trip from Glasgow to Lawson Bottom used to be a dawn-to-dark ride in a horse-drawn wagon. Even in a car in the thirties, it was a half-day trip. Bobby and Alex made the journey many times as boys, traveling back to where their mother and father had lived before migrating to Glasgow in the 1920s. Years ago, the men could hunt just about all the land on the way to Lawson Bottom. Years ago, everybody let you hunt their land. No more. Today, even way out here, you must know people. The towns still have a lovely rural cadence to their names—Eighty-Eight, Marrowbone, Summer Shade. Alex says he used to see great blue herons standing on one leg in the shallow rapids at the curve in Marrowbone Creek. We watch for them this morning, but no herons. Alex says he has never seen smoke rise from chimneys as straight and slow as it does from chimneys on the way to Lawson Bottom.

"Like a picture," he says.

On the drive, as usual, Bobby brings us up to date on the news: the path of the recent tornado to hit Glasgow and the scandal involving a prominent Baptist preacher. "They couldn't even get the votes to throw him out," Bobby says with amazement and to utter indifference among his friends. The men tell stories I haven't heard before: Lewis claiming he parachuted from an airplane once, although nobody believes him; Bobby riding to Scottsville, Kentucky, and back in a taxi at age fifteen to pick up a case of whiskey to bootleg in dry Glasgow and being stopped by a cop who saw the cache but let him go. The men tell stories I *have* heard before: F.B. going to the store to buy those oysters; the white man asking Carl to kiss his infant daughter. We laugh as if we'd just heard the stories for the first time.

We hunt Lawson Bottom every fall although we haven't killed many rabbits here in years. This morning, Matt, at my insistence, has skipped the trip to do schoolwork. I think Bobby, Lewis, Carl, and his brother Milford, who has been nicknamed Goat since childhood and who has joined us from out of town this morning, would just as soon skip the trip, too, especially since Burkesville's C&J Restaurant has been torn down. A single-story building in a wide-angle parking lot, the C&J had big windows across the front that just before dawn gave the place the melancholy radiance of Edward Hopper's *Nighthawks,* country style. You walked in the front door and almost ran into the stools at the counter. We always sat at the booths to the side, where the lighting was dimmer and easier on the faces of the waitresses, who were past the bright-light stage of life. You couldn't eat at the C&J if you were counting grams of fat. You might as well have been counting ladles. The men pretty much ate everything on the menu—eggs, sausage, ham, bacon, fried potatoes, pancakes, and biscuits smothered in gravy that reminded your taste buds why grease is a hard addiction to kick. I always had to unbutton my pants and rely on my belt for the next few hours. I once used the C&J's bathroom, an experience I won't share. Every year, though, I looked forward to breakfast at the C&J. I always had the feeling I was in a place that existed nowhere else in the charted universe.

Even without the C&J, I still enjoy the drive through the countryside to Lawson Bottom, and Alex enjoys the journey back to his roots. Although he never lived in Lawson Bottom, Alex has always thought of it as his symbolic home place. In 1865, his grandfather Berry Lawson was born in a house that stood near where we have parked our trucks. Today, the two hundred and fifty acres are owned by Alex's elderly cousin Reid Lawson, who lived in the now-abandoned farmhouse for nearly seventy years until he moved in with relatives in Burkesville. Since Reid stopped beating back nature with tractor, plow, and Bush Hog, the land has gone rough except for a small tobacco patch, a field that has been cut for hay behind the tobacco barn, and a tractor path that runs to the handful of graves in the old Lawson family cemetery. The man-high briars, weeds, and saplings everywhere else are great rabbit habitat but good luck chasing a rabbit out of the thickets to get a shot. In this tangle, a rabbit can run the dogs in circles all day.

"Ouch! Goddamn it!" I say, as a briar cuts my ear.

I've ventured into a thicket along a narrow branch that flows past Reid's farmhouse. It's a spring-fed stream with water year-round, flood or drought. Reid has dubbed it the Everlasting Stream. I pass Reid's house and push through the edge foliage of an intersecting little stream, and step down onto its rocky bed. A bois d'arc tree has scattered green fruit, each about the size of a baseball, on the bank and the streambed and created a vaguely sweet scent as the fruit decomposes. The land behind me on Reid's farm is flat. But just across the stream, three wooded mountains rise to seven hundred, eight hundred, and nine hundred feet. Two dogs cross the stream and trail in a zigzag up the seven-hundred-foot mountain. I don't see a rabbit but, even if I did, I wouldn't shoot. I could never get up the rise to collect it. I sit on a fallen tree on the bank and enjoy the scenery. I think of a poem by R. P. Dickey: "I am talking / to the man who takes time / nineteen minutes / to look at a chrysanthemum." I hear a gunshot, two, three. I hear Bobby holler, "Dead!" and know he is dangling a dead rabbit above the dogs as they dance on their back legs sniffing and nipping at the corpse. I hear Carl holler, "Yo! Yo! Yo!" to fire up the dogs. In the long silences I also hear songbirds dancing in the brush and a crow cawing. I hear the jostling of water coursing over rocks. At such moments, I can even hear a single leaf as it repeatedly nicks naked branches on its fall to the ground.

In my first few years of hunting, these quiet, magical, contemplative moments in the field screamed out at me because they were so rare in my life back in Washington. Keran and I lived at the cutting edge of modern life. As I had moved up the ranks in journalism, she had moved up, too, becoming a manager for a giant insurance company in Baltimore. I never imagined that she wouldn't have a career, and we earned about the same incomes. So we tried to split the difference between Baltimore and Washington and bought a house near Annapolis, Maryland, giving me a thirty-mile commute, Keran forty miles. Figure two hours a day for each of us on the highway—that's about a thousand hours of commuting a year, forty or so twenty-four-hour days. But we considered ourselves lucky. Keran started work early and got home early, while I could start work late and get home late. That meant I had several hours to dress, feed, and play with Matt and Kyle before bundling them off to day care at 9 A.M. In the afternoon, Keran could pick them up, be home by five, and have dinner ready by the time I got home at seven.

We never had debates about whether it was a man's job to change diapers, take cookies to some event at day care or school, get up with a sick kid in the middle of the night. We took turns. Or we calculated child duties by whether I was on deadline for some story and needed the sleep, or whether Keran had some big project due. Equity in our jobs and incomes bred equity in our home. But our love life went to hell. And we ran ourselves ragged coordinating around children's sporting events, dance and music lessons, accidents on the beltway, snow storms. We put as many as 30,000 miles a year on *each* of our two cars. When car phones hit, we had 'em—and our bills ran to hundreds of dollars a month just from checking in with each other.

Buzz-buzz.

"Hi."

"Hi, I'm stuck on 695. Don't think I can get the kids on time."

"I'm on 495, traffic's good. I'll cancel my appointment, cut over on 50, and get 'em."

Sometimes we'd both get stuck in traffic and neither could get to day care by closing. But we had a contingency—a wonderful woman who worked at the center and who would take Matt and Kyle to her house and feed and entertain them until one of us could pick them up. During one blizzard, I didn't get to her place until after ten. The kids were asleep. It all sounds horrid now but as long as we ran our lives like efficiency experts, we were fine. I think the kids barely noticed. When they got into school, they took a quick bus ride to after-school day care. In the summers, neighbors with kids our kids' ages would take them during the day. Matt and Kyle never seemed the worse for it, seemed to enjoy their lives immensely. It was their parents who were worn to the bone. But we were making more money than I had ever imagined, $165,000 a year. That's loose change for truly rich people, but for most Americans it's a truck load of money. I agree with most Americans: mine was the good life.

Our house sat high on a wooded bluff overlooking the mouth of two wide waterways—Beard's Creek and South River, which led into Chesapeake Bay a few miles downriver. In the 1930s, the community had been a summer shore retreat for people from Washington. The houses were scattered haphazardly along the waterfront, and large tracts of community-owned land assured that houses would never end up packed cheek-by-jowl. From our deck, you looked out across a half mile of water. Giant tulip poplars enshrouded our house, which was a shack when we bought it. But over the years, through several renovations, it became like a cottage out of *House Beautiful:* whitewashed cedar siding, red-shingle roof, oak floors, soaring ceilings, skylights, floor-to-ceiling windows facing the water, decks wrapping three sides. From the house, you walked down a steep pathway, along the edge of a teeming wetlands, across a wooden catwalk to the pier where I kept my speedboat, a maroon, twenty-one-foot Formula Thunderbird inboard-outboard with a six-cylinder Ford engine. That baby could fly.

I remember walking around outside my home at dusk one summer evening. The last bit of sun was glistening off a boathouse far across the water, my boat and a few others were bobbing gently at the pier, our basset hound, Hannah, was chasing a toy that Matt was tossing in the yard, and parked at the garage was a new Dodge Intrepid and a new Mustang convertible. I was sipping a glass of my favorite wine, a Sokol Blosser Pinot Noir. Suddenly, a rush of overwhelming satisfaction shot through me, shocked me, really. The moment the sensation struck, I thought: What has happened to me? I didn't start out looking for this *stuff.* I thought about how I had once told Keran that I would never earn more than $20,000 a year. It was the *work* I had loved, the excitement, the passion, the respect it brought me.

Yet I had come to savor *things,* even to take pride in them—not just our beautiful home on the water in the woods but the rare Theophile Steinlen poster on my living room wall; the Miró lithograph and those by African-American artists Charles Bibbs and Bernard Hoyes; the Hopi kachina carved by Elliott Selestewa Jr. from a single piece of yellow cottonwood; the lush Oriental rugs; the odd assortment of handmade wineglasses bought two at a time for Keran as Christmas and birthday gifts over the last fifteen years; Keran's baby grand; the Stickley couch and Morris chair; the burled-cherry library cabinet handmade by craftsman Michael Seward; the Joe Clearman free-blown glass lamp I had bought for five hundred dollars but which was by then worth perhaps two thousand. It dawned on me at dusk that particular evening that my acquisitions had become a symbol of my accomplishments—not only for other people but even for myself. I had no illusions about the source of this prosperity and identity: Ambition. Work. Achievement. A new thought hit me: I love my work but what if the day comes when I don't? What happens to all of this? What happens to me? Will I be trapped in my affluence for the rest of my life?

In the streambed, sitting on the log, I'm recalled from the moment by Carl's deep voice.

"You see the dogs, Walt?" he hollers from somewhere behind me.

"I see 'em up the mountain," I holler back

Carl knows that's no good and whistles for the dogs to return.

"Walt, you better come on back," he says, hoping they will follow.

I climb out of the streambed and find Alex posted nearby behind the ancient tobacco barn, a picturesque Kentucky barn that is itself in the throes of reverting to nature, sagging in the center, gray and splintered poplar wall planks crowning and twisting, holes gaping where boards have lost faith and fallen to the ground. Chunks of roof have been replaced with sheets of rusting metal weighted down by old tires. With a strong gust, the metal sheets rumble like a bad muffler at idle. I notice a spot just past the barn that is part of our hunting folklore.

"Hey, Alex," I say cheerfully, "right up here is where I shot you."

The place looks entirely different, thick with bushy foliage, instead of clear-cut, as it was a decade ago. I can't even see the rocky ground that I should have noticed before I fired. I should have let that rabbit keep running until he was off the ledge, or just let him go, period. Out of character, Alex doesn't say anything about how bad his leg hurt, about how I was after his inheritance, about a man shooting his own father-in-law. No audience to hear the riff, I suppose. Or maybe Alex is just gone in thought, as he often is when we come out to Lawson Bottom. Naturally, I know my father-in-law better than the other men, and I know that country life and hunting and this place are deeply encoded in his social genetics.

For all his gruffness, Alex is a sensitive man. Only Alex notices that smoke rising gently from a chimney is as pretty as a picture. I've seen his eyes tear up when he tells even funny stories about his dead mother or brothers. Even when he tells a story about a favorite buddy from decades ago, he will often have to dab his eyes dry. Alex's wife, my mother-in-law, Celeste, once told me Alex has to let a cleaned carcass sit in the fridge for a day before he can bring himself to cook and eat it. The men always say Alex wants to kill just one rabbit each hunting trip. That way, he's off the egg but must clean only one rabbit. Alex once told me that one of the most wrenching moments of his life was when he shot his four-hundred-and-seventy-five-pound black bear in the deep Washington state woods, a feat that he has boasted about many times to his friends. The bear had risen up on his hind legs and bellowed a mournful howl like nothing Alex had ever heard. Alex can still throw back his head, grab his chest, and imitate the wail.

"That bear stood up and cried," he said. "I felt awful."

Alex and I make our way along the dry bed of still another branch back toward the farmhouse. Rising on either side of us are thistles taller than a man. A shotgun blasts from maybe a hundred yards away, its echo trailed by a burst of birdsong and fluttering wings. A grasshopper, or something like it, flitters in the air across our path. The ground is littered with bum-burst rocks—limestone geodes, the geologists call them. Alex remembers his mother collecting them when he was a boy visiting the farm and teaching him to smash them on larger rocks to expose the bum-burst's beautiful, silvery quartz interior. Alex once shattered one of the rocks on a flat outcrop, picked up a hand-sized piece, and showed me its white-glitter works. When he tossed it away, I went over, picked it up, and put it in my pocket to take home as a memento for my son, a bum-burst from the place of his ancestry and carved by the force of his grandfather's hand.

At the farmhouse, we turn onto the tractor path toward the Lawson family cemetery. Around us is a rabbit paradise, the snarled winter remnants of savory blackberry, purple vetch, and beggar's tick. Alex and I end up at the little cemetery, where the graves of his grandfather Berry Lawson and his grandmother Ada Flowers Lawson are guarded by towering elm trees and the ground is laced with stalks of broom sedge. I sit on a headstone and Alex talks. He has always loved to talk about his life, and I have loved to listen. At first, out of respect. Then curiosity. Then, finally, a dawning realization at the remarkable richness of Alex's experience.

As a boy on the Fourth of July, Alex picked blackberries near here. The Lawson farm was thick with rabbits and bobwhite quail with their *pup WAAAYK* whistles, as well as numerous chattering birds—sparrows and wrens but also the more exotic yellow-throated warblers with their melodic song descending from nests hidden atop the tallest trees, white-eyed vireos that lived and sang in the scrub brush foliage near the ground, and the inconspicuous Acadian flycatchers that always made their nests in low branches jutting out over the streams. And honeysuckle—the boys would suck the sweet nectar from the white and pink and yellow flowers, and the girls would squeeze the blooms in their hands and rub the juice on their necks and chests as natural perfume.

As a boy, Alex and his friends believed that any stream water that ran over ten feet of rock was pure to drink, and so they did. He learned to tell beech trees and pawpaw, ash, oak, cherry, walnut, poplar, maple, and hickory. He learned that north was revealed by moss growing on the sides of trees. He picked young pokeweed that smelled like spinach for salads and scoured the plowed fields for flint arrowheads that were easily found after a hard rain. He learned how to twist the neck of a chicken and clean the bird for Sunday dinner. He learned to tell a fox's rounded five-pad paw track from a groundhog's sharp-clawed print from a raccoon's elongated five-fingered mark, which always reminded him of a child's handprint. He caught terrapins, salamanders, and tree frogs. He cut out red sassafras roots that were boiled for tea. He took off his shoes and socks and sat on the many streams' rocky banks and let the running water tickle his feet. On cloudy nights, Alex learned just how dark the dark could be. Deep in the woods, his boyhood explorations took him to where the Lawson property met the mighty Cumberland River, where he stood looking out from a towering bluff across at the low, rich farmlands called Irish Bottom. Alex once took me to the very spot, where he couldn't resist a gibe.

"See that corn?" Alex asked.

"Yeah."

"You know what they're doin' with that corn?"

"What?"

"Making Irish whiskey. You Irishmen are the original bootleggers."

Alex never hunted Lawson Bottom as a boy. He and Bobby were born in Glasgow and lived in the town's black neighborhood, nicknamed The Kingdom. But even in town, Alex's life was like a chapter out of *The Adventures of Tom Sawyer.* His dad bought him a Red Ryder BB gun at about age eight. He got it taken away twice—once for shooting a kid in the arm and once for shooting a cat in the eye. Alex insists the cat was an accident. The boy, well, he wasn't.

When Alex was ten and Bobby was eight, their father, a prominent bootleg liquor dealer and a jack-of-all-trades at the Spotswood Hotel on Glasgow's square, died. That changed everything. Their mom worked as a maid in the Glasgow hospital and with five sons times were tough. Although Alex rarely mentioned race directly, it was always an undercurrent in his stories about his boyhood because his poverty and opportunity were so shaped by the limits of the era's discrimination—the hand-me-down books in dilapidated schools, the whites-only drinking fountain in Glasgow's square, the menial jobs. It was never racism that Alex emphasized, though. It was the nature and rhythms of rural life. As was the tradition of necessity among black and white poor people in those days, Alex and Bobby went to live with relatives or friends for long stretches. Family friends—Ms. Carrie and Leon—lived on a hundred-acre farm six miles southwest of

Glasgow. Alex lived with them for a couple of months but then went home, while Bobby stayed with Ms. Carrie and Leon until he went into the military. Years later, Ms. Carrie sold half the farm to Bobby, and Bobby eventually cut out three acres and gave them to Alex, meaning that Alex and Bobby first hunted sixty years ago on the land where they now live.

Leon didn't hunt rabbits, only quail. He had bird dogs, which are ruined if they're allowed to break their pointer discipline and chase willy-nilly after rabbits. So Leon took Alex squirrel hunting with a .22 rifle. In no time, Alex was taking the .22 out alone. Shells cost a penny each then, and even a boy could buy them at the hardware store. In all his times squirrel hunting in those days, Alex can't remember shooting a squirrel. He does remember getting a shell jammed in his gun and putting the barrel in his mouth to try and blow it free.

"Don't do that! Don't do that!" Leon screamed.

As Alex told the story on himself, he shook his head in disbelief.

Almost all the men Alex knew in those days hunted, and he began going out with other family friends, using his Uncle Troop's ancient shotgun. "It was a sawed-off shotgun that would kick your toenails off," Alex said, laughing. On one of those trips, he got caught by a barbed-wire fence and tore an eight-inch gouge in his leg, a scar he still brags about. In those days, a boy didn't need a hunting license, but Alex always saved up fifty cents to buy one so he could wear it in his cap like the men. It was a long time before he killed a rabbit but, finally, he did. Glenwood Ferris picked it up and put it in his bag. Later that day, Glenwood came by Alex's house and dropped off his rabbit, which had been nearly obliterated by Uncle Troop's cannon.

"Here's Alexander's rabbit," a deadpan Glenwood told Alex's mom.

"There wasn't much rabbit," Alex recalled. "In fact, there was *no* rabbit."

Then he laughed until he wiped away tears.

"Did the older men give you advice about how to hunt?" I asked.

"Yeah," Alex said, "don't put that gun in your mouth."

Then he laughed some more. Even then, the ribbing was the same. "Leon would laugh you silly if you missed a shot. He'd say, 'Goddamn, you missed that one!' That's always been. The fun was being out there and laughing and talking after the hunt, even if you didn't kill anything. That's what was fun about it. Just being out there with each other."

A few blocks from Alex's boyhood house, near what was then the city dump, across South Fork Creek, just before what was then a bootlegging neighborhood was a wooded bump in the ground called Snoddy's Hill, which was the stomping ground for Alex and his buddies. They caught fish and turtles in the South Fork, built forts in the woods, carved their initials into the tree trunks. Once, Alex and his friends Eugene Lee and John William Bradshaw—nicknamed Boogerman—were out hunting with slingshots they'd made. They remembered elderly people talking about eating brown thrasher and robin pies in the old days. So they killed a few of the birds on Snoddy's Hill, cleaned them, and fried them up at Boogerman's house. The boys even went to the store, bought flour, and made brown gravy to go along with their feast.

"Man, they were tough!" Alex said. "But they tasted good."

"How'd you know how to clean a robin?" I asked.

"It's like cleanin' a chicken. Everybody knew how to clean a chicken in those days."

"You ever know anybody who got hurt hunting?" I asked

"Yeah," Alex said somberly, hesitating. "My son-in-law shot me in the leg."

Back down the tractor path toward Reid's house, Carl's truck comes bumping along and parks halfway to the cemetery. By the time Alex and I walk over, Bobby, Lewis, Carl, and his brother Goat, a tall, lean, elegant man whom Matt says always strikes the perfect hunter's silhouette on a ridge line, are spread around the tail-gate eating "crackle"—fried pig skins.

"This'll make a man's blood pressure right," Bobby says.

"You're not supposed to be eating those, are you?" I ask Bobby.

He takes a chomp. "Anything good in this world, Walt, is immoral, illegal, or fattenin'."

It has turned out to be another warm, blue-sky morning. Beautiful. But a bad morning for hunting. The men have killed only a few rabbits, and I have killed none.

"I guess Matt didn't miss much," I say.

But, really, I know that's not true. How many chances does a man get to eat fried pig skins on a tailgate under a high sky fifty miles from anywhere? I'm getting hungry and suggest we head to Sproule's store a few miles back toward Burkesville. I don't need to suggest it. We always stop at Sproule's, which was our trip's back bookend to the C&J Restaurant. Sproule's is a gas station and one-room, cinder-block store that sits with a handful of old houses at a barren crossroads. The place has a couple of beat-up stuffed chairs usually occupied by old men smoking cigarettes; a sitting counter with round-topped stools; and a practical mix of items: soda, milk, juice, Moon Pies, baked beans, S.O.S. pads, shoe polish, trash bags, batteries, motor oil, Red Man chew, twine, and fuses galore, in fifteen, twenty, thirty, and sixty amps. Like the C&J, Sproule's is unique in the charted universe. I once took off my cap and put it on the counter while I ate, then forgot it. The next season, a woman at the counter asked, "Did you forget your hat?" and retrieved it from a hook on the wall.

The unrelieved sameness of the place is always simultaneously oppressive and refreshing to me. God, imagine living near Sproule's! No *Esquire, Atlantic,* or *Vanity Fair* on the rack. No Leinenkugel's beer or Napa Valley wines, not even Boone's Farm—the good church folks of Burkesville and its environs have voted to outlaw alcohol sales. Nobody, I suspect, within shouting distance of Sproule's has read Thomas *or* Tom Wolfe, or listens to *All Things Considered* or watches

Jim Lehrer, maybe not even *ER*. But then I come once a year and the proprietors remember me, the guy who forgot his hat, the guy who buys the Moon Pie, Alex's son-in-law. I like that even while I know I could never live here. Sproule's is the unattainable flip side of my modern life. When my kids were little, for instance, I took them to a McDonald's near my house for breakfast at least a couple times a week for years. Every few months, the friendly people at the counter who knew our names would disappear, and we'd start all over again, blank slates. The universe has an abundance of such places. In the field this morning, it strikes me that when I visit Sproule's I always order ring baloney and American cheese with Miracle Whip on Sunbeam white bread, the only bakery choice. I'm getting downright predictable. I'm thinking that maybe I'll sass up my sandwich with a slice of raw onion, as Alex always does. Just then the dogs start howling in the thicket to the southeast of us.

"They's rabbits in there," Bobby had said earlier. "Dogs just can't get 'em out."

"He ain't comin' out unless he wants to," Goat says.

When the dogs ratchet up their howling another notch, Carl and I finish our crackle, wipe our greasy hands on our pants, load shells into our guns. He suggests I cover the path toward the house. Carl later says he was trying to get me out of his way so he could get a better shot. Then, about thirty yards down the path, a rabbit breaks from the thicket and runs straight at me.

One shot—a good shot, if I do say so myself—and I'm off the egg.

The Everlasting Stream

I have a picture, a decade old, from the day I believe I first came to realize something important about these men. It's a typical hunters' photo: men and their kill, in this case somewhere between seventeen and twenty-seven rabbits, depending on who's telling the story of that day's hunt. We're stretched out like suspects in a lineup, looking right into the bright sun, our dead rabbits spread out on the ground before us. It's probably eleven or so in the morning, about the time we usually finish hunting in Lawson Bottom. Everybody but me has the bill of his orange hunting cap pulled down to shade his eyes. We all look so young in the old picture. For some reason, I'm not wearing my hat, and the sun has washed my balding head bone white, making it almost glisten. I'm squinting. Goat, tall and straight with a fresh cigar in his mouth, is on the far left of the camera, which Bobby must have been holding because he's not in the picture. Next to Goat is Lewis, his hunting jacket off and just brushing the grass as it dangles from his right hand. Then me, resting back on my left heel, my head tilted oddly. I must have done some shooting that day because about half the shotgun shells are missing from my vest's shell pockets. Then Gerald, the city brother-in-law of Carl and Goat. He's the only man smiling broadly. Then Carl, short and dense but quite a bit thinner than he is today. Then the tall, gangly Ed Lee, who's too frail to hunt anymore. And, finally, Alex, who looks shorter than he is next to the rest of us because the ground beneath him is angling downhill. I have taken a magnifying glass and tried to count the dead rabbits in the picture, but

I can't see them all clearly. They are too small and, sometimes, stacked in piles that defy counting. The picture itself is unremarkable. It matters only because it was snapped minutes before what became my most memorable hour of hunting. You can't anticipate memorable moments in life, can't will them to happen. My daughter was a restless sleeper as an infant. At first, so Keran could get some needed sleep, I'd get up and take Kyle from her crib and into the living room, where I'd lie on my back on the couch in the dark with Kyle sleeping facedown on my chest. She would calm quickly while I dozed. Then I'd put her back to bed. The first week or so that she cried in the night, I'd think, *Oh, no, gotta get up.* But pretty soon I found myself sleeping lightly, waiting for her to fuss. I'd get up, take her to the couch, tuck her head beneath my chin, and feel her warm breath gently brushing my neck. She was so small that my open hand covered her entire back. I don't believe I have ever felt so powerful in my life. Kyle would be asleep in minutes, but I didn't put her back to bed. I slept all night holding her, knowing even then that this miraculous time that I had stumbled into would not last. After six months, Kyle began sleeping through the night in her crib, which made me sad. Fifteen years later, I can still feel her breath gently brushing my neck.

Such memorable moments are like waking versions of lucid dreams. We are within them and outside them at once as they are happening. The time I hit an inside-the-park home run in Little League. Racing into third base where my father was coaching, everything slowed down as I approached, tagged, and rounded the bag while my dad swooped his left arm in what seemed like giant slow-motion circles waving me on home. Past third base, life picked up its normal pace again. The moment when the Justice of the Peace was asking me if I would take Keran to be my wife, and I noticed out the window how beautiful the park across the street was in the falling snow and said, "I do." The moment when I was eating dinner with my sister and her husband and my eighty-year-old parents in a Mexican restaurant in Yuma, Arizona, and amid the jabbering of voices and jangling of silverware and passing of hot sauces I saw my mother reach out and straighten my father's collar and him acknowledge the gesture with his eyes. No, you can't anticipate memorable moments.

After the hunters' photo was snapped, we carried our rabbits back toward Reid's house to where the spring-fed Everlasting Stream crosses the narrow drive. No matter the season, no matter how little rain, an inch or two or three of water spread a few feet wide is always running south across the drive, which is made of russet creek gravel spread who-knows-how-many generations ago. The water moves so slowly you'd think it was stagnant until it meets a little bank on the far side of the drive. Detouring west at a right angle, the water picks up speed in a miniature, foot-wide rapids convulsing over gravel the size of Alex's slingshot ammunition that years of truck and tractor tires have corkscrewed to the drive's edge. After a few rustling feet, the water drops through a wash in the gravel, making a light musical tinkling as it falls, and then continues south. In the summer, the stream is obscured by pretty roadside junk plants—tall milkweed with white silky stalks; wild onion in pink bloom; partridge pea with yellow, anomalous petals on flowers that are easily lost in the taller foliage. You can barely see a stream.

When we arrive the day after Thanksgiving, it's all changed. The bushy summer growth has retreated and you can see the water cascade over the wash onto a mossy outcrop that juts from the earth along the stream's eastern bank. The water is clear and you can see the tawny rock shelf descend in steps into a triangular pool of calm water that is about eighteen inches deep, ten feet long at the bank edge that is the triangle's hypotenuse, and a few feet wide at its apex on the opposite bank. The pool's slate bottom turns to gravel when the branch becomes a narrow cut and disappears into low tree branches that meet over the stream like the roof of a dark tunnel.

73

Carl pulled his truck up the drive just past the stream and opened the tailgate. The dogs were tired and quiet in their cages, and our guns were unloaded and stored. It was warm, and we had all taken off our coats. We were probably passing around a bottle of whiskey— Early Times if Carl brought it, Wild Turkey if I brought it, Ten High in a Wild Turkey bottle if Alex brought it. With no water faucet under which to soak our rabbits, Carl led the way and laid his rabbits on the triangular pool's slate outcrop, where they half rested, half floated. Other men followed and, when the ledge got crowded, I laid my rabbits in the gravel rapids at the edge of the drive. The men dug in their pockets or went to their trucks to fetch their knives. A little ritual always follows. After each man opens his folding knife or unsheathes his stationary blade, he absently feathers his thumb over the cutting edge to check its sharpness. Goat and Carl had their cigars going. Lewis took off his hat. I had never seen Lewis without a hat and was surprised that he had a full head of hair. The men didn't talk much, and I could hear the shuffling of gravel underfoot.

Remember that I didn't own a knife in those days and always had to wait for somebody to get done before I could skin and gut my game. I stood off to the side of the men and looked at all those rabbits, the most we had ever killed in a hunt. I didn't yet know much about Bobby, Lewis, and Carl, except that they were Alex's friends and, as I said earlier, men I saw initially as quaint country characters. The water in the rapids poured over and around my dead rabbits, making the stalks of their fur flitter like short hair blowing in a wind. The fur on the rabbits half resting, half floating on the slate ledge was billowing out like fibrous tentacles, making the rabbits appear larger than they had when their fur was matted on their bodies and looking as if it had been brushed and styled that way. The men began cleaning and, in a few minutes, were done. As they were rinsing their bloody rabbit carcasses in the pool, I borrowed Alex's bear-head knife but got only one rabbit cleaned before Carl had finished the rest for me. I was the last man to stoop over the pool and rinse blood from my hands. God, the water was cold. When I stood, the men were sitting on Carl's tailgate or gathering themselves in the drive and the short winter grass along its southern edge. I took up a spot on the drive facing the tailgate maybe fifteen feet distant.

That is when the waking lucid moment came. I was watching the men, not talking myself but laughing with them, when time elongated, and I was standing in the field, on the drive and yet standing outside the place, already realizing that I would remember these moments not only as a collection of facts but as pure sensation, just as I remember Kyle sleeping on my chest, the falling snow outside the window at my wedding, my father's eyes acknowledging my mother as she straightened his collar. Athletes talk about entering the "zone" when playing with perfection; actors, artists, and writers describe being lost "in the moment" while absorbed in their work; psychologists use "flow" to describe moments when a person's mind and body are in perfect sync. All are inadequate words struggling to describe sublime human moments.

To this day I don't believe I have ever seen men so at ease, so thoroughly enjoying one another's company, so satisfied with exactly where they were at that instant. As I stood listening to the men at the Everlasting Stream, I realized I hadn't shared that sensation of camaraderie with male friends for nearly twenty years. I had such good friends as a boy and as a young man. When I was ten, I screamed out the secret Indian howl as a fat boy named Timmy sat on my chest and pummeled my face, and my best friend, Johnny, came flying and sent Timmy sprawling. We pounded on him until he managed to get up and lumber off. Then we sat on the grass and told the story of what had happened again and again, making it better every time. And Joey from junior high. We once hid behind some bushes and hollered obscene words at a gang of girls, one of whom recognized my voice. Her parents called my dad and I was in big trouble. I had to visit all the girls' houses and apologize to them and their parents. But I wouldn't—I didn't—give up Joey.

In high school and summers during college, Martin and I were attached at the hips. He called me Twerp. I called him Dipshit. He was a star basketball player. I was a scrub. He always had the prettiest girlfriend. Let's just say I wasn't always in demand. God, we had fun, doing nothing and doing something. We could play Nerf basketball in his garage for five hours straight. Once, good fortune landed us in the second-story bedroom of two adventurous young women. But Grandma got home and began pounding on the locked door with a cane. I remember the panicked look on Martin's face. We had no choice. We climbed out a window onto the garage roof, counted to three, and jumped. Then we stood up, waved heartily to the girls smiling down at us, and took off. After that we called ourselves Butch Cassidy and the Sundance Kid. In college, there were Max and Pete and Frank. In graduate school, Joe and Roger. I loved those guys. Over the years, however, as I moved from city to city, the phone calls and visits got fewer and fewer until the men disappeared. Nobody knew anymore that Martin had called me Twerp, not even Keran.

I and my generation of men became Mr. Moms. That was better for my children and Keran. It also brought unimagined joys such as my nights with Kyle on the couch, moments I would never have known if Keran were the delineated homemaker and I the breadwinner. I wouldn't give those moments up for anything. But to get Mr. Mom, something had to give, and my family and my demanding work at the *Post* couldn't. So what gave was my life with men: no golf, no card games, no afternoons at ballparks or gatherings in front of a big-screen TV on fight nights. Every spare minute away from work went to my family. I made new men friends, of course, but in my circles by then we were all on the career chase, and we ended up spread around the country and the world. In the workplace caldron, friendships are tricky. Someone who's your friend in the beginning may not be your friend years later, may even be an enemy. So you must be cautious, keep your secrets wisely. At the *Post*, I made plenty of casual men friends but only three I trusted deeply enough to talk to with real honesty. These days, Pete and John each live nearly a thousand miles away, Mike two thousand. We e-mail.

Watching and listening to Alex, Bobby, Lewis, Carl, and their buddies, thinking about my old friends I had left behind, it dawned on me that something more was going on with these men than a gathering of quaint country characters. I thought of Alex's words: "The fun was being out there and laughing and talking after the hunt, even if you didn't kill anything. That's what was fun about it. Just being out there with each other." The hour at the Everlasting Stream seemed endless, an hour floating in time, disconnected from the rest of our lives. I don't believe I spoke or was spoken to. I don't recall any words said. I'm sure the men retold the familiar stories of their lives together, and added a few from that day. I remember feeling, well, satisfied. Or maybe I remember not my own satisfaction but the satisfaction of the men. And one detail: Carl, in an old, red-checkered shirt with his hunting hat off and his face open in the bright sun, laughing. Over the years, I have sometimes wondered if I was the only man touched by that hour at the Everlasting Stream. So, recently, I asked. It turned out that Alex, Bobby, Lewis, and Carl all remember the hour distinctly, although it was only one of thousands they had hunted together.

"'Bout the best day of huntin' ever," Lewis said.

"I remember it, yeah, like yesterday," Alex said.

"Glad I took that picture," Bobby said.

Carl, usually parsimonious with his thoughts, remembered the hour so clearly because the hunt went well, the weather was beautiful, cleaning the rabbits in the Everlasting Stream was something we had never done before—and the cold spring water in the pool made him think of the spring his daddy had laid two wooden planks across so Carl could dip water as a boy.

"I reckon that's why it stands out in my mind," he said.

Yet why does it stand out in everybody else's mind, too?

As I've learned, hunting is filled with pristine moments—when you hear a leaf falling through naked branches, see the tableau of a rabbit racing fifteen feet ahead of a dog that is not barking, see the sun lay a pink blanket over trees on the eastern horizon, cut a rabbit's belly open on a cold day and suddenly feel its innards warm your freezing hands. But that hour at the Everlasting Stream . . . I don't want to sound flaky, but I think of it as an hour of near human perfection among men, a slice of time when the stars just line up right and you are in the zone, the moment, the flow, whatever inadequate words you choose to describe the sublime. But this didn't happen only in the mind of one athlete, artist, actor, or father lying on his couch with his infant daughter in the middle of the night. It wasn't only a personal experience. It was a social experience, a set of emotions and sensations felt almost identically by everybody present. Even as an outsider I knew it. And the men knew it, too. That was something to think about.

Behind B.C. Witt's Farm

There is no sway in Carl's walk. He holds his gun at his side and parallel to the ground in his right hand and walks through a wide field that the sun is revealing in shades of sand to ginger to bronze to henna and, a good half mile away, gunmetal gray that demarcates the tree line along Skaggs Creek from a silver horizon that becomes a stunning delft-blue sky. As he walks, Carl's body stays perpendicular to the ground and his legs seem to move only below their knees. His thighs, huge torso, even his arms seem to remain still. It is the most sedate walk you will ever see. The morning is bright and cold, one of our rare hunting mornings below freezing, twenty-six degrees. When we met at the dog kennels behind Bobby's house at six-thirty this morning, the grass was coated with a misty glaze of ice and the blades were curling under the weight. At the land behind B.C. Witt's farm—the place the men took me my first morning of hunting twelve years ago when I didn't know where I was or even what was north, south, east, or west—the icy glaze has melted and distilled into tiny dollops of water that are sticking to our hunting pants like burrs and glistening in the sun. The dogs are hopscotching in the weeds, sniffing and gusting steam. Earl stops, stretches, puffs his chest, peaks his nose, emits a loud, long "arrrr*rououououou*," drops his head, and tears off on a trail with the other dogs howling behind him. A rabbit bounds between Carl and Matt, and before Matt even lifts his gun to his shoulder Carl shoots, lowers his gun to his side, and begins that sedate walk toward the dead rabbit.

"Matt, you let that rabbit get by you," Alex says.

Matt looks at his grandfather, smiles, doesn't speak. He knows it's no humiliation to be beat by Carl. For my money, Carl's the best hunter of the bunch. He's not the undisputed best hunter, because Alex, Bobby, and Lewis dispute it all the time. They insist that hunting skill is measured not by the number of rabbits a man kills but by the ratio of shots taken to rabbits killed. So if a man takes eight shots to kill four rabbits and another man takes one shot to kill one rabbit, the man with one rabbit is the better hunter. Like a batting average in baseball. I get the logic. Because the men don't keep stats, it also means that each of them can argue that he is the best hunter. But I think Carl misfires less than anybody else, and he must take home twice as many rabbits. One year, when the legal limit was eight rabbits a day instead of the four it is now, Carl killed a hundred and thirty-seven rabbits. That's pretty strong logic, too. Carl's the champ. I declare him so, knowing I will never hear the end of it from Alex, Bobby, and Lewis.

The dogs scare up a covey of quail, Alex shoots, kills a quail.

"I'm ready to go home," Alex says.

"We'll never hear the end a that," I say, and Carl chuckles.

The dogs scare up a rabbit, Alex shoots, kills a rabbit.

"Glad I'm not sittin' on that egg," Alex says.

This morning, we have parked our trucks at the unpainted barn where we parked on my first hunting trip years ago. In the cold, the drive's gravel has a crisper, harder sound under our boots. After all the years, I now know where I am. The sun is rising slightly off the eastern edge of the old tobacco barn, meaning it sits northwest-to-southeast. A new wire fence runs along the northeast side of J. Carter Road, which is the name of the narrow macadam road that cuts from the main two-lane drag where Alex and Bobby live a few miles back, past fields of harvested tobacco, corn, and wheat, past B.C. Witt's farm. The small pond that was as dark and smooth as a smoked-glass tabletop still sits to the northwest of the barn, and the tall forest rises high to the west. To the north-northeast, the field that was filled with weeds on my first visit still rolls away in compound inclinations, but it has been buzz-cut by grazing cattle. The shadow of a hawk gliding high overhead slides across the bare pasture.

"They cleaned it up," Carl says of the land.

"It was all overgrown last year," I say. "We got some rabbits."

"We did," Carl says.

Goat walks over. "A lot cleaner than it was last year."

"Yeah, they cleaned it up," Carl says.

"Remember, we ran 'em all over the place last year," I say.

"Yeah," Goat says, and we all nod at the memory.

I'm hunting with glasses for the first time this morning. My vision far away isn't too bad, but in middle age my eyes just can't see close up very well anymore. I've been wearing reading glasses for years but finally bought a pair of multifocals—the progressive kind that hide the reading lens in the larger lens for vanity's sake. I was shocked at what I had been missing. Not only can I read the odometer in my car and see the hairs on the back of my hand again, but in the hunting fields this morning my glasses have reminded me of my father's admonition that the world is best perceived from either long distance in a beautiful blur or on hands and knees, one petal at a time.

The beautiful blur is all around me. Looking across the fields and forests, I see an infinite array of shades in the palette of cool-season colors—grays, tans, yellows, browns, reds. *Grays:* gunmetal, stone, pewter, moth. *Tans:* sand, cinnamon, ocher, wheat. *Yellows:* bronze, copper, camel, gold. *Browns:* ginger, mocha, amber, dun. *Reds:* henna, russet, salmon, plum. When I stop and look, I realize there are as many shades in nature's narrow band of fall-to-winter colors as there are points between the ends of a line. With my new glasses though, the petals now come into anatomical focus. I see the crease that bisects the length of a blade of johnsongrass. I see the cottony hairs on the stem clusters of broom sedge and realize why its genus name from the Latin is Andropogon—"bearded like an old man." I see what looks to be blackberry briars and realize they're actually dewberry—their stems are round, not square, although I'm still not very good at telling the difference. Just now, as Carl and Alex and I walk through a field of weeds and briars on our way to hunt the tall forest, I say, "Blackberry bushes. Ought to be a rabbit nearby."

Alex glances at the bushes. "They're dewberry. I used to eat dewberry pie as a boy."

I bend over and examine the stems. Alex is right. They're round, not square.

Alex posts outside the forest, and Carl and I enter the tall wood, where poison ivy and Virginia creeper ensnarl the trees, as they do the trees at the old Collins place. I now know that if the roots grow into the tree in thick, hairy tendrils, the vine is poison ivy. Don't lean against that tree. If the roots lack tendrils, it's Virginia creeper. Lean back, relax. Among the trees, I see only one pine. It looks like a hemlock. But now, using my new lenses, I can see that the backs of its needles aren't white-striped but yellowy green: it's an American yew.

In the beginning with Alex, Bobby, Lewis, and Carl, I had no multifocal insight. My time with them was an entertaining diversion, no more. I brought my shotgun, shells, orange cap, rubber boots, insulated socks, and brown jersey gloves, but I relied on Alex to outfit me from his castoff hunting gear with pants, vest, and jacket. I couldn't see spending a couple hundred bucks on a diversion. Besides, I enjoyed mostly just standing back and listening to the men rag on one another. I thought of them as a comedy routine going on before my eyes. Then came that day at the Everlasting Stream. I couldn't get it out of my mind. I found myself thinking about that hour and the men and the hunting off and on all year. I kept the snapshot of us tacked on my bulletin board in my study at home. I sometimes looked at the picture and zoned out, thinking about the day it was taken. Next thing I knew, I'd be thinking about the spring at the old Collins place, or about standing behind Bobby's barn passing the Wild Turkey, or Carl laughing in the sun.

I'd long had a way of relaxing myself when I was on a writing deadline or stressed out about something. I would lean back in my chair, close my eyes, and think about something soothing—rocking Matt or Kyle to sleep when they were infants, or the time my father taught me to skim flat rocks off a pool of water near our house, or the time years ago when Keran and I made love on the back porch at night during a gentle rain. One day during the year after the hour at the Everlasting Stream, when I leaned back and closed my eyes to relax, I saw myself standing in the earthen bowl with my foot up on that tree stump and my elbow on my knee. That surprised me. Soon after, I was poking around at the library one day and decided to read up on rabbits.

The little creatures are pretty remarkable. They go back fifty-five million years to the Paleocene epoch and are native to Asia, Africa, Europe, and North America. They come in thirteen species. The rabbits that Alex, Bobby, Lewis, and Carl hunt are Eastern cottontails, which are found just about everywhere east of the Rockies. Rabbits must be among the most hunted animals in history. The ancient Greeks hunted them. The oldest English-language book on hunting—*The Master of Game* written in the fifteenth century—rhapsodizes about hunting them. Animals, too, feast on rabbits. In Kentucky, they're a staple for coyotes, crows, minks, snakes, badgers, weasels, foxes, skunks, raccoons, opossums, great horned owls, barred owls, red-tailed hawks, red-shouldered hawks, and bobcats. Before hunting season even begins in the fall, three-quarters of all rabbits born that year are dead, making them pristine examples of what the celebrated environmentalist Aldo Leopold called "meat from God." To ensure the bounty, nature made rabbits into reproductive marvels. A doe can bear up to seven litters of seven babies a year—forty-nine offspring. In ninety days, those babies can bear babies, too.

Rabbits that look so helpless aren't. Amazingly, half of all cottontails that hunters scare up escape their pursuers. A cottontail can swivel his long ears like twin periscopes individually manned to hear sounds of danger from different directions at once. His eyes bulge on the sides of his head so he can see literally forward and backward. His back legs are so muscular he can take two long leaps in a single second. And those back legs are strong enough that he can kick and stun even a skunk. But a cottontail rabbit's best defense is his sense of place. A rabbit lives his entire life on a few acres, and he comes to know every inch—every brush pile, wolf tree, hedgerow, stack of rocks, tree snag, hollow log, bramble, and hole in the ground. Game biologists describe the rabbit world as a series of "microenvironments." I don't like to be too obvious in drawing an analogy, but that sounded to me a lot like the world of Alex, Bobby, Lewis, and Carl.

Not long after my library visit, I was walking into a little strip-mall store where I went occasionally to buy Matt basketball jerseys for cheap, and I noticed Marty's hunting and fishing shop next door. I started wandering into Marty's to browse. I talked to Marty about shotgun shell loads and figured out that with my poor shooting I should be using heavy Number 6 shells. I anted up for hunting pants and jacket. I decided I needed to be a better shot, found a skeet range, and began killing clay pigeons, as I had done as a boy with my dad. In the summer that year, I kept asking Alex if he was seeing many rabbits in the fields. I didn't give any of this too much thought, though. It was all inauspicious counterpoint to my life in Washington.

I was having a blast, with great assignments and plenty of time to do them. But I also was learning lessons that had nothing to do with journalism. Raised as a blue-collar kid, I had come into Washington's world of power and influence with no training in the social niceties. Fortunately, by the time I had arrived at the *Post*, its tradition of hiring mostly Ivy Leaguers had waned, and informal ways of training self-made climbers like myself had emerged. My editor told me the story of the young reporter from the slums who'd been assigned to the *Post*'s fashion editor for a wardrobe makeover. By the time I met the man, he'd replaced his burnt-sienna suits with elegant, finely striped dark blues. I was told the story of the man who arrived his first day of work wearing a lime-green suit. He was told not to worry, he would be placed at a desk next to an electrical outlet. He never wore that suit again. In my case, a well-bred colleague took pity. She was a news aide and nearly a decade younger, but she started bringing me cataloges from Jos. A. Bank clothiers. She said Bank was a cut-rate Brooks Brothers. I took her advice.

The reeducation of the working class seemed to be going on all around me. I knew a reporter who collected a library of books on sailing, hoping to use his knowledge to weasel an invitation sailing on the Chesapeake with Bob Woodward. He succeeded. An Ivy League editor who was shocked that I'd never eaten steak tartare took me to the elegant Montpellier restaurant in the Madison Hotel and insisted I eat the dish on the *Post*'s expense account to remedy this cultural gap in my education. Our lunch cost fifty dollars. Woodward, who was Metropolitan editor then, balled out my editor for the extravagance. My editor later told me his dressing down from Woodward was worth it to him for me to have had the dining experience.

At the *Post*, I was introduced to the oh-so-sophisticated language of foreign phrases—*c'est la vie* and *je ne sais quoi* and *joie de vivre*, all of which I looked up after figuring out how to spell them. I learned to make *bons mots* and *beaux gestes*. Once, an editor I eventually came to like and admire corrected me when I told the woman who took phone messages for the newsroom that she needed some aide-de-camps to help her. "It's aides-de-camp," said Robert Kaiser, a Yale man with a vague archness forever in his voice. He later became the *Post*'s managing editor.

"Thank you," I said, actually meaning it.

For a time, I had an editor named Shelby Coffey III, who later became editor of the *Los Angeles Times*. He was a brilliant guy with the unusual habit of working the word "peregrinations" into as many conversations as possible. "Tell me about your peregrinations today, Walt," he'd say. I looked that one up, too, and henceforth told Shelby all about my travels. I gravitated toward colleagues from similar working-class backgrounds, and we chattered endlessly about these people and their affectations. A few of us even had a lunch club I dubbed "the BCBs," named ostensibly after Benjamin Crowninshield Bradlee but actually after our common pedigree: Blue Collar Boys. We'd eat, drink a Bud, and bitch about the *Post*'s prep-school brats, who, truthfully, were almost always hardworking and brilliant. I knew people at the *Post* from poor or working-class backgrounds who seemed unaffected by the cultural divide, who were, I suppose, confident enough to do their work well and leave it at that. But I also knew people who became obsessed with the social-class fissures, who were eaten up by resentment, who left the paper. I didn't know why at the time, but I had a good sense of humor about it all. I figured, well, when in Rome . . .

I began wearing seven-hundred-dollar Tallia suits, a considerable step up from Robert Hall's $49.99 merchandise. I gave up Thom McAn for Bally. I wore hundred-dollar Ike Behar shirts. A colleague told me he had his shirts handmade for about that price and gave me the name of his tailor. When wacky neckwear swept New York City, I began buying flashy ties that cost a good hundred bucks a pop. With Keran's help, I built a store of socks with intricate color patterns that picked up on the subtle stripes in my suits. I made sure I had several ties and pairs of socks that went with each suit. I didn't want to run the risk of lacking in variety. Finally, I began getting manicures. I had noticed that many of the men I wrote about displayed well-kept fingernails. If I noticed their nails, weren't they probably noticing mine? I had been at the *Post* nearly a decade when I realized one day that it had been years since I'd had one of those nattering conversations with the Blue Collar Boys about the *Post*'s prep-school brats. I realized I no longer attracted those kind of discontented people. I had crossed over to the other side.

About that time, I began mentioning to folks at the *Post,* to neighbors, and to people I knew around Washington that I'd taken up rabbit hunting—and it brought the craziest reactions. Mostly, people were appalled. I mean *disgusted.* You should have seen their contorted faces. Anybody who killed an animal for sport had to be unhinged or culturally retrograde. People's vehemence was nearly universal. I tried to explain but, at the time, I really didn't understand hunting's emerging appeal to me. I tried to tell about the Everlasting Stream, the men's friendship, Alex's boyhood, the moments of sensory alertness that seemed to make time stop. Still, people who had no problem eating ground raw beef tenderloin looked at me blankly, as if they'd just discovered an evil flaw in my character. Most people didn't even want to try to understand. They clung militantly to ignorance on this subject as if it were a virtue. I understood. I had thought that way myself only a few years earlier. A handful of people were vegetarians. But most who contorted their faces were happily dining on some of the 400 million chickens, 300 million turkeys, 85 million pigs, 35 million cattle, and 7 million sheep slaughtered in America every year. It wasn't slaughter that bothered them; it was hunters.

"Do you eat meat?" I asked people who insisted that hunting was wrong.

"Yes, but eating an animal and killing one for fun are two different things."

To such folks, a hunter's heart seemed unimaginably dark: "What kind of *person* enjoys killing an animal?" I was asked over and over. It didn't matter that I cooked my rabbits all sorts of ways—southern fried like Keran's mother had taught me; or slow-cooked with red wine, mushrooms, onions, and honey; or baked with potatoes and carrots and dusted with parsley and oregano; or Hawaiian-style with pineapple slices; or roasted in Middle American fashion and smothered with Campbell's mushroom soup; or boiled, baked, and de-boned for barbeque. What mattered was that I had admitted that I enjoyed going out into the fields with other men and, as a piece of human ritual, killing the rabbits myself. A man who touches the electric prod to the head of a hog in the slaughterhouse was forgiven because he killed for commerce, without emotion. To people who ran the city that ran the nation, the millions of Americans who hunted or accepted hunting were sadistic brutes. Behind all the moral posturing about the evils of hunting, it was really men like Alex, Bobby, Lewis, and Carl that my friends feared, distrusted, and disparaged.

When I wrote a short Sunday magazine article about going hunting—a quick throwaway story to help my editor fill an empty page—he got a disapproving note from the *Post*'s publisher himself, Donald Graham, a fine man who over the years sent me many notes of praise for stories I'd done. This time, though, he said my article was offensive. My editor told me, "Don doesn't like you this week." Not over a story on George Bush or Jesse Jackson or Jerry Falwell. Don Graham was miffed over a story on *rabbit hunting*.

Carl is a quiet, determined hunter. He doesn't like to chat. He wants everybody spread out, concentrating, ready to fire. But this morning behind B.C. Witt's, the dogs are working the tall wood casually, and even Carl's guard is down. Except for Earl, with his distinctly deep voice, and Alex's dog, Red, who is pretty much all red, I still can't tell one dog from another. Carl says it's easy and then amazes me with the precision of his knowledge: Earl has a dark back that turns brown at his shoulders and continues like a helmet over his head and ears. His white front legs are specked with brown spots. Bullet's back is black to the middle of his head and nearly all the way around his stomach. His legs are brown almost to his ankles, where they turn bright white. Shorty's back is black-saddled but turns stark white at the middle of his ribs and stays stark white to his toes. Rowdy's back is black, too, but she has a white spot behind her collar and a white girdle that separates her black back from her brown rump. Earl has that carnival barker voice. Bullet whimpers when he's searching for a trail but opens his lungs when he finds one. Rowdy's voice is squeaky but strong. Shorty has a weak, timid voice but that dog can hunt. Carl says Red's voice is of no matter. "He ain't worth a damn and he never will be." But Alex, stubborn as any dog, isn't about to admit he paid fifty dollars for a worthless hound and get rid of him. Carl thinks Red is teaching young Rowdy bad habits. About this, Carl is confident: "I know my dogs."

Early on, I decided Carl was the man to teach me something about hunting. Alex, Bobby, and Lewis always said Carl was stingy with his hunting knowledge because he didn't want anybody getting an edge on him in the rabbit count. I never found that to be true. I think Carl doesn't give men advice because they don't ask properly. Certainly, Alex, Bobby, and Lewis would never ask. Too proud. The men always say that if another hunter stands too close to Carl, he'll move away quickly, again so nobody can learn his hunter's secrets. Carl does joke a lot about how men who can't shoot worth a damn are often good shots when they hunt next to him and fire at the same rabbit at the same time, meaning of course Carl is doing the killing and they are doing the taking. With Alex, Bobby, and Lewis, I figure I'm about as likely to have shot the rabbit as any of them. If I get to it first, it's in my bag. Not with Carl. If we shoot at the same time at the same rabbit, it's Carl's rabbit. I'll even pick it up and hand it to him. I think Carl believes a man should show quiet respect for his betters. I have always done that with Carl, and he has taught me a lot about how much there is to know about something seemingly as simple as shooting a rabbit.

Even a novice rabbit hunter knows that a rabbit scared up and chased by dogs will usually circle around his few acres of territory and end up back where he started. If you wait patiently at one spot during the dogs' pursuit, good chance you'll get a shot. That's what everybody told me anyway. By hunting near Carl, however, by watching him, and, mostly, by asking questions, I learned plenty of variations on that theme. Some dogs track faster or slower, for instance, and if fast dogs push a rabbit too hard, he might panic, duck into a hole, and be gone, interrupting his natural circle. Or he might be scared out of his normal territory and run helter-skelter. Or, late in the hunting season when rabbits have been chased by dogs and coyotes and foxes, those that survive seem to learn to vary their instinctual pattern and run more unpredictably. Carl told me he once watched a rabbit run along the row of a harvested field with dogs in baying pursuit and saw the rabbit stop, jump sideways, land a couple rows over, reverse direction, and run right past the dogs. Because beagles trail by scent, they didn't even see the rabbit pass.

"I've actually seen that with my own eyes," Carl said.

He once saw a rabbit lay down a confusing spaghetti pattern of scent by running in crazy circles, dart out and back in several directions, and then, finally, take off, forcing the dogs to waste long minutes unraveling the snarl of scent. He saw a rabbit stop atop a hill, look back at the trailing dogs, and calmly lick his paws again and again, Carl believed, to weaken the scent he would leave on the ground behind him. He saw a rabbit run in a straight path the dogs could easily follow at full throttle. But then the rabbit stopped, hunkered down, let the dogs barrel past and tumble over one another while the rabbit bounded off in the opposite direction.

"A rabbit is a lot slicker than you think he is," Carl said. Just think about it: a gang of men with shotguns and a pack of howling dogs. "And the rabbit still gets away!"

When Carl was a young man, despite the common hunter's wisdom, he rarely posted after a rabbit had been jumped. He kept an eye out for the rabbit on the run but also kept doing his own dog's work by kicking brush piles and fencerows and walking through the thick edge growth that always separates fields from forests. "Even when the dogs was runnin' a rabbit," he said, "I never quit stompin'." Carl figured that doubled his chances of getting a shot. Now that he was old, Carl more often stood and waited for a shot. But I was young.

So I took Carl's advice and fared well. Once, as the dogs were chasing a rabbit, I kept stepping in and out of the edge foliage and scared out and shot two rabbits before I also shot the rabbit already up and running. I noticed how Carl almost always carried his gun in two hands across his chest no matter whether the dogs were running a rabbit or not. Carl said that was because probably a quarter of the rabbits killed are simply scared up unexpectedly as a hunter walks the fields. Keep your gun always ready, and you'll give yourself an extra shot or two every hunt.

"But mostly," Carl told me, "you got to listen to the dogs. When you learn your dogs, it's just like somebody singin'. You and me wouldn't sing alike. And once you really, really know your dogs, you know which dog is doin' the barkin'."

A man then must learn which barking dogs he can trust and which he can't. Some dogs are leaders. When they speak, you listen. Earl and Bullet are leaders. Ignore worthless Red. Rowdy's a good young dog but she'll yip on a cold trail, an old rabbit scent, which calls the other dogs over, interrupts their search for a hot trail, and sends you a faulty signal. And some dogs are what you call jump dogs. They just have a way of finding and scaring up rabbits, while some dogs aren't good at jumping but are fine at running trails. Know which is which, because recognizing the trustworthy voice of a good jump dog like Earl over the voice of the other dogs gives a hunter a second or two of early warning that a rabbit is up and on the run. Dogs also track better with moisture on the ground. A lot of hunters don't like to go out in heavy mist or light rain. That's a mistake. And remember the converse. Dogs have a hard time trailing in dry, warm weather. On those days, plan to do more stomping in and out of thickets and fencerows. If a strong wind is blowing, the dogs will be even more off their scent. Stomp harder still.

Carl's most profound advice seemed at first contradictory: Stay relaxed and alert at once. Relaxed enough to see the sweep of the foliage for flashes of movement within your wide field of vision.

Alert enough to see the foliage intently square foot by square foot. But remember that a man who relaxes too much will miss the motionless rabbit blending into the brush. A man who looks with too sharp a laser eye will miss the flash of a white tail at the edges of his vision.

"How do you do both at once?" I asked.

"You heard a sleepin' with your eyes open?" Carl asked.

Around my lessons in hunting, I also came to learn the story of Carl's life. He began hunting at an age when boys these days are still playing with unisex dolls. "I was born in the country," Carl told me. "The first huntin' I remember is Daddy ordering a single-shot .22 rifle from Sears, Roebuck for seven dollars and fifty cents. I've got a brother two years older. He carried the gun. I carried the game, about age seven. We'd walk around lookin' for rabbits, and if we seen one sittin', he'd shoot 'im and I'd bag 'im."

Hunting wasn't a pastime for Carl, his brothers, or his daddy, who eked out a living on a thirty-two-acre farm with a wife and seven children. Carl's daddy could sell a dressed quail to Glasgow's lawyers and doctors for a dollar each. In those days, the 1930s and early '40s, Barren County's sprawling countryside was wide open for a hunter, and Carl's daddy, carrying his nickel-plated Winchester shotgun, took his bird dogs out every day of the season. "The quail he killed, we didn't eat," Carl said. "We sold 'em. You'd take the money and buy somethin' else to eat." It was the job of Carl and his brothers to kill rabbits for the dinner table.

"We was huntin' to eat," Carl said.

Hunting, fishing, slaughtering cattle, chickens, and hogs were everyday life. Late each fall, Carl, his brothers, and father would go to their Uncle Virgil's house near Goodnight, a wide spot in the road six miles north of Glasgow, and slit the throats of two or three hogs, gut them, boil off their prickly hair in a giant black-iron scalding kettle, and chop and slice them into pieces that were then hung in the smokehouse for curing before warm weather in the spring. A boy got used to being slathered in blood. At age six Carl could twist the head off a chicken. At age nine, he was trapping opossums and skunks and skinning them for Daddy to sell their furs for a quarter and fifty cents each. A black skunk's fur was the prize of prizes: it brought a dollar.

"What'd you do about the stink?" I asked.

"You let it wear off."

This was premodern life. "Where we lived, they didn't have no refrigerator. Whatever game you killed, you ate." The banter among men was even more biting in those days. "If you missed a shot, you was gonna be punished with humor." So it was always good to have one feckless hunter along to make fun of. But the men never got angry. Carl remembered a time his uncle and his friends got into a dispute about who'd shot a particular rabbit. They finally decided his uncle had killed it. As Carl and his uncle walked away, the man laughed and told Carl he hadn't even fired his gun, which he never did tell his friends.

"Do you remember the first rabbit you ever shot?" I asked.

"Well, yeah, I do," Carl said.

Carl was eight years old and visiting Uncle Virgil, who let Carl hunt with his ancient Belgian 10-gauge double-barrel shotgun, as much a cannon as the sawed-off shotgun Alex's Uncle Troop had let Alex shoot as a boy. Carl got to go with the men, and when they came upon a sitting rabbit they were going to let Carl shoot it. "But there was this one guy, died about ninety-three years old. Anyway, the old fellow found one and called me to shoot it. I shot the rabbit, and he went and put 'im in his pocket. You know, for a little fellow, that really makes you sick. I'll never forget that. But everybody got to know what kinda guy he was. If you shot, he would take off runnin'. And if he got to the rabbit before you did, he might shoot in the ground and pick the rabbit up." The old man wasn't goofing with friends as was Carl's uncle when he kept that rabbit he didn't shoot. The old man was deceitful for real. "They finally cut him out of the huntin' crew," Carl said. For decades, Carl ran into that old man occasionally. They'd have a few friendly words. Every time, though, Carl remembered that the man had stolen his rabbit. For Carl, the lesson at age eight and today is the same: "You learn to stay away from guys like that."

By age thirteen Carl was hunting two, three days a week. He preferred rabbit hunting, because quail hunting was a lot of walking and not much shooting. A man also needed bird dogs and bird dogs were expensive. Rabbits were so plentiful then, you didn't need dogs. In the early fifties, out of high school and hunting with Lewis, Carl saw a man's rabbit dogs work a field for the first time. "I'd heard talk of how a rabbit would circle and come back, but I didn't believe it. The first time I seen a rabbit comin' back with dogs runnin' him, I thought that was about the most amazing thing I'd ever seen." Carl got himself a beagle pup—Joe. Then Lewis got a couple of pups. Bobby and Lewis had hunted opossum together as boys, but Bobby was gone to the army then, and Carl and Lewis hooked up. All year long, they'd take their pups out in the fields at dawn or dusk, when rabbits are feeding, and let the dogs run the rabbits, learn their trade. Sometimes, the young men would be out until ten at night trying to get those damned pups back to the truck. Carl, unlike most men, never hunted simply for companionship and relaxation. He hunted like his daddy, seriously. For Carl, hunting was a test of knowledge and skill by which he measured not only himself against other men but also the efficacy of his philosophy of life.

"In years back, I used to try harder is what it amounted to. You'll find some men drag assin' and some hustlin', and the hustlin' man usually does better. The last couple years, I ain't got the energy I used to. Times now I'll be by myself, and a rabbit will surprise me and get plumb away, and I ain't even got a shot off. I get tired faster. I noticed this year most of the times I went out I hunted two, three hours and quit. I used to go out early in the morning and stay out till dark.

I haven't done that in years." His friends just didn't take hunting that seriously. "Myself, I don't shoot near as good as I used to. But up until about twenty years ago, I was pretty tough in the field. I do think I intimidated other hunters. I had a reputation."

"Did you like that?" I asked.

"Oh, yeah. I earned it."

The day Carl first took me to the spring in the earthen bowl at the old Collins place, he mentioned the spring where he'd dipped water as a boy, and I said I'd like to see that spring someday. Carl remembered my request and sheepishly asked if I'd like to take a drive with him to find it. The place was a couple miles south of Temple Hill on Lyon School Road, just west of Shoal Creek. It was still country but the landscape looked nothing like Carl remembered it. The open fields and thickets, following the progression of all Kentucky farmland left to nature, had become forest. From the blacktop Lyon School Road, which was a dirt wagon-cut when Carl was a boy, he could discern the drive that had once led back to his house only because he knew where to look. We parked Carl's truck and walked the mile or so through the woods that led to the rear of the house. "It's funny how the place don't look just about at all the same," Carl said as we hiked along. "These woods is grown up to where I don't recognize nothin'."

We came to the house. *Good Lord!* I never imagined how hard Carl had grown up until I saw the house, a two-story, four-room shack built of unpainted, irregular oak boards probably milled from trees right off the land. The wide slits between the perpendicular planks were there even when Carl was a boy. The tin roof still looked pretty solid but the house was listing badly. The widows were popped, the doors gone. The house made the decaying tobacco barn at Lawson Bottom look shipshape. Inside, the place was a mess, a wasp hotel. Patches of decaying cardboard that had served as drywall and insulation were still tacked to the walls. Most of the wood flooring had been torn out, revealing the hay-covered crawl space where the dogs had slept. I didn't see any plumbing. Carl said there was none. At night, the family of nine used bedpans or went outside. No electricity, of course. The family burned a kerosene lamp, went to bed early, got up early. A little wood-burning stove was the house's only heat.

I thought of Carl's words: "We was huntin' to eat."

"I didn't know it was still here," Carl said of his house. "It's been many years."

"This was rough living," I said.

"At the age I was, I got nothin' but good memories."

In one of his rare references to the undercurrent of race in his life, Carl said that in his father's day a black man couldn't secure a $500 bank loan without a white person to co-sign. "It was hard," was all he said. We dawdled at the house, Carl not saying much. Then we headed down what used to be the drive from the front of the house to Lyon School Road. About a half mile along, down a gentle hill, just before the forest turned into a field somebody was keeping cut, we came to where Carl remembered the spring had been located. Sure enough, pushing aside the foliage that masked it, Carl found his spring, still making water. The planks Daddy had laid across it so Carl could dip were long gone. Carl said his father had dug the heart of the spring out so its pool was about waist deep, making it easy for Carl to submerge an entire bucket. I grabbed a stick and confirmed that his father's handiwork was still waist deep.

"Whew, that's cold water," I said.

"We didn't have no ice. That water was as cold as you were gonna get it."

As we drove back to town, I said, "You don't do that every day."

"No, you don't," Carl said, falling silent. Then he repeated himself. "No, you don't."

This morning, behind B.C. Witt's farm, Carl and I seem light-years away from his boyhood home. And I seem light-years away from life in Washington, which is yet another quantum distance from Carl's childhood. The men and I have worked our way out of the forest, east across the buzz-cut field, and then southeast to a pasture of timothy and orchard grass just northwest of Skaggs Creek at the far corner of another wood. At the ground beneath the young cherry, ash, and poplar trees is a jungle of succulent foliage so thick that only the dogs venture in. In seconds, three rabbits are up and running, and the shots begin.

"Toward you, Walt!" Carl hollers.

A rabbit breaks from the wood at a diagonal across and toward me. Goat shoots and misses. Alex shoots twice and misses. At the peak of one of the rabbit's long bounds I fire, and the rabbit drops. It's pretty rare that I kill a rabbit when the other men have missed, but I'll take the glory. When I get to the rabbit, it is lying on its side atop a bed of brown leaves, its front and back legs outstretched as if it were frozen just at the peak of its jump's arc. No blood. I stand and look at the rabbit and its legs and the leaves for a moment, knowing that I must pick it up before the howling dogs arrive and pounce. I've been hunting long enough now that I rarely feel any hunter's guilt. But sometimes, when a rabbit looks so animated, so alive, its eyes still moist with expression, I am reminded that I have made it dead, in truth, for my pleasure. Not for the pleasure of killing but for the pleasure of being with these men, in these fields and forests. And I feel guilty. Clearly, I haven't yet got the moral tangle of hunting unknotted in my mind. I pick up the rabbit by its hind legs, dangle it above the dancing dogs, and say, "Good boys."

"You get 'im?" Alex hollers, surprised.

"Of course," I say with feigned confidence and without a hint of what I was just thinking. Then, from the direction of Skaggs Creek, two young hunters, maybe nineteen or twenty years old, walk toward me. They're quail hunters without dogs, a hard go.

"Morning," one young man says. "Ya'll havin' any luck?"

"One bird, half a dozen rabbits."

"You got a quail?" the other young man asks.

"Yeah, we saw a bunch."

"Thanks," he says, excited, and they head off across the pasture.

Carl walks up. "Who were they?"

"Don't know. Two young guys. Like we used to be."

"Yep," Carl says, and he laughs out loud.

The Square

Now that I have learned about the childhoods of Alex and Carl, I'm curious about those of Bobby and Lewis. I try to imagine them as boys. This morning they stand together in the field, Bobby with his shotgun hitched up onto his left shoulder and parallel to the ground, his left hand wrapping the neck of the gun's butt, his right hand in the pocket of his hunting pants, the corner of his open jacket hanging heavy with a rabbit. He looks straight ahead through his tinted glasses, softly whistling some tune. Lewis stands a few feet to Bobby's left, his body turned slightly toward his friend, his gun in his right hand at his side, his left hand in his pants pocket, the corner of his hunting coat, which is empty of game so far, tucked behind his arm in the way gunslingers tucked their coats behind their holsters. Lewis is a talker, and he's looking at Bobby, talking. Lewis, too, wears tinted glasses, trifocals he bought recently. He believes they're why he isn't shooting well this year, but he hasn't told his friends because they'd laugh and moan and say he's making lame excuses. Bobby and Lewis, like Alex and Carl, look young for nearly seventy years old, their faces smooth and supple, their eyes bright. Haggard and frail they aren't. But when I try to conjure them up as boys in the fields near here, I get no image at all. Too long ago.

"Bobby and I been huntin' from about the beginning," Lewis once told me.

The beginning goes back to 1944, when Lewis's family moved across the street from Bobby. In the winter on Fridays and Saturdays, the boys, with Lewis's older brothers, headed out to hunt opossum on dark nights, which folklore claims are better than moonlit nights for hunting nocturnal opossum. They almost never *killed* a opossum, but they walked the woods many nights waiting for their farm dogs to announce that they had trapped one in a tree. On those rare nights, the boys would trace the barking, hold their lantern high behind their heads, and see two coal-hot eyes burning back at them. It was a while before Bobby realized that Lewis and his brothers always ended the night in Spillman's Woods, just behind their own house. That meant Bobby had to walk home a good mile in the dark. But Bobby didn't mind. He was a little boy packing it hard; he carried not only his .22 rifle but also a bayonet his older brother Shed had sent him from Europe.

"Bobby was *loaded*," Lewis said with awe. "I didn't have a gun yet."

This morning, we're hunting our way toward the Square, a few acres of tall forest bordered by Needmore School Road to the southwest, a Bush Hogged field to the southeast, an unkempt field rich in rabbit habitat to the northeast, somebody's yard to the northwest. We're walking through the Bush Hogged field that last year was so thick with the residue of prickly jimsonweed, floppy elephant's foot, and blackberry briars that we could barely yank through it. Carl says that while hunting alone last year he scared up quail here, shot two, but couldn't find them in the thicket.

Lewis rolls his eyes.

I change the subject. "I forgot my glasses the other day."

"Is that what the trouble was?" Carl asks, referring to my poor shooting.

I alter course again. "It's a little chilly."

"It's always chilly when you ain't gettin' nothin'," Carl says, persisting.

A rabbit suddenly scares up from the low grass at my feet and startles me—my punishment for not taking Carl's advice always to sleep with my eyes open. I get off a shot that kills dirt.

Damn! I think to myself.

"You get 'im?" Alex hollers.

"Winged 'im," I say.

Son of a bitch!

The rabbit bounds into the Square. I cross a garden of dormant mountain mint that boasts almost microscopic purple-flecked flowers in the summer and step up onto the four-foot rise that carries Needmore School Road past the Square. The dogs are wild in pursuit but through their ragged chorus, because of Carl's tutelage, I can now discern Earl's guttural yowls and Rowdy's shrill cries. I can also distinguish the voice of a pup Bobby has brought along to begin his schooling. My schooling has gone far enough that I can now hear the dogs' language complete with punctuation: the declarations of Earl and Rowdy, although in different intonations, end with exclamation points, while the yelps of the pup always finish with question marks.

The Square is important to me. It's where I got my first inkling of what Carl meant when he told me that I needed to hunt relaxed and alert at once. The Square is where I first began to recognize the difference between the way I usually go about sensing the world and the way, if I got my mind right, I could sense it as a hunter. This morning, the dogs in the Square have gone silent, and I step down off Needmore School Road into the wood. The forest on the land behind B.C. Witt's farm is mostly an upland wood, high and dry. The Square is a wetland wood, damp and populated by towering sycamores with their peeling white trunks rising more than a hundred feet, water elms with scaley bark curling in long bacon strips up their sides, a solitary sweet gum tree with gray and furrowed elephant hide. Almost all the sapling sprigs at the ground are spindly box elders, which love the moisture. The Square isn't my favorite forest. It's dank and dour and threatening, a place where the evil stepmother might have abandoned Hansel and Gretel.

I'd been hunting three or four years when one season I found myself walking the Square alone, the men somewhere behind or ahead of me. No dogs were howling. Except for the crackling of twigs under my boots, it was stone quiet, no distractions. The silence in this gloomy wood probably helped unwittingly create in me the simultaneously sedate and intent cast of mind Carl had described. Not the sensation of being deep in prayer or thought or meditation when you hear and see nothing around you. More the cast of mind when you are bearing down at sixty miles an hour on a traffic accident that has just happened ahead of you, when you have time enough to think about what you should do but not time enough to ponder it, time to glance quickly to the sides and into the rearview mirror, time to take a couple clicks to decide how hard to hit the brake or the gas or how sharply to turn the wheel, a long moment of heightened acuity, clarity, and oddly calm.

The rabbit appeared to me as a blur of motion at the left edge of my vision about twenty-five yards distant. I didn't turn my head to see it, but let the rabbit enter my field of sharp focus as I raised my gun. This is the kicker: I *heard* the rabbit as it hit the ground with each bound. I know that's impossible. I know it was my imagination. But I heard it. Several seconds seemed to run a minute. My gun followed the rabbit like the turning beam of a lighthouse, and I fired and killed the rabbit. I stood still for few moments because I realized something fresh had happened, that I had entered a room of sorts outside my experience, stood in that room, and stepped back out. I didn't know what had happened, but I knew it felt not exactly good but all-enveloping, a kind of sensory baptism. I had killed many rabbits by then. I knew the feeling of excitement, the rush of adrenaline, the momentary sense of pride after a good shot. The involuntary cheer. Not much different from the feeling I had rooting for my favorite ball team. This was different. Everything was quiet and clear and magnified—acuity and calm not as extremes but of a piece.

I thought of a time a few years earlier after my father's heart attack. I had traveled across the country and found him in the hospital unconscious and wired to every imaginable contraption, with electronic graphs running and beepers beeping. I'm not a deeply religious man, but that day I found myself in the hospital's tiny, darkened chapel on my knees, asking God to please spare my father's life. It was a moment of emotional nakedness I had never known. Whether spiritual or psychological, it was a moment of grace. In the Square that morning, I had reexperienced something like that moment, which baffled me. Only after a few days of contemplation did I realize that my moment in the hospital chapel also felt like the quiet moments I had spent with my wife and children, my hour at the Everlasting Stream, and all the other sublime moments of my life. Killing an animal as a moment of grace. Even I was taken aback at the thought.

I went home after that Thanksgiving and began reading about hunting. Hunters from Socrates onward have described an ethereal hunter's state of mental and emotional clarity. What nature writer James Swan calls the Zen of hunting—"a state of awe and reverence, which is the emotional foundation for transcendence." I thought of the philosopher William James on the instant of religious conversion: "The mysteries of life become lucid." A mindfulness that is easily comprehended through experience but hard to grasp through second-hand telling. Like prayer and love, joy and grief—you've got to be there. The psychologist Erich Fromm wrote that hunting frees a man from the "existential split: to be part of nature and to transcend it by virtue of his consciousness." The Spanish philosopher José Ortega y Gasset wrote that hunters experience the world as "an imitation of the animal" with heightened alertness to sounds, images, wind on the skin, scents in the air—what he called the "particular richness" of nature. By acknowledging that he has no idea what will happen in the next instant, by presuming nothing and remaining open to the unpredictable, a hunter enters a state of "universal attention, which does not inscribe itself on any point and tries to be on all points. . . . The hunter is the alert man." The Navajo's hunting wisdom, as evoked by writer Terry Tempest Williams: "Walk lightly, walk slowly, look straight ahead with the corners of your eyes open." That sounds pretty much like Carl's advice to sleep with your eyes open. Good advice for hunting, and for living. Yet all this Zen of hunting would have sounded ridiculously stilted to me—a rationalization for a blood-thirsty pastime—before the morning I killed that rabbit in the Square.

Imagine trying to make my friends in Washington understand.

The gap between my world in Washington and the alternate world of Alex, Bobby, Lewis, and Carl was by then awfully striking. I'd always been drawn to writing about the lives of ordinary people. Between articles on political notables, I'd done stories on the day-to-day life of a retarded man, a husband and wife whose son had committed suicide, a Christian fundamentalist family, a high school genius. I enjoyed writing about these people more than I enjoyed writing about the famous and the powerful. They had no product to sell, no votes to court. They didn't weigh every word for how it would sound in quotes. They weren't slick. When I wrote about ordinary people, I always felt I was giving readers something near the bone. My daddy didn't raise a fool, though; it was my stories on the famous and powerful that had gotten me attention, pay raises, and the freedom to do more or less what I wanted. Washington *is* power and politics, and the place and its way of thinking are seductive and addictive, or at least they were for me.

A small example: In one of the millions of internecine struggles over turf that went on between section editors at the *Post,* an editor on the National staff had argued that I, as a Sunday magazine writer, was too inexperienced a political reporter to be trusted to write about Vice President George Bush, then the next likely GOP candidate for president. I was told later that some nasty things were said about me. Ben Bradlee, however, decreed that I would do the story. After it ran, Ben called me into his office and asked, "So how's it feel to stick it to those guys on National?" I calmly told Ben I tried not to worry about such pettiness. He waved his hand to brush away my false piety, and said, "Yeah, yeah, but what's it *really* feel like?" There was no denying it. Ben knew exactly how I felt. I leaned forward and in a raspy voice said, "It feels fucking great!" He leaned forward, too: "I knew it did."

The town and town's ethic were growing on me. After George Bush was elected president, I wrote him and said I wanted to follow him through his administration and write a book about what it was like to be president of the United States. To my amazement, the president-elect invited me to his vice president's residence at the Naval Observatory to talk about my idea. I knew he wasn't just being polite. No one in Washington does anything just to be polite. As we sat in wing-backed chairs before a burning fireplace, George Bush told me that although I probably didn't know it, my profile of him had mattered in his run for the presidency. The story had dug deeply into his life and concluded that he wasn't the cartoon caricature that "Doonesbury" and Democrats made him out to be, that he was an accomplished, decent man. Bush told me that my article in the *Post* had forced other journalists around the country to rethink their takes on him. He had earlier mailed me a *Vanity Fair* magazine profile of him by journalist Gail Sheehy and included a handwritten note: "They're all going to school on you!! Amateur night though." I didn't take it all that seriously. Clearly, he did. George Bush said he would consider my proposal.

For months he considered. In the meantime, Keran and I were invited to the White House for Bush's first State Dinner in honor of Egyptian President Hosni Mubarak. I sat at a table with Secretary of State James Baker. Keran sat at a table with Bush's White House chief of staff John Sununu and Lynne Cheney, wife of future vice president Dick Cheney. The mingling portion of the evening brought us around to Chrysler's Lee Iacocca, Wall Street's Carl Icahn, starlet Cheryl Ladd, Supreme Court Chief Justice William Rehnquist, jazz legend Lionel Hampton. The first lady wore a silver-white Bill Blass. Keran wore an elegantly beaded ecru gown she'd bought at Lord & Taylor on half-price sale for six hundred dollars, more than she'd ever paid for an article of clothing. When she was at the mirror in the White House ladies' room, Lee Iacocca's date, Darrien Earle, said to her, "Oh, I love your dress." Keran, swept up in the moment, answered, "Yes, I'm so pleased with it." In the receiving line in the White House East Room, President Bush told Keran she was lovely, then looked at me in my tuxedo. "Walt," he declared, "you clean up real good."

At dinner, we drank La Crema Reserve Chardonnay, ate smoked salmon mousse, rack of lamb persillade, and asparagus with noisette butter, which I cut with my knife and began eating with my fork before noticing others who were using their fingers. It turned out that etiquette allows asparagus stalks firm enough to lift without bending to be eaten with the fingers. My little faux pas reminded me of a time I had eaten lunch with George Bush at his vice president's mansion, and I had mistakenly taken salad from the server's bowl and placed it on my dinner plate. When Bush took the tongs for himself, I thought I could see him momentarily wondering if he should follow suit to keep from embarrassing me. He put his salad on his salad plate.

I said nothing. *C'est la vie.*

President Bush and I met again and again to talk about my book idea. I had a power breakfast at the elegant Hay-Adams Hotel across Lafayette Square from the White House with National Security Adviser Brent Scowcroft, White House Counsel C. Boyden Gray, and the president's son and future president himself, George W. Bush, to talk about the project's details. The president invited Keran and me over for a picnic gathering in the White House East Garden, where we ate tamales. President Bush asked what I had been doing lately, and I mentioned that I had been skeet shooting the other night, trying to bone up so I could shoot better when I went cottontail rabbit hunting next Thanksgiving with Keran's father and his friends in Kentucky. President Bush said he had hunted jackrabbits when he lived in Texas, but that he'd never hunted cottontail rabbits. He asked what kind of gun I used, and I said a 12-gauge shotgun. He said that jackrabbits, which sit still at a long distance, were hunted with a rifle. Then we talked about which gun required the greater marksmanship, and he decided it was the rifle. I decided to agree. After dinner, we all watched *When Harry Met Sally* in the White House theater. It was a little strange being at the White House while sitting through Meg Ryan's fake-orgasm scene.

As Keran and I were about to leave later that evening, President Bush pulled Keran aside and told her to tell me that he had decided to allow me to do the book and would be in touch. For days, I was riding on air, planning to get a couple-million-dollar book advance, leave the *Post,* and spend at least the next four, probably eight years, shadowing the president of the United States. Talk about seductive. But President Bush later changed his mind. He decided too much confidential information was floating around the White House to give me free rein.

"I am very, very sorry," the president wrote to me.

I was sorry, too. Very, very sorry.

The last time I saw President Bush was more than three years later at a party during his final White House Christmas season. Toward the end of the evening, George W. found Keran and me in the crowd of several hundred people and said that his father wanted us to come up to the residence after the party. As Barbara Bush gave us a tour, President Bush and I fell behind a few steps in the foyer outside the Lincoln Bedroom, and I took the opportunity—even though I knew I wasn't being an impartial journalist—to say I was sorry he had lost his reelection bid. He stopped and looked straight at me. "You know the worst thing about it, Walt?" he said. "The embarrassment. It's just so embarrassing." That night, President Bush told me that during his years as president, he had sometimes thought to himself while making a decision, "I wish Walt were here to get this down." I didn't say it, but by then I had thanked God that President Bush hadn't let me do that book.

Bobby joins me in the Square, which he has been hunting for decades. He once shot a rabbit bolting along Needmore

School Road with his .22 pistol—third shot, right front shoulder. "Me and old Lewis, on a Sunday," Bobby said. "I don't know if Lewis remembers it." What Bobby meant is that Lewis might not *want* to remember it and have to admit Bobby made a good shot.

Bobby began hunting when he was eight. He remembers exactly because when he and Leon, the family friend with whom Bobby lived after his father died, got home from the field that first day of hunting—December 7, 1941—Ms. Carrie said the Japanese had bombed Pearl Harbor, which Bobby at first thought was a woman's name. Leon, like Carl's daddy, was a quail hunter. But in Bobby's house they ate the quail, which Leon's mother plucked. When Bobby went into the field with Leon, Bobby carried Leon's .22 rifle. As it was for Alex and Carl, Bobby's real job was to fetch and tote dead game. Once in a while, he got to shoot a walnut off a tree. But Bobby practiced and got to be a crack shot at popping beer cans laid on their sides.

"It only counted if you hit the spout hole, not the can," Bobby said.

When Bobby was twelve, he bet Ms. Carrie's brother, Lindsey, that he could beat him shooting cans. Poor Lindsey put up his new .22 rifle. Bobby won that gun, and more than a half century later he wheezed with laughter at the memory. "Lindsey didn't have but one eye," said Bobby, who still has the rifle today. Bobby loved living on the farm with Ms. Carrie and Leon. Bobby laughed and said the only strange thing about living in the country instead of Glasgow's segregated Kingdom was that when he walked along the road to get to school every morning, white kids would ride past in their bus and holler obscenities at him. About age twelve, Bobby began hunting quail with Leon, carrying his old double-barrel shotgun. The first quail Bobby killed, he accidentally pulled the triggers of both barrels at once. All Bobby found amid the feathers that fluttered to the ground were the quail's legs. Leon later gave Bobby his first beagle pup, Gal, who became the best jump dog Bobby has ever seen work a field. "If she barked three times, you knew she'd started a rabbit," Bobby said. Leon knew his dogs and he knew hunting. "I never learned everything Leon knew," Bobby said with reverence. "I never did get as good as Leon."

When Bobby was home visiting from the military as a young man in the early fifties, he was hunting with Leon up near Coral Hill, and they ran into Lewis, who was hunting with Carl. Bobby knew Carl, but not well. The chance hello got the men hunting together. Even then, Bobby was what he called a lazy hunter, which made him the perfect partner for the peripatetic Carl. Bobby didn't like stomping through briars, climbing fences. He didn't care if Carl got more rabbits. He enjoyed being in the fields and woods because they made him thoughtful. No doubt, Bobby's always been the thinker of the bunch, a man with an informed opinion on just about everything. The men tease him about being a know-it-all, but they don't very often debate him. On my visits over the years, Bobby always grilled me about politics in Washington. He often wanted to talk about whether I believed the experts who believed in global warming. Bobby was a news junkie. He once asked me if I'd felt the mild earthquake back at my house a couple of days earlier.

"What earthquake?" I asked.

Bobby was incredulous. "It was all over the news."

As Bobby and I walk on through the Square, the dogs howl outside the wood where the other men are hunting—two shots. Alex hollers that he has killed a rabbit.

"I missed 'im," Matt says when Bobby and I reach him and Carl.

"Never say you missed 'im," I say. "Say you slowed 'im down."

"No," Carl corrects. "Say you got 'im before the next guy who claimed 'im."

We hunt across the unkempt field to the northeast and then across a pasture that used to be a cedar forest. You can tell because every year fledgling cedars sprout up from the root nation that lives beneath the deceptively clear ground. We're spread out in a flying-V formation that allows everyone the most room to shoot. Birds rise and settle, rise and settle as the dogs work ahead of us. No barking.

When I now scan the landscape with more than a decade of hunting behind me, I see collections of details, not washes of color. I've learned, as the men say, "to read the land." The language of the land tells me the ground before us is prime rabbit real estate. Its foliage is diverse— goldenrod, ironweed, deer tongue, honeysuckle. In the middle of this rabbit restaurant is an island of tall cedar, cherry, and willow trees that protect rabbits from airborne predators. Beneath the trees are blackberry brambles that protect them from ground predators. The island then rises to the top of a steep hill where a plentitude of sumac saplings will always feed rabbits during long and snowy winters. The dogs enter the thicket at the foot of the island. Matt and I take the eastern side of the slope ahead of the dogs, hoping they will drive any rabbits out front. By the time we hike to the top, I'm winded. Matt looks as if he isn't even breathing.

Alex shoots. "I think I clipped 'im," he says.

Matt, who has learned from the masters, says, "He was runnin' pretty fast for wounded."

The dogs trail the rabbit to a pile of old tires. I've never heard dogs so mutually frenzied, at least not since my first morning years ago when the bunch of dogs now long dead was atop that pile of cedar logs, digging, scratching, and yowling. The dogs are beyond barking. They're screeching, fingernails on a blackboard. But through the noise I notice that I can still hear birds chirping nearby. Somehow, they know that all this violent commotion is not threatening to them.

"The dogs can see that rabbit," Carl says, just as the rabbit breaks from the pile.

Matt fires.

"Got 'im!" Matt hollers, showing the most animation I've seen in him in a long time.

"Quickdraw!" Alex shouts, in about the only hunting compliment I've ever heard him give.

Another rabbit bolts—*shot, shot, shot.* Lewis puts the dead rabbit in his bag.

"Me or Bobby got 'im," Goat says, laughing. "Lewis picked 'im up."

"Lewis didn't shoot," whispers Matt, who was standing next to Lewis.

"Hey, Lewis," I say, "now you're killin' rabbits just lookin' at 'em."

"I tell ya what, everybody shot my rabbit up, that's what happened."

There is laughter all around.

"Matt," Lewis says, appealing to the wrong guy, "you heard me shoot, right?"

Lewis grew up about as hard as Carl. His boyhood house is still standing thirty miles southeast of Glasgow, just past Marrowbone where Burkesville Road meets Mole Hill Road. The field around the place is still thick with chigger weeds in the summer, as it was when Lewis was a boy. When he and I visited, I wore Off! on my socks and pants legs. When Lewis was a kid, he rubbed lamp oil on his ankles, which worked fine against the chiggers and cleared his sinuses, too. I parked in front of the big house where the land's owner, a white man, had lived when Lewis was a boy. He walked up to the front door and asked permission for us to inspect the old house. When he got back, Lewis said that even after sixty years he still felt uncomfortable knocking on the front door—as blacks, he and his family had always known to knock on the back door. Lewis's single-story house is a mess, its tarpaper faux-brick siding peeling and its roof rusting. It's maybe twenty-by-thirty feet. Lewis and his four brothers slept in one room. The house sits beneath a small mountain where Lewis's daddy hunted rabbit, groundhog, quail, and dove. In the winter, Lewis and his family lived on hunted game. The family had one shotgun, and only Lewis's father used it. His daddy, a sharecropper who raised tobacco, couldn't afford to waste shells. As did his friends when they were boys, Lewis tagged along behind and fetched and lugged the game.

Like Carl's family, Lewis's had no refrigerator. His daddy shot only what they could eat. Some days he didn't shoot at all because their dog Dusty, a German shepherd and collie mix, would catch rabbits in his mouth and drop them at Daddy's feet. Dusty chased a rabbit so hard once the rabbit ran into a tree and knocked himself out. When Lewis moved near Bobby and they started opossum hunting, Bobby had the necessary .22 rifle. So Lewis and his brother Paul pooled their money and bought an old 12-gauge shotgun from the Reverend Bransford, who was minister at Glasgow's First Baptist Church. After that, Lewis began hunting rabbits with his dad.

"My dad was a good hunter," Lewis said solemnly. "I learned to hunt from my dad."

Then Bobby went off to the military, and Carl and Lewis took up hunting together. Lewis got excited just talking about those days. "Me and Carl used to go out and the rabbits didn't have a chance. We been huntin' fifty years. I been huntin' with Bobby and Carl longer than I been married." Although Lewis couldn't really afford it then, he bought himself a new Remington 12-gauge. "Carl had old Joe for a dog, and I had Judy and Lady. Everybody brags on their dogs, but we had some dogs—Big Foot, Bingo, Whitey, Queenie. Carl had a little dog, Jack, oh, he was good. And that basset hound Carl raised for Bobby when he was in the service, what was his name? Bo. We had good dogs then, 'cause me and Carl used to run 'em all summer. In winter, they was *ready.*

"I got a dog now, Trouble, that me and Carl was talkin' 'bout the other day. If we were able to hunt him like we used to hunt, we'd have a heck of a dog. Trouble'll go another five, six years. When old Trouble goes, I won't have no more dogs. Look, we were out huntin' the other day, and Carl got his foot hung up in a barbed-wire fence, and I had to get the fence off 'im." Lewis paused to laugh. "I don't feel too old to hunt, but huntin' makes you feel too old to hunt."

Then Lewis surprised me. "Why do you like to hunt, Walt?"

I thought for a moment. "It's the story within the story of my life."

At that, Lewis went uncharacteristically speechless, only nodded.

It has gotten warm this late morning, maybe sixty degrees, not a cloud. We've hunted through the island of trees. I've killed two rabbits and a quail, my first ever. Bobby, Alex, and Goat have each killed a rabbit or two. Lewis has his contested rabbit. Carl has two. Matt is high man with three. Matt and Alex are still laughing about Lewis claiming that rabbit.

"Lewis ain't fired a shot yet," Alex says.

We head out on the long walk across the fledgling cedar pasture toward the trucks. I pass a tree beneath which the ground is littered with walnuts turned black and mealy. I pass parched animal bones strewn randomly across the hillside by scavengers. I hear birds chirping and my own breathing and my feet scraping against the short weeds, and my breathing and stepping fall into sync. At the trucks, we take off our jackets and empty our guns, which *sha-shunk* as each shell pops into our hands or onto the ground. Carl whistles for the dogs, but Bullet is still hunting, and we settle in around Bobby's tailgate. Alex passes around a Wild Turkey bottle that I know he has secretly refilled with Rebel Yell whiskey. Nobody notices. Or at least nobody mentions it.

I think about my quail, the first I've ever killed. "How do you clean a quail?"

"Same as a rabbit," Carl says.

"Or you can pluck it," Bobby says.

"What's the difference between plucking and skinning?"

"The flavor," Bobby says.

"More flavor in the skin?"

"Like a chicken," Bobby says. "Didn't I tell ya Leon's mother plucked his quail?"

I nod yes and then lift a mangled rabbit from the tailgate. "Who shot this rabbit?"

"That's the one everybody but Lewis shot," Matt says.

"That rabbit is *dead*," Alex says.

Everyone goes quiet.

Then Alex notices what only Alex notices. "Have you ever seen a sky this beautiful?"

Carl scans the stark blue heavens. "We're havin' some good weather."

Bobby jumps in. "It's global warming."

Nobody speaks. Nobody will debate Bobby on global warming.

"I'll get Bullet," Carl says, and he ambles off to collect his dog.

Lewis's Garage

Lewis's garage should be in the Smithsonian. Think of a replica of Abraham Lincoln's law office with the inkwell and fountain pen atop his desk; or the workshop of the Wright brothers; or a nineteenth-century prairie schoolroom with McGuffey's readers on the desks, a paddle on the wall, the alphabet written neatly on the chalkboard. Living snapshots. Life as it used to be, frozen, so to speak, in mid-sentence. Lewis's garage looks pretty much like any garage on the outside—room for two pickup trucks, a peaked roof, old clapboard siding. But enter through the side door, step down onto the dirt floor, let your eyes adjust to the shades of darkness that expand from the bare lightbulb, and you've entered a lifelong conversation in mid-sentence.

"Is this your clubhouse, Lewis?" I ask.

"Yeah, yeah," says Lewis in that accelerated way he speaks.

"This is the huntin' lodge," says Gerald, Carl's brother-in-law visiting from the city.

"I don't know which rabbit is mine," I say, "but I'm cleaning this one. Matt, pitch in."

"Matt didn't get a rabbit," Carl says. "No use a man cleanin' if he didn't get a rabbit."

"I thought low man cleaned," Alex says.

"Rules change," says Matt, who's leaning against a post holding a Pepsi.

"That man is finally sharpenin' up," Carl says, and everybody laughs.

I have come to love hearing the men laugh. After all the years, if I were blind I'd still know the men by their laughs. Carl's bass laugh booms from his ribs and vibrates the room like a big truck down-shifting gears and rattling the windows. Alex's baritone laugh ema-nates from about his Adam's apple and then squeezes brightly through a tight throat. Bobby's higher-pitched tenor laugh is faster and more insistent. Lewis's laugh, a countertenor laugh, the falsetto of laughs, the most infectious laugh of all, makes a piercing instrument of his sinuses. When the men all laugh together, as when their dogs hunt, they are a choir of still distinct voices.

This morning, Lewis's garage is bathed in a golden hue because, after better than a half century of seasoning, the oak wall planks and oak studs, the oak six-by-six post that shoulders the oak ceiling beam, the oak joists, and the oak roof have all deepened to a mellow amber about the color of the cigar tucked in the left corner of Carl's mouth. My friends have aged as gracefully as the oak beams, although Carl and Bobby do seem to be aging in reverse directions: Carl's body has got-ten thicker and his face rounder; Bobby's body has gotten leaner, his face narrower. The bodies of Alex and Lewis seem unchanged, still fit, although age has settled deeper beneath their eyes and in their voices. This morning, with all the brown hunting pants, jackets and overalls, the men's brown hands and faces, and the brown dirt floor tramped down as hard as rock, Lewis's garage glows like an Indian summer. In the middle of the floor, sitting on end, is a two-foot-high chunk of cedar log a foot or so in diameter. A piece of plank is nailed across the log's top for use as a makeshift cutting board. Nearby is a water bucket for soaking rabbits before cleaning and a water bucket for rinsing carcasses after cleaning. Next to the buckets is a silver aluminum pail, the gut bucket, streaked with dried blood inside and out from years of skin-ning and gutting. We stand in a circle around the pails, rabbits dangling from our hands. As we work, we dip our knives into the water and, with a few jerks of the wrist, splash them clean, which sends tiny rockets of water exploding onto the dirt and our boots, spotting them. As the water turns bloody, the spots get darker. The garage soon smells of guts, which I must now think about to even notice.

In a matter of minutes, the carcasses are rinsed and bagged and set aside, and the silver bucket is heavy with skin, fur, feet, heads, ears, eyes, and innards in about a dozen glistening shades of red. The bucket sits center stage as the men rinse their knives one last time, wipe both sides of the blades on their pants, fold them shut or sheath them, and settle in, leaning against posts or workbenches or walls, Gerald sitting on the cutting stump. I head to the fridge.

"Any you guys want some a Lewis's beer?"

When the men get rolling and I am listening, I no longer feel lost inside a Frederick Wiseman film—all detail and dialogue, no context. I now know the context. Listening to the men is like watching a pinball bounce around its board. The action is impossible to predict but it isn't random. The point is to relax and let my time with the men wash over me in the way that a Christmas midnight Mass with candles and organ and incense would wash over me as a boy. The meaning of that Mass was never in the priest's words but in the unchanging and unspoken sense of it all. The meaning of the men's time together isn't really in their words either but in what is also unchanging and unspoken: the affection and lilt and sweet indulgence of their friendship.

As I hand out cans of Busch, I say, "Lewis, did you check the size a that shot?"

"Oh!" Lewis says, frowning as if he's sorry he forgot.

Hunting this morning, Alex and Lewis shot at a rabbit at the same time. Alex got to the dead rabbit first and claimed it over Lewis's objection. Lewis shoots a 12-gauge shotgun and Alex shoots a 20-gauge. Lewis swore he could tell which man hit the rabbit by examining the shot pellets in the dead rabbit's body. All morning, Lewis and Alex went back and forth about who shot that rabbit. Matt kept track of the contested rabbit so the men could settle the debate later. Then Lewis supposedly forgot about it, probably because neither man really wants to know who shot the rabbit, which would end the dispute; now it can go on for years.

"That rabbit's *not* in dispute," Alex says.

"It is! It is!" Lewis says.

"When I shot," Alex insists, "that rabbit tumbled."

Carl frowns. "It's pretty hard to hit a rabbit in the back when he's comin' straight at you."

Alex wisely moves the spotlight. "Walt, you have any long shots today?"

Everybody laughs, and I think of how Carl's daddy and his friends always liked to have at least one feckless hunter along in the field so they'd have somebody to make fun of. This morning, when a rabbit broke between Goat and me, Goat shot. I was just then pulling my trigger, and at the instant the rabbit fell dead, I shot, killing Goat's rabbit, well, twice. I didn't try to claim the rabbit. I even apologized for tearing up its meat, but I got laughed at plenty.

"Walt," Alex said in the field, "you shot Goat's rabbit."

"Goat and I almost shot together," I answered, which wasn't the best reply.

"Don't get too close to Walt!" Alex hollered. "He'll shoot *almost* when you do."

Bobby takes me off the hook with a story. He once knew a man who ran so fast he could catch up to a deer, stick his finger in the deer's ass, crook his finger, stop the deer cold, then reach around and cut its throat. By the time the man was ninety, he'd slowed down. He could still catch up to the deer and get his finger in its ass, but he was too old to crook his finger, and the deer always slipped away. After the laughter, Alex says, "Walt allows Matt to hear that stuff. I don't." Matt, who knows his grandfather is a maestro of foul language, smiles but stays quiet.

I study Matt, so much a man now, and think of the times I've found myself looking at him and absently whistling the old Harry Chapin song "Cat's in the Cradle," about a father whose ambition causes him to miss most of his son's childhood and leaves them distant and the father lonely and regretful when the boy is grown. In my rational moments, I don't really feel that way about Matt. Despite my hectic schedule, my career and affluence allowed me to spend many more hours with him than my working-class father could spend with me. When I was a young man, my dad once wrote me a letter that said, "If I had it to do over again, I would somehow find more time to spend with you. It seems we never realize this until it's too late." My father rarely gave me direct advice, and I heard what he was saying. Not only did I coach Matt's ball teams, but we had good seats for the Washington Wizards and Baltimore Orioles. In nice weather, we took walks every morning before I dropped him at school, stopping to examine flowers and leaves, bringing home rocks he found interesting. When it snowed, we built snowmen with gravel eyes and mouths, carrot noses, and stick arms. We spent hours throwing balls, shooting baskets, racing around in the speedboat. We hunted rabbits every Thanksgiving. Now that Matt's nearly grown, though, I still feel the way my father felt a generation ago: it wasn't time enough.

The years from when I gave Matt his BB gun at age eight to today in Lewis's garage have passed in a blink. But I don't think any set of memories I have of Matt and me together are stronger and clearer than my hunting memories. Matt was just ten when I first let him shoot his grandfather's old single-shot .410. He'd been target shooting with Alex's .22 rifle for a couple years. I had Matt shoot sides of cardboard boxes with the .410 so he could see the wide pellet pattern a shotgun made and realize how lethal it was. I had him walk along as if he were hunting, his gun held in two hands across his chest, and then I'd yell, "Rabbit!"—and he'd turn to the target, raise his gun, and fire. Alex had a portable trap machine like my dad had when I was a boy, and Matt got so he could easily hit a clay pigeon arcing away from him. He learned to click off the trigger safety as he raised his gun to shoot and then always, no exceptions, to flick it back on as he lowered his gun after firing. Then we ventured into Bobby's fields and forest, where I played hunting dog and kicked briars and brush piles to scare out rabbits.

Matt was a quick study. He listened attentively, didn't show any of the skeptical cockiness that sometimes crossed his face when I told him how to hold a baseball bat or shoot a free throw. Like most kids, Matt cut corners when he cleaned his room, washed the car, or mowed the grass. He fussed and whined when I made him pick up the toys he'd stuffed in his closet, wipe away missed dirt on a fender, trim closer around the trees. Yet he never fussed when hunting. He seemed to understand intuitively that a shotgun in hand was a scary business. His maturity seemed to rise to what was demanded of him. The first animal he killed was a red squirrel. We took it to the taxidermist and had it stuffed and mounted, put it on his bedroom shelf. The last Thanksgiving with the .410, the year before Matt graduated to his 12-gauge, I didn't hunt with the men. I knew it was the last year of hunting alone as father and son. I knew that next year Matt would have four teachers who knew much more than I.

That Thanksgiving, I left my gun behind and took Matt out on Bobby's farm every day. Matt wore an orange cap and one of his grandfather's old hunting jackets that had shrunk when it was washed. Matt's once lithe, angular body had by then taken on the thicker, rounded contours of the last stages of prepubescence, but his grandfather's shrunken coat was still too big, and he looked puny tucked inside, like a boy play-dressing at being a man. But he could shoot by then, and he killed three rabbits. I used the outside faucet at the rear of Alex's house, filled a bucket with cold water, grabbed an empty gut bucket, and lugged them over to the wood behind Bobby's house, where I turned a trash can upside down and plopped one of the carcasses atop the can's bottom. Matt had an expectant look on his face, and I knew he was wondering if I was going to clean his rabbits. I took out my knife and handed it to Matt.

"You want me to clean 'em," he said, not as a question but as a statement.

"You killed 'em."

Without defiance, Matt said, "Okay."

Matt had cleaned rabbits before, but always with Alex, Bobby, Lewis, and Carl hovering like a collection of gruff mother hens, giving directions, reaching in and pulling out the anal tube over which Matt had hesitated, grabbing the carcass and cutting slits over buried pieces of shot, digging them out with their knife tips. "Here, let me show you," one of them would say, and Matt would gladly hand over his rabbit for the demonstration. Which meant Matt had never cleaned a rabbit by himself. I got a beer from the antique Coke machine that Alex keeps outside next to his old-timey garage, sat down at a picnic table, and lit a Fuente. I tend to be a talker, don't like long silences among people, figure folks ought to have something worthwhile to discuss. Matt's more like his mother, who can go for long stretches without her or anybody uttering a word. But I'm sometimes keen enough to recognize times when I should shut up, and that was a time.

Matt never spoke, never asked advice. He worked slowly but insistently through the mess, twisting off the rabbit's head, pulling off its fur garment, shaking down its innards, poking the tip of the knife through the soft skin at its rectum and skimming the knife up to its chest. It was as if the blade were slicing water, so smooth. Matt paused but didn't gag, reached his fingers into the cavity above and behind the heart and scooped the warm organs down and into the bucket. Relieved and confident that he had mastered the logistics, Matt began to talk: "Dad, remember when you were on top of that big brush pile at Bobby's property line, and I could see the rabbit under you but he wouldn't flush, and I asked, 'Should I shoot 'im?' And you said, 'As long as you don't shoot me instead.' And that long shot I had back by the pond at the pig fence?" Matt then tossed an exclamatory nod my way: "Good shot, eh?"

"Not bad for a beginner," I said.

"Grandpa says you can't hit the broad side of a barn."

"You seen Grandpa shoot lately?"

"He says he used to be a better shot."

"'Used to be' is the operative phrase there."

It went on like that through three rabbits, Matt chatting and laughing while his hands glided through the gruesome motions of turning an animal into food. When I look the word "contentment" up in the dictionary, I find a picture of me watching Matt on that morning. A few lines of poetry by Raymond Carver come to mind: "Happiness. It comes on unexpectedly. And goes beyond, really, any early morning talk about it." I suppose the same sensations could have been as powerfully evoked in me while we walked back to the car after a Little League game, or while standing in the chow line at a Washington Wizards game, or while flying over waves on the South River. But they weren't, at least not for me. I don't know exactly why. The cold air on my face, the isolation, the wretched stench, the gory refuse, the baffling exaltation that comes with the killing, the acquired ability to be cheerful in the face of that disturbing knowledge—it all adds up to a kind of human riddle without a certain answer, perfectly imperfect. In those moments, I always felt I was as fragile as the rabbit I had killed and just as small in the big scheme of things. I felt as close to being without smugness as I've ever felt. Being at the nexus of life and death made me humble. I wondered if it made Matt humble, too. After he had cleaned his last rabbit, Matt got a bottle of Coke from his grandfather's machine, pushed the brim of his hat high on his head, sat down at the picnic table, anchored his elbows, and unleashed an ironic smile: "Bring your gun next time, Dad, and let's see who shoots better."

Those years just before Matt turned fourteen and began hunting with the men had been years of yearning for him. We were men. He was a boy. Matt has his own parallel memories of my memories of Alex and me getting ready to hunt in the mornings. Yes, Matt remembers climbing out of bed and walking through the dark house to the kitchen where Alex and I were lacing our boots, drinking coffee, and eating breakfast. When we were gone, he thought about us constantly. He always played in the den, where the big French doors assured that he would see us when we returned. He'd throw on his jacket and race out to the barn. Whatever it was that occurred during the hours we were gone, in Matt's mind, was the difference between being a boy and a man. I didn't realize how strongly he felt the distinction, and I don't remember feeling it so strongly myself as a boy. Even when Matt was killing rabbits with his .410, he still felt the stigma of being a boy instead of a man. He once went with me to buy .410 shells at Kmart, where a man at the counter said, "I don't know about hunting rabbits with a .410, that's a really hard shot. I don't know if I could hit it." I told the man that Matt had killed two rabbits with his .410 that morning. Matt didn't say anything but he was trying to figure out his place: "I'm twelve and you're forty, and I can hit shots you can't. But I'm a kid and you're a man."

When I took Matt out and bought him his Mossberg 12-gauge, he was cool about the whole deal. But inside he was excited as hell. "Finally, I was going to get a chance to hunt with the men." He knew he was going to be hazed for wearing new clothes without bloodstains, for missed shots. "I was going to be the butt of most of the jokes, but that was okay because I was going to be going to Lawson Bottom." Matt, who in the year before he began hunting with the men had sprung up several inches and begun to go from round to lean, got up even before Alex and I on his first morning, dressed in his new hunting clothes, went outside in the dark chill, looked up, saw the constellation Orion, and knew even then that it was Orion the Hunter.

Matt thought to himself, "I'm going to have a good day."

As soon as we got to Lawson Bottom at the Everlasting Stream near Reid's house, somebody told Matt the story of the day we killed somewhere between seventeen and twenty-seven rabbits and cleaned them in the stream. Bobby told Matt the story about how Alex had once fired three errant shots at a rabbit coming straight at him near Roseville Road, then swung his empty gun like a golf club trying to hit the rabbit but missed. Matt looked calm, but he was afraid to shoot and miss because he knew the men would joke about him, and he was cautious for fear of shooting somebody. He got no rabbits that morning, and Carl and Bobby kept saying that low man cleaned. "I thought I was actually going to have to clean all the rabbits." Of course, low man never really cleans all the rabbits, but Matt didn't know that yet. Besides, he figured cleaning all the rabbits was fine with him: "I was finally hunting with the men."

For the first couple of Thanksgivings after that, I was always suggesting that Matt take off his jacket in the heat or be careful not to cut himself with a gutting knife. I asked if he'd brought his hunting license, if he'd flicked his safety back on after a shot. I reminded him to point his gun at the ground or the sky, suggested where he stand to get the best shot as we surrounded a field where the dogs were working. In his third year of hunting with the men, Matt told me he really didn't mind me suggesting where he stand, because he knew I was trying to help. But now that he usually killed more rabbits than I did, maybe he should give me a few tips. I took the hint and shut up. Of course, the men teased Matt mercilessly about shots he missed. Matt smiled, laughed shyly, took it all cheerfully. I think he had just the right attitude.

"Beautiful weather," I said to him early one morning as we hunted.

"Yeah, the sunrise," Matt said.

"Tomorrow it's supposed to rain," I said.

"It's all part of it," was Matt's reply.

Mostly, Matt listened. Like myself, he couldn't help but learn the stories of the men's lives—what it had been like to grow up dirt poor, rely on hunting game to feed your family, sleep five children to a bedroom; to value recognizing a dog's voice; how to twist a chicken's neck, or how to tree a opossum over understanding what Herman

Melville was telling us about vengeance in *Moby-Dick;* how to talk your parents into that sixty-dollar Tommy Hilfiger sweatshirt, or knowing the mathematics of whether to guess at a question or leave it blank on the SAT exams.

"Do we know anybody at home like the guys?" Matt once asked.

"I doubt it," I answered. "Can you think of anybody?"

"Nope."

Matt listened to the stories the men told and quickly realized they often repeated the same stories over and over. "Nobody ever gets tired of the same stories," he told me, amazed. Even when the men told new stories—tales of events that had just happened—the new stories became old stories overnight, Matt marveled, because the men repeated them so many times. Then Matt became a character in the stories, too. The first year he hunted with us, we were walking across the Barren River Lake bed that had dried up for the winter. Matt stepped into a patch of wet muck and began to sink. Instead of jumping out quickly, he stood there for a second or two or three and kept sinking. He was up to his ankles when he finally yanked his feet out of the goop and got to hard ground. The men laughed and laughed. Then they talked about it later, how Matt had stood there with no expression on his face, just sinking and sinking, and they laughed some more. At last, Matt, too, had become a shard of legend. One morning, I realized I didn't have to worry anymore about him fitting in with the crew after I had taken two shots to kill a rabbit.

"I hate it when I have to take two shots," I said.

"You mean instead of three?" Matt quipped, and the men roared with laughter.

Matt had at first been afraid of the men, especially Carl, because of his size and deep voice. Matt wondered how Carl could manage *never* to have a fresh cigar in his mouth. He wondered if Carl carried boxes of cigar butts. "The first time I hunted with Carl, I was frightened. He had those huge sausage fingers, and you'd think that he'd fumble around gutting a rabbit. But he slit open a rabbit's belly more deftly than any of the other guys." Matt quickly figured out what I had figured out before him: Carl was the serious hunter; Bobby, Lewis, and his grandfather were along for the camaraderie. Matt realized this one morning when the dogs were barking in an indecipherable chorus on a rabbit trail, and Carl said, "Old Earl's got the lead, Bullet's just behind." Right then, Matt decided to hang close to Carl in the field. "I'm in awe of Carl," Matt told me later. If Matt never learned anything else hunting with Alex, Bobby, Lewis, and Carl, that respect for a man so different from himself, so outside his experience, was enough for me.

I came to be glad that President Bush had nixed my book because, if I'd done that project, Matt would have been grown and gone before I had even realized it. He was seven years old when I was negotiating with President Bush. At the time, I assumed the president would be in office for two terms, which meant that I *should* have been thinking about how Matt would have been seventeen by the time I was able even to raise my head for breath a decade later. I might have done an important book. I might have won an award. I might have gotten rich. But I soon realized how blindly ambitious I had been. Only a few months after President Bush had killed the idea, I was in the field for hunting season when it struck me that I surely would not have been able to make that trip—or any other Thanksgiving trip after that—if I had taken on the book. If providence had allowed me to pursue my ambition, none of the years of hunting with Matt would ever have occurred. Not the BB gun or the .410, not the times I kicked brush piles to scare out rabbits for Matt to shoot. I never would have learned that he could recognize Canis Minor and Canis Major, seen him sink in the muck of Barren River Lake, heard him make fun of my poor shooting, or been there when he realized Carl's knowledge was worthy of respect. I thought of psychologist Carl Jung's notion of synchronicity, how sometimes events and insights occur in eerie concert, giving meaningful coincidences the shape of predestination. Good for synchronicity.

By that Thanksgiving, at nearly forty years old, I had become wise enough to realize that my stop-time moments in the fields and woods had become representations of all the stop-time moments in my life that I had walked blithely through, the sublime moments of *being there* that I had missed. I thought of a line by the novelist Graham Greene: "To me the present is never here: it is always last year or next week." I had done my duty, spent time with my son and family, but I had too often done so in the way that I had attended that springtime feast at the home of my friends Nina and Joe twenty years earlier. I was there, all right, but going through the motions, not savoring the moments. I too often scheduled time with my family in the way I scheduled lunches with sources—efficiently and graciously but without passion. I hope Matt didn't know the difference. I had come to know the difference, however, and to realize that it wasn't Matt or Kyle or Keran who suffered most from my distraction, but me. I no longer wanted to live that way.

Back home after that Thanksgiving, I shared my thoughts with a friend, also an obsessively ambitious man. In a voice lowered so that no one else in the newsroom could hear, he told me that every time he heard the song "Cat's in the Cradle," he cried. Couldn't help himself. He had covered a presidential campaign and then the White House while his son was young. He said he had no choice, really, couldn't pass up the perk assignments. Then his son was gone.

"What would you do if they wanted you to cover the White House?" he asked.

"I'd say no," I said.

"You would not!"

"I would now."

Back in Lewis's garage, Carl lights his cigar. Goat and Lewis and I light up, too, and the garage is soon soaked in a dreamy mist of rising, looping, swirling smoke that's good for nobody. The smoke and the men's movements and laughter are going in slow-motion for me: Carl's head bobbing with his deep "he-he-he" laugh; Lewis slapping his thigh and kicking the dirt for emphasis; Goat holding his cigar up to the light to see if it's burning evenly; Matt taking off his cap and scratching his head. The feeling I have is by now familiar to me. No place else exists. We are in the zone. Time is distended. The room is without tension. We belong here. No one need say it: we know we are liked, even loved. We are in a safe place.

"Lewis," Alex says, "you got eight-foot garage doors."

Lewis glances at his doors. "What's yours gonna be?" he asks, referring to the old-timey garage Alex has been building at his usual pace, which means for about the last two years.

"Nine foot," Alex says.

I hold the men's coats. "So he's got bigger doors than you, Lewis."

Lewis's voice goes dead serious. "Alex, no playin'. Is your door as big as mine?"

Matt spits out his Pepsi, Alex laughs tears, Bobby wheezes, Carl rattles the windows, Gerald laughs so hard he falls off the cedar cutting stump onto the dirt floor. After the laughter fades, Carl nods toward a burner where Lewis is heating water to clean his rabbits better.

"Lewis cleans his rabbits more than anybody," Carl says.

I risk making a modern joke. "That's because he's in touch with his feminine side."

A momentary silence—then hoots of laughter.

"That's what it is!" Carl yells. "Yeah, yeah!"

Carl keeps pin-balling. "I'm gonna tell you a story. Gerald used to come down here, and he'd always stay close to me, and we'd both shoot, and he'd holler, 'I got 'im!' And one day, me and him and my brother-in-law Robert went huntin', and me and Robert's on one side a the ditch and Gerald is on the other side, and the rabbits are comin' out on Gerald's side." Carl hesitates and laughter starts to ripple through the room because everybody knows the punch line. "Boom! Boom! Boom! Rabbits kept on runnin'. Boom! Boom! Boom! All gone. And I said, 'How in the hell do you shoot so good when you're close to me and can't hit nothin' by yourself?'"

Through the laughter comes Gerald's plaintive reply. "That's been years back."

Lewis seizes the moment. "Ol' Carl didn't tell the whole story," he says and then again tells the tale of Gerald coming in from the city with a new shotgun years ago, and how Carl and Bobby conspired to tell Gerald he needed to take his gun by the gunsmith's and have it zeroed in.

"I don't know where that story came from," Gerald insists.

"Did you do it?" I ask.

"*No!*" hollers Gerald.

Everybody groans. True or not, Gerald will take that story to the grave.

Out of nowhere, Alex asks me, "You ever seen snake shit, Walt?"

"No," I say, perplexed at this one.

"I've never seen snake shit *directly,*" Carl says, purposely taking Alex's bait.

Alex and Bobby laugh so hard it's tough to understand them. But the drift is that they once took snake feces and held it right under Carl's nose to ask him what he thought it was.

"Carl," Bobby says, "tell me what snake shit smells like."

"I told ya," Carl says. "It don't smell like *nothin*'!" The men laugh and laugh.

Lewis gets a worried look. "Hey, Carl, you think Matt should hear all this?"

Leaning against the post, Matt smiles a goofy smile. It's way too late for that question, although I still sometimes worry that Lewis is right. I believe these men's friendship is beautiful, although I can just hear them laughing if I were to tell them that. I also know their lives together could be interpreted many ways. A boy could see them as a model of manhood he should emulate instead of as an example of humanity in one of its many guises. A boy could think that to be a man he must be crude and rude, curse, take joy in ragging on his friends' weaknesses, be insensitive and downright mean. But a boy might also read the more subtle messages.

Somehow, Alex, Bobby, Lewis, and Carl always know when enough is enough. For instance, Carl believes the other men, who dropped out of high school, are sensitive about that, so he rarely brings it up. The men believed Alex was a bit touchy about the toupee he wore for years, and they went pretty light on that. The men know Bobby doesn't like to be corrected too strenuously by his older brother Alex, and they stay away from jokes about that. The men were never regular churchgoers, but when Lewis began attending church every week after his heart attack, nobody made fun of him. Like everyone in the world, the men have gone through troubles with some of their children. Nobody jokes about that. The men don't always agree with the opinions of each other's wives. But in all my years with them, I've never heard a man make a biting remark about another man's wife, at least not to his face. I've been surprised at how seldom the men even talk about any women at all, how rarely they make a lewd remark or tell a fiercely dirty joke. The men's time together just isn't about women; it's about themselves.

I've seen Alex get miffed at Bobby, Lewis, and Carl for not putting up a fence or building a shed to his technical standards. I've seen Bobby, Lewis, and Carl get ticked at Alex for doing what they see as a trivial job—say, building a doghouse or installing a new trac- tor light—as if their lives depended on the work being done to tool- and-die-maker tolerances. I've seen Bobby get mad at Alex for telling him how to take care of his livestock when Bobby has been taking care of livestock since he was ten, and Alex has never owned a cow. I've seen Carl get miffed at Lewis for deciding to go to bed early and not show up to gig frogs as the men had agreed.

After listening to the men go back and forth for years, I've finally decided I know what they have that I don't: they are friends in a way that has nearly vanished from our modern, transient lives that begin in suburbia and end in distant retirement in the Sunbelt. The men love one another and dislike one another like folks who stayed in the old neighborhood. They can't reinvent themselves in the way of immigrants, traveling salesmen, and climbers like myself. They can't discard one another for great or small failings. Like brothers, sisters, fathers, mothers, daughters, sons, committed husbands and wives, they're stuck with one another. I think of Matt's words as we walked out to give the day's garbage to the dogs almost a decade ago: "Grandpa and the guys don't always like each other, do they? . . . But they're still friends, aren't they?" The men are family. They aren't friends in the way of so many of my Washington friends, associates with like interests as long as those interests last. A few years ago, Carl came home from a trip to discover that Lewis had suffered his heart attack. Carl hurried to the hospital, worried sick. "Losin' Lewis would be like losin' a brother," he said. Then he caught himself: "'Course, then I wouldn't have to listen to him no more, either." For reasons I don't yet grasp, this blend of toughness and affection among men feels right to me, makes me realize I won't understand my fascination with Alex, Bobby, Lewis, and Carl, my desire to have Matt spend time with them, if I don't break away, travel back, and unearth the roots of my own sense of what it is to be a man.

I think of a time when Matt was a baby. It was late at night and only the light in the hallway was alive, pouring a shower across my knees as I sat in the dark of his room, rocking him through some unknown annoyance. Rocking to the hum of the air conditioner, the flutter of the cat scurrying on the stairs, the hollow groan of the water turning on and off in the apartment upstairs. I watched his face grimace and flex in the shadows. And then, in time so short it passed only in my mind, Matt was gone and I was the boy annoyed, and my father was me. I could feel the mannerisms, the voice, the phrases that would be mine someday. Just as suddenly, I was gone again, and the light was falling across the knees of Matt, who was grown, who was a father, who was me. All in time so short it passed only in my mind.

Back in the garage, Alex says, "Well, we gotta get on home."

"Lewis," I say, "thanks for the beer."

"Yeah," Lewis says. "Anytime."

Skunk Hollow

It is the snow that I remember. Not deep but luxurious, laid over the flat three acres in front of our house as if it had been painted there, always white and undisturbed in my eight-year-old's memory, although I know that must be wrong. Dirty snow would have been piled along our hundred-yard drive that ran from the gravel country road inappropriately named Broadview, and footprints from me, my sisters, the neighborhood kids, our dogs Teddy and Romeo, as well as sled tracks and snow angels would have pocked at least the snow just in front of the house, where we played every day after trudging the half mile home from the school bus stop at the corner where Broadview met Loomis Street. In my family, we called our house, our land, and the few ramshackle houses around us "the country." When we moved into a nearby village a few years later, I would learn that people in town called it Skunk Hollow, which they didn't mean as a compliment. I have no idea how often my father came home from work and found me bundled up in my snowsuit and wearing black galoshes, stiff mittens, and a hat with earmuffs that snapped either over my head or under my chin, depending on the day's temperature. I have no idea how often he disappeared into the garage and returned carrying his ancient single-shot .410 shotgun and wearing his own black galoshes, World War II overcoat that he'd cut off and hemmed at hip length just below the side pockets, and brown hunting cap with its warmer flaps, like my own, snapped either up or down for the day's weather. It could have been ten or it could have been a hundred afternoons. For me, the trips have all blurred into a single memory.

"Butch," my father said, calling me by my boyhood nickname, "let's go hunting."

Teddy, a mix of collie and German shepherd, and Romeo, some kind of black Chow blend, always raced ahead of my dad, who walked ahead of me as we rounded the house and crossed the backyard and the narrow slat-wood walking bridge that spanned Deer Creek and led to our seven acres of land behind the stream, a shallow, noisy, icy winter run. It was my game, my challenge, and, when the snow was deep, my saving trick to step long into my father's boot prints. I suspect he knew enough to take short strides. I don't remember ever talking. Only an hour of winter daylight remained by the time my dad got home, and we wasted no time.

I remember the first shot because Teddy always ran home after the first shot, making my father laugh and say, "There goes old Teddy." He always said that. I turned and watched Teddy run away. I remember more shots. I remember rabbits seeming to sleep in the snow and blood splattered in patterns never repeated exactly. I remember the beating of wings and the silky, incandescent greens, blues, and golds of ring-necked pheasants fallen to ground. I remember my father's shotgun snapping open, barrel cocked at a diagonal to its butt, empty shell being removed and discarded, new shell being inserted, barrel snapping shut with a definitive *click*. I remember the smell of gunpowder and blasts echoing off the trees that lined Deer Creek. I remember that we never hunted long and we never took more than a few animals. I remember velvety drops of blood marking the snow as I—like Alex, Bobby, Lewis, and Carl when they were boys—carried the rabbits and pheasants by their legs a few inches out from my sides. I don't remember feeling queasy about the blood or the dead animals in my hands, but I must have because of something I remember my father telling me more than once.

"You shoot an animal, Butch, and it bleeds."

I can't remember the last time I thought about any of this, but while walking the long drive from Broadview toward the boyhood home I left nearly four decades ago, the memories come easily. The house is now obscured by giant trees. The three front acres are still nicely trimmed, but the place looks naked in the summer sun without the red geraniums and pink cockscombs my father planted along the drive every spring, without the flower boxes beneath the windows. The one-story ranch house, stark white when I was a boy, is brown today. The paint is peeling. I knock. No sign of life, except for a garter snake sunning itself in the yard just off the concrete steps, the same steps where I fell as a boy and chipped my front teeth, chips I still wear. I walk around to the back, the same path my father and I took on our way hunting, where I see that the foliage along Deer Creek has grown wild and that the bridge is gone.

I'm wearing hiking boots and jeans, and I step into the mess, clearing away brush down to the creek. I cross on a fallen-tree bridge and climb the fifteen-foot embankment on the creek's back side. As a boy, I once swung on a vine from this bank while wearing my blue serge First Communion suit. A dare from my best friend, Johnny. I push through the dense foliage on the far bank where Johnny and I always had a fort hidden, expecting the thicket to break into the open fields where my father grew oats and corn and raised chickens, chinchillas, turkeys, minks, goats, cows, even a bull. Instead I'm reminded of Carl's remark when he visited his boyhood home: forty years later, just about nothing looks the same. The foliage beyond the creek never breaks.

I make my way along the bank and come out on a neighboring property where the back land has been cleared. What was once our pastureland is a fortress wall of trees and thickets. It has become what Lawson Bottom will be in a couple of decades if nobody fights it back. I navigate my way around the outer reaches of our back acres that are now the province of butterflies and bumblebees and birds, a covey of quail I scare up, a groundhog I see, a skunk I smell, daisies, clover, and thorn bushes, one of which leaves a two-inch needle gouged into my forearm. I finally come out at the other side of our land at Deer Creek, where a frog jumps into the water as I cross. I think about taking a souvenir, a pebble from the creek, but decide against it. It's not the material remnants of this place that matter. It's the meaning I've made of them.

My father built our cinder-block house in the years after he returned from fighting the Japanese in World War II. He worked ten hours a day, six days a week at the dairy and built the house in his spare time—nights and Sundays. My folks bought the ten acres for seven thousand dollars with a thousand-dollar down payment borrowed through the dairy's owner. They lived paycheck to paycheck in the land's dilapidated cottage—four rooms heated by a fat and brown oil-burning stove. The outhouse was out back. They were so poor that about all they ate for the first six months in the country were the chickens my father raised and the eggs they laid.

"Leonard, how do you want your chicken or eggs cooked?" my mom asked every night.

"Surprise me, Catherine," my father answered.

If they were to have a decent house, my dad would have to build it. He went to the library, borrowed a batch of books, and started digging the foundation with a shovel. My mother was, as she boasted years later, "the hod carrier," hauling the cinder blocks in an old wheelbarrow. She wasn't built for the work, not in body. She was a slight woman, milk-skinned with a natural pinkness in her cheeks, raven hair, placid laughing eyes, and delicate lips that always creased her face with the trace of a smile. But she was a pioneer. She and my father, who was lean, dark-haired, and handsome with a touch of John Wayne's theatrical hitch in his walk, dug the septic field themselves and then stayed up all night in a rainstorm burying it with stones so it wouldn't wash out. They worked on the house for years, some weeks able to afford only a few dollars in shingles that my father would dutifully nail to the roof. Even when they finally moved into their home, the walls were two-by-fours still gathering flesh on evenings and Sundays.

"Tough days," my mother once said of those years. Then she laughed.

"Man, oh, man," said my father, who laughed with her.

"But we did it," said my mother.

"I don't know how, but we did," said my father.

My dad, who like Alex could fix anything, got the old iron-wheeled tractor that had come with the place running and the field grass in front of the house was trimmed. He planted the senatorial rows of geraniums and cockscombs along the drive. He built a green-house and became an amateur horticulturalist. He grew a night-blooming cereus whose huge white blossoms would remain open only a single night that and my sisters and I always got to stay up late once a year to see it. He thought the land around the house was beautiful so he got canvases, brushes, and oil paints and taught himself to paint the landscape.

My dad was a town kid. He had never raised livestock or farmed, and it was learn as you go. When the first time came to slaughter thirty turkeys to sell at Thanksgiving, he realized it was going to take two hours to pluck each turkey's feathers. He took a five-gallon ice-cream drum, poked rubber pilings through the metal, hooked up a motor and pulley, and built a feather-plucking machine. It worked like a charm, plucking a turkey in three minutes flat.

I remember one day when Teddy and Romeo treed a family of five racoons in the backyard. I suppose most people would like to hear that my dad tied up the dogs and let the racoons go. No, he got his .410, killed them all, and gave their carcasses to a poor country family on his dairy route. "A treat for them," he said. My dad had bought his .410 at age sixteen from his friend Bernie Mack for two dollars. Actually, he traded an acetylene tank worth two dollars, be-cause he didn't have two dollars. Even in 1935, the Bridge shotgun was old. Its barrel was bent at the tip, and my dad had to saw off two inches. He scraped the varnish off the butt with glass and oiled the wood. Good to go. It's pretty obvious my dad rarely sat still, and he really wasn't around much when I was a boy. He was working, building our house, tending his animals, painting his pictures. But I have plenty of warm memories—stepping into his footprints in the snow, sitting on the couch together watching the Saturday night fights, riding the tractor with him, walking Broadview at dusk, coming home at night in the darkened car singing "The Red River Valley" as the car bounced through the dip in Ashland Avenue just past Virgil Gray's house.

He was a good man, my father, and I knew it then. He laughed easily and was the life of the party, playing the guitar, singing, organizing the games. He also was a rugged teaser, and it was during his teasing that I always sensed his great, unspoken love. Always, my dad had a way of smiling at me, a way of tossing a backhanded compliment that let me know he was proud and watchful of my achievements. He was no bully. I teased him back plenty, imitated his way of showing affection by telling him his nose was too big or his tie too ugly. When I was older, I learned that this is how men of that generation showed affection without acknowledging vulnerability. What I remember most about my dad is that he made me feel safe. He could, as I said, fix anything, which made life seem manageable. But he also fixed more profound matters.

I hated elementary school, hated getting on the bus and riding into the strange suburban world where kids wore different sets of clothes every day, while I had two sets that were rotated day in, day out. I wanted to stay home and run the woods. Anyway, my third-grade teacher once had us write an essay titled "My One Wish." I wished that we didn't have to go to school, and, as I read the essay to the class, she grabbed me by my ear and dragged me down to the principal's office, hollering at me the whole way. My parents came to the school and my father told me that what I had done was wrong and that I would be punished. Only many years later did my mother tell me that my father also went into the principal's office with my mom and teacher, said that if my teacher hadn't wanted to hear a child's honest opinion, she shouldn't have asked for it. Then he told her she had better *never* lay a hand on me again, or there'd be hell to pay. My father didn't harp on it, but more than once I heard him tell my mother, "They look down on people from the country, but they're not gonna mistreat our kids." As a boy, I was proud of my father. I knew even then that he didn't let the world take easy advantage of him or his family.

There was a time when I yearned to be with my dad more. But the day came early when I also dreaded his presence. Even when at work, he was the taskmaster in absentia. Infractions were added up and at night my father dispensed punishment, which was usually a threatening voice and never more than a spanking. In time, though, my father's masculine warmth paled next to his feared judgment. When he was around, I was in trouble more, there was less silliness, more attention to correct behavior. I, like so many kids in the 1950s, saw the tender way Ward Cleaver disciplined the Beaver. My dad came up way short in the tender competition.

Of course, there were things a boy couldn't understand. I didn't understand that we were poor. I didn't understand that my father had worked in the steel mill for eighty-five cents an hour before I was born, and that he was fired when he refused to work nights, refused to leave my mother and my older sister home alone. I didn't understand that he got up at 3:30 every morning to deliver milk because he had little choice. I didn't understand that the hours and hours of labor he put into our house and the farm were my parents' only hope of achieving affluence. I just knew that he was a kind of stranger in our house. He appeared occasionally, announced decisions, passed judgment. It was the way manhood went in my father's day. On top of that, the workingman's world my father occupied required yet an extra dose of grit in mind and spirit. I knew as a boy that my dad went to work no matter how sick he was. He delivered milk when his back was so sore he couldn't stand straight, couldn't sleep. To my father and men like him the world wasn't a friendly place where good things necessarily happened to good people. A man hung on by his fingernails. He was tough or he was in trouble. To a boy, the message was clear.

My dad and I didn't talk about *feelings*. We talked about action—a soapbox cart I was building, a White Sox game, a Red Skelton skit we found hilarious. We worked in the yard, installed the furnace ductwork in the attic, played catch. If I was angry at my dad, I told my mom, knowing she'd pass it on. If my father was sorry he'd yelled at me, my mother would relay his apology. "Dad didn't mean it," she'd say. "He's just tired." I can't recall a time my father ever hugged me or kissed me or said he loved me. I remember climbing into bed next to him on Sunday mornings, the only mornings he was home. I remember the strong, warm feeling of him holding me as I dozed off in his arms. But men, even little men, didn't kiss or hug. They shook hands. There would be times much later, when I went off to college, with the car packed and my parents and me standing on the driveway in those final few seconds, times I wanted so badly to hug my dad. But my muscles wouldn't move with the emotion. I hugged my mother. My dad and I shook hands, and I said, "Well, take care." In such moments, I always remembered my father's words: "It's not what a man says but what he does that counts." That was his and his generation's ethic. Words and promises, displays of emotion, declarations of love were suspect. They were easy; action was hard. That ethic was our bond. It was our barrier.

The last few years we lived in the country I had a BB gun. I could take the gun out by myself but was under a strict code of killing conduct: I could kill only starlings, which were pest birds. I did. One day, my blood lust got the best of me though, and I shot a cardinal that fell dead into the creek and began floating downstream with its red wings elegantly outstretched. I was riveted with guilt. I ran down to the creek, intercepted the bird, got a shovel, and gave it a burial complete with the "Lord's Prayer." Eventually, my dad taught me to shoot the .410, taught me on clay pigeons. He walked the fencerows with me a couple times but we never scared up a rabbit, and I never did get to hunt with my dad. The world intervened.

In the early 1960s, the suburban revolution intruded on the country when houses went up in the empty field across Broadview, their foundations dug quickly with backhoes and bulldozers. In short order, Teddy and Romeo, who had been used to roaming the open land, were found dead. The little houses weren't so bad but the septic tanks never worked. After a summer storm, when the fragrant evaporating moisture was fresh in your lungs, and the sound of water trickling from upturned leaves was amplified a thousand times, and the sunlight suddenly arced in a prism above the dark clouds, all your senses could accommodate was the stench across Broadview. My mother was despondent about having to leave the country.

"Things change," my father said, which was something he said often.

They sold the place, and we moved to a pretty little suburban town nearby. With the $19,000 they had made on their house, my parents built a magnificent home with three bedrooms, huge living room with a vaulted seventeen-foot ceiling, balcony dining room, rec room, greenhouse, and an apartment for my grandmother. In town, my father went about his independent and eccentric ways. He painted his house yellow with turquoise and brown trim. The place looked like a castle, but the neighbors were in a buzz about it, which delighted my father. The home milk business was dying by the 1960s but my dad's route prospered. He was a hard man to quit. If he thought, say, an old wooden wagon wheel would look good in front of your house, he'd look around until he found one somebody wanted to throw out, clean it up, and drop it off at your house. When the blizzard of '67 dumped twenty-four inches of snow and the milk trucks were stranded in the dock, he put chains on his car, drafted me, and we spent the entire day trudging through snow drifts to deliver bottled baby formula to the few women my dad knew would need it. He had long ago taught himself to play the guitar, and he began writing songs, which got him interested in writing poetry, which got him interested in writing eulogy poems for his friends' dead pets, which got him interested in crafting animal gravestones into which he inscribed his poems. The words are lost but they'd go something like this: "Here lies ol' Eddie / The hound always ready / To meet Joe, Babe and Freddy / At the bus / To bring them home safely to us."

I was fifteen. I thought the man was weird.

Twenty years later, when I was a man and Matt was four years old, I still thought my father was weird. By then, that made me proud. I remember once sitting with Matt in my father's living room with his song lyrics, scrawled into homemade booklets, spread out all over the floor and his music stand. His guitar had his name printed immodestly in three-inch iridescent letters on its body, and they glistened as he tuned up to play. In old age, my dad still looked much as I remembered him from my boyhood: hair full and brown, body trim, face tanned, eyes sharp. As my dad thumbed through his children's song collection, Matt bounced on the couch, furtively strummed the guitar he wasn't supposed to touch, and talked incessantly.

"You know 'Give Me a Home Where the Buffalo Roam'?" my dad asked in the high-pitched, teasing voice he reserved for kids and, on occasion, my mother.

"No," Matt said. "We gotta find some I know, right, Grandpa?"

"How 'bout 'I Been Workin' on the Railroad'?"

"Yeah! I know that one. You know why? One time I heard my daddy sing it." Then with a fierce pride that shot through me unexpectedly, Matt added, "My *daddy* taught it to me!"

I thought to myself, *And so it begins.*

At age fifteen, I despised my father—and I made sure he knew it. All the classic stuff, the painful yet gleeful realization that he didn't know everything, the shouting matches, the strange clothes and music. It all seemed surreal after Matt had come along, after I had recognized my two great revelations about my dad. The first came some time in my late teens when I suddenly realized I was *not* my dad and that I could stop trying to prove that I wasn't. The second came soon after Matt's birth when I realized, in apparent contradiction to my first revelation, that I *was* my dad, like it or not. By then I'd come to like it. I didn't have my father's voice—we shared a voice. I didn't have my father's eccentricity—we shared eccentricity. I didn't have my father's resistence to the opinions of others—we shared a resistence to the opinions of others. But I didn't exactly grow up to *be* my father. He tried to teach me to fix engines and repair rusted automobiles, to enjoy working with my hands. Didn't take. We had moved to affluent suburbia, and I became a suburban kid. I enjoyed driving around in my car, not working on it. That was for grease monkeys. I enjoyed shooting hoops, not hunting. That was for hicks from Skunk Hollow. I planned to be a lawyer, was president of the student council one year, editor of my high school paper, an Illinois State Scholar. Like an immigrant, I was determined to leave it all behind to make my way in the world. It's difficult to face even decades later, but what I most wanted to leave behind was my father's place in the world, which I thought I had come to understand living in that nice town of school-teachers, businessmen, insurance agents, and lawyers. My father's labor had allowed me to live among these people. It also had allowed me to look down on my own father.

I remember how mortified I always was when I had to fill out the forms in school every year that asked how many years of educa-tion my dad had completed. Circling the 10 always made me want to disappear. Maybe it was a peculiar motivation for a youngster, but I remember thinking to myself that someday I would have a job that my children would be able to talk about without embarrassment, even with pride. Thirty years later, I wonder: Can the roots of a man's obsessive ambition go back to so simple and painful a motivation? I blamed my father for the shame I felt. It got snarled up with my teen-age rebellion, because I had come to realize that for all of his competence, confidence, and mastery, the world considered my father small. So who was *he* to tell *me* what to do? Thank God, I never told him any of this. And thanks for the day when I was home from college my freshman year and sitting in the living room reading when an encyclopedia salesman came to the door, and my folks let him in to give his pitch. He asked my dad what he did for a living and my father said, "I'm in the milk business." In our nice home, the salesman probably thought he was making an appropriate leap. "Oh, you own a dairy," he said. My father hesitated and said, "No, I'm a milkman." For the first time, it hit me. My father, too, knew that the world believed he was small and, at some level, he also believed it.

I won't pretend that I can remember how I connected all of this in my mind. But I was almost uncontrollably angry. I was angry that some lousy door-to-door salesman had the power to shame my father. And, suddenly, I was angry that anybody, no matter their status, could shame my father. He worked ten-hour days. He had dug a foundation with his bare hands, posted red geraniums and pink cockscombs along our drive, built a machine that plucked a turkey in three minutes flat, let me watch a flower bloom just one night a year, saved me from a crazy third-grade teacher, irked the neighbors with a yellow castle's turquoise trim, delivered bottled baby formula to the few women who needed it, carved poems into animal gravestones. In a flash, I was ashamed for ever having felt ashamed of the man. In a flash, I was again able to feel the pride I had felt in him as a boy. I was fortunate to come to so sharp an insight so young. I don't believe I was ever again embarrassed by my roots. To this day, when the dentist suggests he repair the front teeth I chipped when I fell on the concrete porch in the country as a boy, I always say, "No, I got this far with these teeth. I think I'll keep them." Looking back, I believe that's why I took the social-class gamesmanship at the *Post* with good humor, why I wasn't embarrassed when I put my salad on the wrong plate, or cut my asparagus instead of eating it with my fingers. None of it mattered, not really. That wasn't who I was, although, for a while, I had lost track of that.

I was, of course, a modern father. I tried not to repeat what I saw as my dad's mistakes, or rather, the supposed mistakes of his generation. I was determined to abandon my father's idea of manhood—his unrelenting masculinity, his unquestioned authority, his emotional distance. I refused to be the enforcer, expecting Keran to take an equal role, because I knew what that had done to my father and me. We raised Matt by the modern catechism. He had Raggedy Andy *and* Raggedy Ann. We didn't buy him a toy gun until he was the only kid on the block without one. When he scraped a knee or an elbow, I told him it was okay to cry. I told him again and again that I loved him. He told me that he loved me. We hugged and kissed good-bye. I used to say, "A boy's never too old to kiss his father." I tried never to be embarrassed about this, although I suspect Matt sensed my occasional uneasiness. This was the new masculinity, and it is as common now to my generation as was the kind of masculinity accepted in my dad's day. I think it mattered some.

When Matt went off to camp or trips to the farm, he hugged me and said, "I love you, Dad" as naturally as I had shaken my father's hand and said, "Well, take care." But, honestly, I was never one who believed that modern masculinity would save Matt and me from what writer Larry L. King once called the "mutual thirst to prevail" between father and son. That prophecy came true on schedule when Matt turned fifteen, despised me, and let me know it. I'm looking forward to the day when he realizes he isn't me and can stop trying to prove that he isn't.

It took my father time to feel proud that I was a journalist. I mean, I didn't even know how to replace my own car muffler. When I came to own a house, I wasted money on plumbers to fix leaky faucets and electricians to repair broken light switches. I hired a nursery to lay down the landscaping and a gardener to trim and tidy it all up twice a year. Even if he could have afforded it, my father would never have ceded so much mastery of his world over to hired hands. But I had done what young men in America are supposed to do. I had risen in society. I had eaten dinner with the president. Funny, but despite my social ascent, my simple and deepest hope came to be that I could teach Matt some of what my father had taught me about being a man.

He taught me that a man kills and eats animals. Animals bleed. Live with it. He taught me that a man strives to master his world, whatever that world is. He doesn't sit and whine—he acts. Most important, a man is never powerless, no matter how powerless he is. Maybe that philosophy is rooted in hard circumstances, but its noble qualities of grace and strength, resilience and eccentricity are self-evident. My parents went the modern retirement route. They sold their beautiful house in town, bought a big Ford van and a trailer, and traveled the country for years before settling into a nice mobile-home retirement park in Arizona. They refused to fly in an airplane or drive in the crazy East Coast traffic, so we visited them once a year in Arizona or when they returned to the Midwest to my sister's house. It was fun, but I always felt the time was disconnected from our earlier lives together. It lacked the moorings of place and people that I felt when we visited Alex's farm. Matt and I just didn't see my father as often as we saw Alex. So by default, he and Bobby, Lewis, and Carl became the living bridge to the old values of manhood I had known as a boy. I grew up to be a man with the tastes and sensibilities of the educated, urbane, upper-middle-class folks around me. Yet my childhood world had been more like that of Alex, Bobby, Lewis, and Carl, if not so extreme in its poverty and deep country life.

I finally realized that my time with the men rubbed that piece of me, stirred old memories, stoked old resentments and hurts, reminded me of the qualities I had so admired in my own father. The time I spent with the men every year was a perennial touchstone to who I was before who I had become. Each year, that sensation felt better and better. It unlocked something in me that I had put away for a long time. It wasn't that I wanted to go back to where I had begun. It was that I didn't want to lose touch with where I had begun—and I wanted Matt to somehow know something of that place and something of those qualities of grace and strength, resilience and eccentricity that are earned facing the world from the bottom up every day of your life. I hope Matt someday judges that I, in my own way, had those qualities. I hope he has them. Finally, along with a grit in mind and spirit, I also hope the displays of affection and declarations of love that never came to my father or Alex, Bobby, Lewis, and Carl, and that came only awkwardly to me, will come to Matt as naturally as I once told my dad that his nose was too big or his tie too ugly.

What I hope is my father's lasting lesson for Matt: When Matt was a boy, he, my father, and I were driving through California's lush Imperial Valley. As we traveled, my dad told us all about gravity irrigation systems. He was so excited when we came upon Old King Solomon, the first date tree imported to California, that we had to stop to see it. He told us the names of countless cacti and grasses, that hornets don't fly at night and that ants don't eat fish. In the desert, he pulled over and made us get out of his van to admire a stunning sand dune. "Look over there," he said, pointing past the dune. "Look at that lonesome mountain." Matt and I looked, and, indeed, way off, a craggy ridge rose from the flat horizon like a hopeful, noisy effort against a dominant, muffling sky. We were quiet until my father spoke the words I had heard so often as a boy.

"Everything's beautiful if you look at it right."

Alex's Pig Feast

The pig is delicious, finger-pulling tender and bar-becued to the bone. Alex spent hours baking and basting it, making potato salad and baked beans seasoned with brown sugar and jalapeños. He has laid out the feast in his basement near the pool table as his antique Seeburg jukebox plays old blues songs on crackling 45s. Alex bought the pig we're eating as a pet for my kids years ago. They've gotten too old to spend their summers visiting the farm, though, and pigs all meet the same eventual fate on a farm. Alex probably won't like me mentioning it because he won't want my daughter to know we ate her pet pig. But somebody was going to eat him someday. Either strangers buying pork in the supermarket or people the pig knew. Carl shot him in the forehead an inch above the line of his eyes, a skill Carl acquired as a boy at his Uncle Virgil's hog killings near Goodnight. We're sipping Rhinelander beer that Alex had me bring from home, where it sells for $7.99 a case. On principle, Alex likes to serve cheap beer to his friends, especially cheap beer they've never heard of so they don't know it's cheap.

Lewis stops chewing. "Carl, when did we first get huntin' together?"

"Oh," says Carl, thinking, "it's been a million years, since fifty-three."

"Remember that time Charles lost ol' Red?" Lewis asks, refer-ring again to the time twenty-five years ago when their friend Charles couldn't find his hunting dog, and they searched for two days before they found him in the trunk of Charles's car, where he'd put him for the short ride home. Charles insisted somebody had stolen Red from his backyard. They went over and interrogated their friend James Ellis and then their friend Buttermilk, who had reputations for, to put it delicately, borrowing men's hunting dogs without permission. The men were back out in the field calling and whistling for Red when Lewis thought he heard some whimpering.

"Charles, that dog ain't in the trunk, is he?" Lewis recalls asking.

The men begin to chuckle.

"Oh, hell, no, he ain't," Charles answered.

Now the men are clapping, bobbing their heads, snickering.

"He opened the trunk, and there was ol' Red!" Lewis says. "Talk about one happy dog!"

And the choir of distinct laughter, from bass to countertenor, rises forth.

On this visit to Kentucky, I'm determined to get a deeper sense of what it is about Alex, Bobby, Lewis, and Carl that intrigues me beyond reminding me of my own roots. As I eat, drink, and laugh with the men, I think to myself that they've become a kind of Rorschach test for me. I look at them and see flesh and blood, but I also suspect that I see an image of something that is missing in my life. I wonder if it is middle-age reflection or knowing these men that has made me ponder that question. I decide it doesn't matter. These guys are my inkblots.

We stay most of the rainy afternoon and goof and shoot pool. We have so much fun that Bobby, who quit beer and liquor a couple years ago, breaks down and drinks a Rhinelander. Most of the men's conversation is familiar to me, like eating a favorite meal. But within each familiar tale is always some new twist, an ingredient that miraculously makes stale bread fresh. I've heard the story of Charles and his lost dog a dozen times, for instance, but I've never heard that the men interrogated James Ellis and Buttermilk. I've heard the story of the time Lewis and Carl were driving to the Fourth of July potluck celebration at Barren River Lake, and Carl pulled over, took his .22 rifle out of the truck bed, and shot a groundhog for the party. But this afternoon I learn that Carl hit that groundhog at a hundred yards, what the men must all reluctantly admit was one of the best shots any of them has ever seen. I've heard the story of how Bobby and Carl tracked down that pack of wild dogs that was killing calves on Bobby's farm. But this afternoon I learn that the vicious black dog that Bobby missed when he killed two of the pack later mauled a neighboring farmer, something Bobby still feels bad about three decades later.

This afternoon, when I think I've heard every story, I learn for the first time that Carl once was about to give his dog Bullet mouth-to-mouth resuscitation after the dog bumped his head and got knocked out, except Bullet regained consciousness just then. I learn that one day when it was cold and sleeting and Lewis refused to get out of the truck to hunt, Carl—knowing that dogs track better in the rain—climbed out and killed six rabbits in ten minutes. And, thanks to Lewis's relentless eye for embarrassing details, I learn that Alex always furtively wipes the mouth of the communal whiskey bottle before he takes a sip, something nobody has ever mentioned before.

"You notice Alex cleans the bottle every time before he takes a drink."

I wonder if Lewis has been saving that barb for fifty years.

"Oh, shit!" Alex says by way of weak denial as he hands off the Wild Turkey.

Lewis won't let go. "Was that top greasy, Alex?"

Everybody chuckles, and we keep munching Alex's pig and drinking Rhinelander. Carl is done eating first, and he grabs a cue and heads for Alex's pool table. Alex can't help himself: "Wipe your hands and get the grease off before you touch the table."

We about split a gut, especially Lewis.

After my George Bush book fell through and I realized soon after while hunting with the men what I would have sacri-

ficed if it had gone ahead, I was cleaning out junk boxes in the basement one Saturday and came upon a copy of a letter I'd sent to a friend
thirteen years earlier when I was twenty-six, earning $175 a week, work-
ing like a madman, and loving it. "I don't want blind ambition to be
my main motivation," wrote the young man I had once been. "It's a
total package of life satisfaction that I'd like. I'd prefer less status and
money in my work to more freedom." I sat down on a step stool and
read the words again and again. Could I even remember being that
idealistic young man? Just barely. By then I had begun to realize what
my ambition had cost me and how my childhood and working-class
shame had fed my obsessive drive. But to realize that even as a young
man I was already wrestling with my blind ambition, admonishing
myself to take care, worrying about balancing success and satisfaction, stopped me cold.

I won't kid you. It was no Saul on the road to Damascus moment.
I had a $2,500-a-month mortgage, bills for kids taking lessons in
everything, summer camp, the Formula Thunderbird, the nice cars,
the car phones, the uppity suits and ties and shoes, the manicures and
wines, the fine collectibles. I had expenses that were the offspring of
my ambition, work, and achievement, of my success. And remember
that my *things* had become embedded in my image of myself. I admit
that I loved to have parties on beautiful Sunday afternoons when
friends who lived in Washington's ridiculously priced suburban tract
houses would come out and ooh-and-aah at my house, swim with
their kids at the beach, sip drinks overlooking the water, take rides in
the boat. I had already realized that hard work was the wellspring of
it all, that if I ever stopped enjoying my work, I'd have to keep laboring anyway to pay for all of it. That I could live with.

What I couldn't get used to was the insight that hit me in the
basement that Saturday morning: I wasn't pursuing the freedom I had
once craved. I was spending my time writing stories that plenty of
other journalists could write. I was writing about men and women
and matters of power for which I had no natural feel. I was faking it.

And I was faking it for the worst of reasons: to succeed. Yet that work could never tap what was deepest within me. So it would never be my best. I thought of a line from the novelist Harry Crews: "Once I realized that the way I saw the world and man's condition in it would always be exactly and inevitably shaped by everything which up to that moment had only shamed me, once I realized that, I was home free." I wasn't a novelist, didn't want to be. If I had a rare quality, however, it was getting people to talk about themselves, listening, being always fascinated at the dignity, complexity, frailty, and strength of ordinary people. That quality was surely borne of my own very ordinary background. My basement epiphany: what I had forever seen as a deprivation to overcome was actually a gift.

Turning points in life are misty, even murky places. It's easy to look back and believe that, *presto,* you were changed after, say, reading an old letter, after a friend or a parent dies, after an illness in a child. You know the insight: *Now I realize what's important in life and will be forever changed.* Maybe it works that way for some people but it didn't for me. Slow on the uptake, I suppose. Or, being more sympathetic with myself, maybe it's just that personal epiphanies are usually like the space your hand takes when you dip it into a stream of running water. Pull it out and the space disappears as fast as a life-changing insight can get lost in the current of daily doings. Changing your life is like battling those forests that will inexorably overtake croplands that have been left untended. It's a day-to-day fight. Wait too long, and you will need a bulldozer.

I thought of a day years earlier just before I began working on the George Bush profile that would so dramatically change my career. As I had eaten a delicious French cassoulet at Au Pied De Cochon in Georgetown, a friend asked me what I would work on if I could work on whatever I wanted. I thought for a moment and surprised myself by saying that I'd get in my car and travel the length and breadth of black America and write a book about whatever I discovered. After reading that letter in the basement, I kept thinking of what I had told my friend. I thought of the freedom I had craved as a young man. I thought of working from my heart. I thought of Carl Jung's synchronicity. And I began the book—not a consideration of grand policy but a 25,000-mile journey that would eventually take me through every social strata of black America. My wife was black, my children were hybrid. Race mattered to me, them, and everybody in a way that, honestly, was more important than what it was like to be president of the United States. The book—*Crossings: A White Man's Journey into Black America*—didn't make me rich or famous. It ended up costing me nearly a year's income. It barely made a ripple, although five years after it had come and gone, *The New York Times Book Review* would name it one of a handful of "vital, if unfamiliar, books about race." My real accomplishment: Plenty of other journalists could have written a good book on President Bush. Nobody but me could have written *Crossings*. Where did I begin my journey? Where else? In Glasgow, with Alex, Bobby, Lewis, and Carl.

I'm always amazed at what I didn't know once I learn that I didn't know it, and it was that way with the men and race. Remember that they rarely even mentioned race. But when I began to ask, to talk with the men alone, away from the hunting fields and pig feasts, their voices changed to monotones and their expressions went monochromatic. As a boy, Alex remembered once being sent on an errand from Glasgow's black school to the white school. It wasn't the better facilities that amazed him, it was the cafeteria bowls filled with fresh apples that any child could take. Remember the whites-only water fountain on Glasgow's square? Alex and Bobby would sneak up at odd hours and spit on the mouthpiece. In 1946, at age fifteen, Alex enlisted in the U.S. Air Force and went straight to shoveling coal into furnaces, doing secretarial work, and later driving in the motor pool. It was a decade before he could get training to become a skilled mechanic. Alex always loved his tours of duty in Europe, where white people treated him and his family like anybody else. When they returned to the States, they would once again have to drive straight through to vacation destinations because no motels would take black people.

It turned out that Bobby launched his career as a child bootlegger after he had learned that white kids were earning more money for doing the same janitorial work at the Glasgow Hospital. Lewis remembered that the police in the old days were all white and that a black man always had to be a little afraid. Carl remembered that he couldn't start school until age nine because the only school near his house in the country was for white children. He remembered that any white could cut in front of a black person in a store checkout line. Many times Carl saw his father stand patiently as whites moved ahead of him. Out of high school, Carl worked as a "wash boy" at the local Texaco station, earning less than the white workers. He was thirty-one when a national factory opened in Glasgow, and he was hired and finally paid a white man's wage.

Maybe you're thinking that this litany of indignities is familiar, old news. We know all about race and racism, don't we? Well, when it came to the men, it wasn't only the racism that got my attention. It was the way the men had reacted to the racism. They had kept their heads. Carl remembered sometimes wanting to punch the white men at the Texaco station who earned more money than he. Just below the surface, all the men were angry and resentful. But they had kept their heads. They were black *and* poor. Yet they realized that even powerless people are not really powerless. They took what opportunities came to them, raised families, enjoyed their lives and one another. I admired that, as I had admired that same stance on life in my father, who was himself deeply resentful of the way affluent town people looked down on poor folks from the country. That was my kinship with Alex, Bobby, Lewis, and Carl. I recall something Jesse Jackson had told me about growing up poor: "You learn to yearn." That yearning goes beyond race. It's a kernel of doubt clothed in resentment that abides in anybody born with less who must always wonder if having *less* actually means they are *less than*.

I once was seated across a dinner table from a successful lawyer, a white man. We talked and I learned that he, too, had been a working-class kid from a small Illinois town. His father was a coal miner. That fast, I knew that I needed only to touch the place where the man kept his kernel of doubt, and I mentioned how I had never met a person who'd attended the Ivy League before I began working at *The Washington Post*. With that, the man began. How, as a boy, he was determined never to work in the mines. How only he and a couple others among his childhood friends went to college. How he had to work while his college pals were out drinking and partying. Then he told me this story: He was putting himself through law school, working or studying day and night. One afternoon, a few of his classmates invited him out for drinks, but he couldn't go, had to work. He felt the familiar emotion rising—the bastards have it so easy, everything handed to them, life a cakewalk. *They* . . . and then he stopped himself in a way he had never done before when he had felt the resentment. He said these words to himself: *Let it go. They are good guys. They don't know what they've got. They don't know what I've been through. It's wrong for me to feel this way about them. And it's no good for me. Let it go.* He did. The man told me he never let himself feel that resentment again. Did I understand? I said I did, and I told him about the day decades earlier when the encyclopedia salesman had shamed my father.

In Glasgow with Alex, Bobby, Lewis, and Carl, I had launched my journey through black America. I continued on that journey off and on for two years. It was in that first week with the men, however, that I learned something important about myself. At the *Post*, I thought I had been writing about people and power. But after months investigating the life of George Bush, I wrote about how being the scion of an Eastern-elite family had shaped him and the public's perception of him. After months with the Reverend Jerry Falwell, I wrote that he had risen from the poor side of town and been powerfully driven to seek respect and respectability for his uneducated fundamentalist flock whom he knew to be every bit as smart as the fancy-pants Episcopalians across town. When Ben Bradlee asked me to profile Jesse Jackson, he mentioned in passing that I wouldn't need to get into all that "social class stuff" this time. I ignored the comment, excusing Ben—himself the child of Eastern privilege—for not understanding what I knew intuitively, that I would need only to touch the place in Jesse Jackson where he hid that kernel of doubt, and the stew of resentments and ambitions rooted in race and class would pour forth, which it did. In Glasgow, I had set out to understand how race had shaped the lives of Alex, Bobby, Lewis, and Carl. I did that and wrote about it. But I also learned this about myself: all those years I thought I was writing about people and power and politics, I'd actually been writing my own life.

It was time to let it go.

Leaning against the wall in Alex's basement, pool cue in hand, I have this thought: Maybe I was wrong a decade ago as I cleaned rabbits with the men and their friends at the Everlasting Stream, when I had the sense that time was standing still, that the hour was endless, that we had entered a place disconnected from the rest of our lives. I know that was the way *I* experienced those moments, but I wonder if the men experienced them that way. It's not that the hour wasn't powerful, wasn't indelibly memorable for them. It was. They later told me it was. But that hour at the Everlasting Stream no longer seems so different from many other hours I've spent with the men—at Bobby's barn when we shot the breeze under a warm blue sky and Matt wouldn't take off his jacket for the longest time, the time we cleaned rabbits in Lewis's untidy garage, the time this afternoon. I have by now come to savor the heightened stop-time moments in the hunting fields when acuity and calm are of a single piece, when time and place are inexplicably experienced consciously and unconsciously at once, when a moment is lived not walked through. Then this afternoon, it hits me. The men's time together as friends evokes that same in-the-moment sensation. The same purity. The same unself-consciousness. That's the ineffable beauty of life for Alex, Bobby, Lewis, and Carl—and the sad truth for me and men like me. I know most people will want to take from my story clear lessons, country wisdom that can make modern men's lives better. I wish I could give them that formula and that hope, simply and neatly. Unfortunately, in the relent-less world beyond nostalgia, just remembering what we have lost doesn't necessarily mean we can get it back again.

I think of a scene from the 1960 movie version of *Inherit the Wind,* a portrayal of the 1925 Scopes "monkey trial," in which Spen-cer Tracy plays a character based on the famous lawyer Clarence Darrow who defends a Tennessee teacher charged with illegally teach-ing evolution in his classroom. Tracy speaks these lines: "Progress has never been a bargain. You've got to pay for it. I think there's a man behind a counter who says, 'All right, you can have a telephone, but you'll have to give up privacy, the charm of distance. . . . Mister, you may conquer the air, but the birds will lose their wonder, and the clouds will smell of gasoline!'" We modern men made a bargain. For more than a century, we've been packing up and leaving our farms and hometowns. We became migratory animals in pursuit of achieve-ment. There was a price. Historians of manhood say men's friend-ships have always been rooted in shared activities—the action of war, work, athletics, hunting, fishing, hobbies. They tell us that women's friendships have been more rooted in the conversational sharing of heartfelt thoughts and feelings. Social scientists tell us that women these days have more intimate friends and more often make new friends than do men. Who could be surprised at that?

Let's face it, the modern world is tough on men's friendships. Upward mobility demands geographical job hopping and leaving friends behind. Corporate culture expects those who are promoted to acquire equally prestigious neighbors and friends, jettisoning the old for the new. The workplace, too, as I learned at *The Washington Post,* is ruthless, not a nurturing environment for friendships. It seems almost unbelievable today but before the twentieth century, before the dawn of dog-eat-dog competition among self-made achievers, men often had deeply expressive and intimate friendships. Even then, though, men still became friends through action—what poet Walt Whitman called "the manly love of comrades." Men hunt, fish, repair the jalopy, play tennis, basketball, golf. A man comes to trust another man after he sees that man handle a Boston Whaler, a socket wrench, a 12-gauge, after he sees whether that man cheats at the baseline, plays dirty with elbows under the basket, nudges his ball to a better lie. Remember, it's not what a man says but what he does that counts. Some social scientists denigrate this as nothing more than childish "parallel play." But I will change my whole opinion of a man if I learn, for instance, that he can't add up strokes correctly on the golf course. I suspect that men are just built to judge one another through action, a kind of primal directive. The trouble is, it takes time—years—to know a man through the mirrors of shared experience. Modern migratory career-climbing men, especially now that married men have more than doubled the hours a week they spend taking care of children, just don't have the time. Sure, a lot of the change has been for the better. But as we now understand, progress has a price. How many men anymore can wait fifty years to tease a friend about always wiping clean the mouth of the communal whiskey bottle?

That's why I was wrong years ago at the Everlasting Stream. In my modern world, time passes on a continuum. My life is laid out before me like a train with whistle stops, moving from farm to town, college, jobs, cities, marriage, births, deaths, joys, disappointments, houses, vacations, always moving away from where it began. I suspect that's how most modern men today see their lives—time passing on an orderly track from before to now to onward. But this absolute conception of time, Isaac Newton's conception of time, isn't the way Alex, Bobby, Lewis, and Carl experience time. The men live in an Einsteinian social universe, where time can race, slow, stop, even reverse. The men have wrinkled and warped time, wrapped it over upon itself, traveling from now to before and back with the ease of the starship *Enterprise* passing through a wormhole. I think of the famous story that tries to explain the relativity of perceived time to laymen: If you watch a movie of two billiard balls colliding on a pool table without seeing which ball was struck by the cue, it's impossible to tell whether the movie is running forward or backward. That's perfect. Watching Alex, Bobby, Lewis, and Carl shoot pool this afternoon, listening to their stories and permutations on those stories, hearing the way they speak in an indefinite past tense that can slip instantly from a minute to eighty years past, it's impossible to tell whether their actions are running forward or backward.

"I lose track of time," Carl once told me, as he tried to remember the year a story he was telling had taken place. "It doesn't matter." Now I know why. The men don't *tell* stories; they *are* their stories. The men don't lose track of time; they defy time. William Faulkner once wrote that there is "no such thing as *was* . . . no such thing as *will be.*" For me, time and memory are solid markings on a yardstick that stretches from past to present. For Alex, Bobby, Lewis, and Carl, time and memory are soluble liquids swirling in a bowl. For me, that hour at the Everlasting Stream seemed outside linear sequence. For them, the hour *was, is,* and *will be,* all at once.

I think of the theorists who say that a man passing through a black hole in space will exit on the other side younger than when he entered, discombobulating time as we know it. The men have at least discombobulated time on earth. Maybe more, too. I think of the avant-garde theories of physicists who take Faulkner's metaphor literally and argue that time itself is an illusion, doesn't exist, and that the instants we believe to be melting away and then gone actually live etched free of all other instants forever, meaning every moment exists for all time. Not as a metaphor but in acuality. It's what the theoretical physicist Julian Barbour calls the ultimate "Now." I think of how I learned over the years to experience my time hunting in fields and forests not as a rolling strip of movie happening before my eyes but as a collection of discrete frames and how much more powerful those moments then were. It's curious to think this may not have been a sensory illusion but instead an intimation of immortality. More curious still, Alex, Bobby, Lewis, and Carl seem to live their lives simultaneously in the "Now" *and* in that strip of rolling movie. I think that thought, and then I think that achieving such simultaneity is a pretty amazing thing.

How have they done it? Well, beyond their shared lifetimes and re-remembering the tales of Old Red, the potluck at Barren River Lake, the pack of wild dogs, the men live and hunt on land they walked as boys. They still fish Skaggs Creek. As his mother taught him sixty years ago, Alex still shatters bum-bursts on the rocks at Lawson Bottom. Every day, Bobby drives by the house where he lived with Ms. Carrie and Leon as a boy. Every time we go to Lawson Bottom, Lewis drives past his boyhood house in Marrowbone. From a back road off the main drag to Glasgow, Lewis and Bobby can still see the house that marked Spillman's Woods. A couple years ago, an old man who had once lived near Carl's boyhood house outside Temple Hill dropped by to tell Carl about his grandfather, who was born before the Civil War. The house on Lewis Street in Glasgow, where Alex grew up, is gone but the street still looks much the same, and Alex occasionally drives it just for memory's sake. The mother and father of Alex and Bobby are buried in Glasgow's Odd-fellows Cemetery. Ms. Carrie is buried next to her parents in Oak Grove Cemetery, where Lewis's dog once whizzed on Bobby's leg. Leon is buried next to his father a mile from the farm Bobby and Carl own near Coral Hill. The men's hunting dogs are often named after hunting dogs they owned as long as fifty years ago. The men's dogs are like the begats in the Bible, with generations of Reds and Joes and Bingos. Carl's Shorty and Alex's Rowdy just had pups. Visiting Skunk Hollow brought me a rush of memories long for-gotten. But the men live daily among the artifacts of their memories. No wonder time is jumbled.

Alex, Bobby, Lewis, and Carl are entwined with this place and its people in a way that is mostly gone from the American scene. Even when Alex and Bobby left Glasgow for the military, they never left emotionally. They returned every chance they got, and they thought of Glasgow as a place they would inevitably live someday. I think of President George Bush—the first President George Bush—once telling me that no matter where he lived, the Bush ancestral estate in Kennebunkport, Maine, was his "anchor to windward," a kind of talisman that reminded him of his own past, present, and future. That's an aristocratic version of the same timelessness that unifies the lives of Alex, Bobby, Lewis, and Carl. Not many of us, privileged or not, have that left in our lives. Many of the men's siblings and friends didn't stay anchored in Glasgow. They left for better jobs and stayed gone. Tempted by the big factory wages, Carl thought about following his brothers and friends to Detroit or Chicago or Indianapolis.

"I'd go visit for a few days," Carl said. "But then I was ready to get home."

In America, we always think of the people who strike out from their homeland for distant shores as more adventurous, ambitious, brave, and intelligent than the people who stay behind. It's an article of faith. But think of those who remain in a different light. Think of them as people who loved more deeply, were committed to caring for their parents and families, looked closer and longer and saw the beauty around them, were willing to give up fatter incomes and nicer houses and cars because they valued human connection and place over prosperity.

A lot of people couldn't stomach staying behind, and I was one of them. I thought of the claustrophobic worlds of Sherwood Anderson's *Winesburg, Ohio;* Willa Cather's rural Nebraska in *One of Ours;* and Sinclair Lewis's *Main Street*—the narrow curiosities, the abiding prejudices, the limited horizons. I wanted out and away. If I had stayed in my hometown, I suppose I'd still be called Butch today. I'm glad I left. But Alex, Bobby, Lewis, and Carl have what I bargained away. I keep telling you about rabbit hunting. Yet rabbit hunting, although an important piece, is only a piece of the men's lives. They all raised families, had sons, who, like me, moved away. The boys all hunted with their fathers and, like me, gave it up. Not much room for hunting if you are a journalist in Washington, a small businessman in Atlanta, an airplane pilot. I keep telling you about rabbit hunting because it's how I know the men, and because it's a window into how they experience their world. None of the men ever took a class on rabbit hunting. Their knowledge of it is what the philosophers call "tacit knowledge." Think of how a boy learns to walk, struggling mightily with each individual motion until, suddenly, his disjointed actions all blur and he is running across the yard. Or think of how we learn to talk without formal instruction. Or think of how a blacksmith, after years of smithing, can tell the temperature of hot iron without a thermometer by reading the spectrum of color as black iron turns red to orange to yellow to molten white. Tacit knowledge is knowledge so ingrained, so second nature, we no longer know how we know it. We just know it. After all the years, that's how the men know one another. Instead of trivializing the men's friendships by labeling them as childish "parallel play," I think of them as friendships rooted in the most sophisticated of knowledge, tacit knowledge, knowledge so deep it's literally beyond words. When I look at Alex, Bobby, Lewis, and Carl as my Rorschach test, I see that depth of friendship with men missing in my life. It's what we modern men gave up. Just knowing it's gone, though, won't ever get it back.

In Alex's basement, the men are still discombobulating time.

"That pig was good," Lewis says.

"Real good," Carl echoes.

"Almost as good as the hunters' breakfasts," says Bobby later. With that he flashes the men back thirty years to when they launched the first day of each hunting season with what they have come to call The Hunters' Breakfast. For most of a decade, Carl's wife, Juanita, cooked a magnificent feast. At four in the morning on opening day, she began preparing the 6 A.M. breakfast for the men. She peeled and sliced potatoes, seasoned them with hog lard, salt, and pepper, and fried them up. She had already thawed and soaked four or five of last season's rabbits the night before. She coated them in flour, salt, and pepper and heated up grease in two giant skillets until it was snapping like miniature explosives. She dropped the pieces of rabbit in for a quick browning and turned down the heat for a slow fry. She mixed flour with Crisco and just enough buttermilk to make the dough stick a bit to her fingers as she kneaded it. She fried sausage seasoned with sage and red pepper and scrambled eggs. She always had a grits casserole she'd done up the day before—grits, eggs, and cheese mixed with milk and garnished with corn flake crumbs. On the table, she put out jars of blackberry and damson jams she'd made from fruit off her brother's land in Hiseville. She always brewed three pots of coffee. I listen to the men talk about The Hunters' Breakfasts and, really, it's as if we are at one of those breakfasts right now. The words of physicist Julian Barbour come to mind like a prayer: "Immortality is all around us. Our task is to recognize it." *Amen.*

Twenty years ago, after a decade of The Hunters' Breakfasts, Alex visited his cousin Reid and got permission to hunt the farm in Lawson Bottom. The rabbits were plentiful then, and the men didn't want to give anybody a chance to clean them out. So on opening day, they began making the hour's drive to Lawson Bottom, which required that they leave Glasgow before dawn and didn't leave enough time for breakfast. They began taking their morning feast at the C&J Restaurant, where they were still eating when I joined the crew, and the action, for me, began running forward. I think of what my father often used to say with optimistic resignation: "Things change." For as much as Alex, Bobby, Lewis, and Carl are rooted in place and memory, they are also easy with change. Maybe that's because, unlike for people like me, the past is never lost to these men. For them, every moment exists for all time. *Now.* Not as a metaphor but in actuality.

At the pool table, Carl says, "I done missed a couple shots I wouldn't hardly ever miss." Dismissive laughter rumbles through the room. "Startin' from here on, I'm gonna tighten up."

Carl does, beating us all again and again.

"You better hope I don't find the range," I say, and then I scratch the cue ball.

"I'm not jokin'," Lewis says gravely. "*Walt can't shoot!*"

I hesitate, getting ready to discombobulate time just a little bit myself.

"This table's out of alignment," I say. "You better call Gerald and get it zeroed in."

Home Place

It was so hot yesterday and the rabbits so scarce that Alex, Bobby, Lewis, and Carl have done something shocking—they've decided not to hunt today. So Matt and I get dressed, take our guns, and head out to hunt Bobby's farm. We haven't hunted the home place alone together for several years, not since Matt was shooting his .410 and I was playing hunting dog and scaring rabbits out of brush piles for him. Matt's taller than I am now. His voice is deeper than mine. He's a better shot. He no longer needs my hunting advice, but I'm still prone to dispense it. The morning is warm, overcast with ominous clouds, and windy. With the chimes on Alex's porch clinking, Matt hands me his gun and twists open the homemade wooden latch on the dog kennel.

"Okay, Rowdy, you wanta get some rabbits?" he asks Alex's dog.

Bobby and Alex walk out to the kennel to meet us.

"Rowdy'll run a rabbit but she don't have no stayin' power," Bobby is saying as they arrive.

"She run like a professional yesterday," Alex replies, defending his dog.

Bobby shakes his head. "She's a good trail dog but she hasn't got no stayin' power."

Alex looks as if he's about to curse but doesn't. "She'll kick in."

As the brothers bicker, Matt and I click shells into our guns.

"Gonna rain," Alex says, nodding upward at the clouds.

Not surprisingly, Bobby disagrees. "Last night the rain hadn't even gotten past Paducah."

I ignore the men. "Be careful shooting toward any farm equipment," I tell Matt, unable to resist giving him advice I know he doesn't need. "Pellets might ricochet."

That catches Alex's attention. "You should know. Shot your own father-in-law."

I sigh, knowing that I will take that story to the grave with me. Matt smiles, and we head off to a blackberry patch just beyond Bobby's barn. Rowdy and I go in on the far side and walk back toward Matt, who posts twenty yards outside the thicket. Rowdy howls, and I see the flash of white tail bounding from the weeds. Matt fires and the rabbit drops. We hunt across a pasture littered with pieces of old clay pigeon that Matt shattered when he was first learning to shoot his .410. We hunt around the pond where he and his sister used to catch catfish a foot long. We pass forty giant rolls of hay Carl and Bobby have laid in as cow food for the winter. Cows stand all around, their bodies motionless as statues, heads dipped to the ground, jaws grinding. When a cow does move, it moves with operatic precision, one step, then another. Elegant, if you stop to look.

"I'm gonna shoot the next rabbit since I gave you the last one," I say.

Matt is unimpressed. "Who's on the egg?"

"I let you have that first rabbit so you won't have to tell your friends you didn't get any."

"What about your friends?"

I hesitate just one beat. "I'll tell 'em I got four."

Matt flashes a big, surprised, boyish smile. I could take a picture.

I cherish these moments. But how do I conjure up their power for you, a man or woman who has never hunted? Do I tell you again that it's like the mystery of love and joy and grief, that you've got to be there? Tell you again that it's like the time in the hospital chapel when I prayed for my father's life, a moment of grace? Tell you again that time seems to interweave with itself in an immortal instant? It must all sound cloying if you don't already get it. Maybe this will help: I think of eating biscuits and gravy at Burkesville's C&J Restaurant and American cheese and ring baloney on Sunbeam bread at Sproule's country store—moments and places that exist nowhere else in the charted universe. I think of a man I knew of who once stayed up late into the night and played the old 1923 Irving Cohn and Frank Silver tune "Yes! We Have No Bananas," because he wanted to know for certain that he was the only person living that exact experience at that exact moment. That's how I feel: *"But yes, we have no bananas / We have no bananas today."* A rabbit breaks from tall grass along a fence line behind Alex's house, Matt fires, and kills the rabbit at thirty yards. I'm impressed and glad and proud.

"Good shootin'!" I holler.

So much is in the way we see, and I was seeing Washington differently by the time I finished *Crossings* and returned to *The Washington Post.* I met a man who mentioned that he gave away his $210 Tasmanian wool slacks to charity after a few dry cleanings because they had lost their soft feel on his skin. In Georgetown's Antonio Buttaro Boutique, I saw a woman calmly trying to decide whether to buy a thousand-dollar alligator purse. One morning, in line for coffee at Francelle's Express Café, I heard an outraged boy, maybe seven years old, turn away from the waitress and say, "She's out of fresh-squeezed orange juice! *During breakfast!*" A man who must have been the boy's father, from the soles of his white canvas shoes to the leather-backed buttonholes of his jacket, seemed equally outraged. I knew a woman, a lawyer, with a baby at home. She worked fifty-five hours a week and felt guilty for not working weekends. I met a woman who worked in the public library. She once told a man that he couldn't check out anymore books until he paid his back fines. The man became enraged, threw down his high-level government ID, and announced with a flurry, "This is who I am!" I had a friend, a best-selling author, who told me about a game he had played at a Washington cocktail party. When asked the city's de rigueur question about what he did for a living, he said, "I'm a garbageman."

"Oh," said someone in the circle of suits, "you own a garbage company."

"No, I pick up garbage." The crowd went edgy. "Yeah, and you know what bugs me—people who put wet grass clippings in plastic garbage bags. You know how heavy that is? Why don't people think?" My friend kept talking and talking while his trapped audience squirmed. When he finally stopped, nobody said a word. In a minute, he was alone.

I could go on and on with this stuff.

None of it, of course, was new to me. Everybody in Washington isn't a status-grubbing snit or a workaholic, naturally. The city has hamburger slingers, schoolteachers, government nine-to-fivers, an army of folks working for little money for what they believe are good public causes. But those people don't set the tone of the city, a place where you are three times more likely to meet a lawyer or a journalist or a public relations man than in the rest of the country. In Washington, people more often drive new convertibles (as did I), buy foreign brandy (as did I), and visit the Caribbean (as did I). On the other hand, in Washington, you're half as likely to run into a man who has installed the muffler on his own car. As a prominent Washington attorney once told me, "It's a constant fight to remember that there is another world out there."

Alex, Bobby, Lewis, and Carl had made that easier for me. I had looked at the men and seen something missing in my life. My travels for *Crossings* had taken me into the homes of scores of ordinary people across the country—a sharecropper in North Carolina, a mortician in Tennessee, high school kids in Arkansas, a beautician in California, an autoworker in Ohio, a trumpet player in New York. They were fascinating to me, so much more fascinating than men and women in pursuit of power back in Washington. When I looked at Washington's people as a Rorschach test, I saw things in myself I didn't like. I had always been blindly ambitious, and Washington was a culture of blind ambition. "So many people in Washington say, 'My life is my work,'" a congressional aide told me. "You can get caught up in that." Indeed. I had come to Rome from the hinterlands and been seduced, willingly. I didn't feel guilty about it. I just didn't feel satisfied.

While writing *Crossings,* I had worked at home and Keran had kept commuting to her office. During that year, I began running the family errands to the dry cleaners, auto mechanic, vet. I took the parent-teacher meetings. I picked up Matt and Kyle after school and got their homework going. During the week, I cooked dinners—spaghetti, chicken, steaks, Dinty Moore beef stew. Not exactly haute cuisine but edible. I kept the house tidy so Keran wouldn't come home to a mess. And with me doing the errands during the week, we suddenly had weekends free. I still worked long hours but, for the first time, I felt as if my life had, I don't know, it's hard to explain . . . as if my life had an organic shape to it. I didn't feel anymore as if I got up every morning and raced headlong through a series of checkpoints until I collapsed late at night. My life didn't feel sequential; it felt interwoven. I got tired but it was a good tired, the tired you feel after a workout or an afternoon in the garden. Actually, it was a lot like the tired I felt after a long day of hunting in Kentucky.

I had an old friend my age who was a corporate executive. He earned a fortune, flew all around the world, lived regally—and complained constantly about how he wanted more "balance" in his life, more time with family and friends. I had begun to wonder if "balance" was the way to think about it. The word implies either / or, weights in separate pans of a scale. I thought of a furniture maker I knew whose workshop was a few steps from his back door. I thought of Alex, Bobby, Lewis, and Carl, who had everything in their lives a few steps from their back doors. I knew a lawyer who had passed on $200,000 a year and eighty-hour workweeks in Washington to live in Helena, Montana, on $75,000. His life there wasn't either / or.

He still worked long hours but he was fifteen minutes from the office. Plenty of parking and no lines in the stores, not even at Christmas. He walked out his back door and went horseback riding with his wife and children. I knew that most people in our life-versus-work society can't live that way. He was a fortunate man. And so was I. As I had stumbled into the joy of sleeping all night with my infant daughter on my chest, I had stumbled into an organic life. I wanted to keep it.

When I went back to writing for the *Post* magazine, I kept working at home. As long as the stories flowed, that was fine. But I knew that being at home would slowly isolate me from office politics, which would hurt me in the long run. When you're away from the corporate water cooler, you don't keep up alliances and friendships that carry power and opportunity, or stay attuned to the ever-shifting political landscape. You just lose touch. I figured it was worth the risk. As it was time to let go of the themes of social class that I had revisited again and again, it was time, too, to let go of stories on political movers and shakers. Although I knew that study after study had shown that life satisfaction is mostly determined by people's happiness in their family lives, I loved my work. I couldn't pretend that away. But I wanted to work again as I had when I was young, with passion and abandon. I wanted to be impelled from within, not by the pursuit of status or respect from without. I didn't want to achieve any more to cleanse myself of shame. I wanted to achieve for the joy of it. It's corny, but I found myself humming Ricky Nelson's old pop song "Garden Party": "See, you can't please everyone / so you got to please yourself." I wanted to take advantage of what was deep within me, what I'd always seen as a deprivation to overcome, and write about people who were just trying to make it through the night.

Over lunch at Washington's trendy Georgia Brown's I told this to my editor, and synchronicity delivered another meaningful coincidence. My editor had been off on a yearlong fellowship, spent a lot more time with his wife and daughters, and returned with his interest in politics tempered by a taste of everyday life. Because plenty of

Post reporters wanted to cover politicos, he was happy to let me go my arcane way. In the next few years, I wrote long articles about an old man who moved back in with his daughter and her family; an amateur gospel singer hoping to break into the biz; a young, working-poor couple with children; a typical thirteen-year-old suburban boy; a runaway teenager; a happily married man and woman; a poet writing a poem; a girl's soccer team; a small-time, small-town stock car racer. *The Washington Post,* an amazing institution, gave me months to do each story. While doing them, I felt what I'd felt years earlier at the Everlasting Stream. When I stood off stage at the Apollo Theater in Harlem as the gospel singer twisted her body into a crouch, flung her arm behind her back, and wailed out a line of gospel . . . When the poet described how she heard the *cadence of thought* in the rhythm of her written words . . . When the stock car driver told me how he became no more than a piece of the physics of motion and mass as his speeding car's inertia bent into a curve . . .

At all these times, I remembered, people are distinct, moments immortal.

"But yes, we have no bananas / We have no bananas today."

Matt has been hunting with the men and me only a few years, and it's already nearly time for him to disappear. Next year, his high school basketball team has a tournament over the Thanksgiving break, and he won't be able to come with us to the farm. The year after that, he'll be in college. He has told me several times that he plans to go to the farm for Thanksgiving that year, but we'll see. Stomping through briars with a bunch of old men may not be high on his list by then. In the decade Matt has been shooting and hunting at the farm, he hasn't had a single friend who has also hunted. Mostly, he has taken grief from kids who, like my friends in Washington, believe hunters are brutes. "How can you do that?" they ask him in moral indignation. Matt, a chip off the old block in this regard, enjoys riling them, contesting their city prejudices.

"Do you eat meat?" he asks. "How do you think it gets on your plate?"

If only vaguely, Matt already realizes that things change. He doesn't like to think about how the men and I will not be around forever. He thinks of the men's dead friend R.C., who taught Matt to load a high-powered shell as the third shell in his gun so that if he missed his first two shots, he'd have extra distance on the last. "One year R.C. is there," Matt told me, "and the next year, he's just not." Matt has mentioned to me with concern that I don't have the energy I did when I was stomping through brush piles for him years ago. He has mentioned how strange it would be to hunt without hearing Bobby once again tell the story of how Alex fired three errant shots at a rabbit coming straight at him near Roseville Road. Or without hearing his grandfather complain yet again about the time my shotgun pellet hit his leg.

"It won't be the same," Matt said.

When Matt was a boy, I worried that he was seeing only the surface of what I believed was going on among Alex, Bobby, Lewis, and Carl and their hunting habits and rituals. One day in the field, when Matt had been particularly quiet, I asked if he was enjoying himself.

"Yeah."

"But are you learning anything?"

"No, but I'm enjoying myself."

"Don't you think hunting has anything to teach you?"

"Nope."

Yet the experiences of the boy are finally beginning to be remembered through the eyes of a man. An insight of poet Rainer Maria Rilke comes to mind: *The power of memory is when it returns to us through experience with new meaning.* I asked Matt recently to please think about what he has learned while hunting and tell me what he thought. A few weeks later, he wrote me a note that amazed me: "I want my son to hunt. I want him to hunt the same places that I did—

Lawson Bottom, the Square, Bobby's farm. Even though it's not socially acceptable to be a hunter anymore, I want him to know his roots. Even if we live in a city, his roots are country, his roots are Glasgow, Kentucky. I want to play dog while he hunts with the .410. Hunting was one of the best things that made me, as a boy, mature. There's nothing a father can do to tell his son that he has the utmost trust in him that can rival putting a shotgun in his hands at the age of fourteen and letting him go out with grown men—cussing, whiskey-drinking, country men. The son will learn so much about people different from himself, things that can't be taught in school. The son will learn that his father trusts him, no matter what arguments happen any other time, because the father has the confidence in his son to send him out into the field with a loaded weapon."

It was eerie reading Matt's words written as if about someone else's father. But I knew what he was trying to tell me, and I appreciated it. I realized, too, that Matt had grasped the heart of it all—James Swan's Zen of hunting, Ortega y Gasset's "perpetual alertness of the wild animal," the Navajo's way of hunting in the manner of a deer, Carl's idea of sleeping with your eyes open, my father's simultaneous alertness to a landscape's sweep and a flower's petals.

"You have to always be on your toes, always alert, always expecting the unexpected. Yet at the same time you have to stay calm. I think the biggest part of being a hunter is being able to see the big picture and detail at the same time. The trick is to see detail and not see detail all at once. It was hard for me at first but eventually I got used to it." Matt then told this story about the first time he believes he mastered something of that blend: A rabbit was running away from him, and, as Matt lifted his gun, he noticed that the foliage was taller and thicker to the rabbit's left. Matt decided that the rabbit would likely jump left, and so he pointed his shotgun slightly in that direction. Sure enough, the rabbit zigged left just as Matt fired. In an instant, Matt had correctly calculated the mathematics of detail and impression. Ortega y Gasset says this hunter's alertness carries into the routine world, and he quotes Socrates speaking to one of his students: "Now then, Glaucon, we must post ourselves like a ring of huntsmen around the thicket, with very alert minds, so that justice does not escape." Matt's less grandiose but he has still gotten the point: "I started applying the 'hunter's eye' to the rest of my life, and I realized how beautiful a place the world is. I'll see the big picture of an amazing sunset. But then I'll notice the way the sun is making the shadows look on the ground and the way the clouds are moving. That's the ability to see detail and not see detail at the same time. I learned that while hunting."

Matt has most enjoyed hunting the old Collins place, where I once showed him the remains of the limestone springhouse Carl had shown me. "I wouldn't be able to find it myself. But I've had the pleasure of stumbling onto it a couple of times. And whenever I do, I just sit and look around. I remember one time I was sitting there, it must have been twenty minutes, and I was zoning out in the simple beauty of the surroundings. I probably would have sat there for an hour except that a gunshot snapped me back to reality. It was almost a surreal experience." I once asked Matt what he believed to be the most important thing he had learned from hunting with Alex, Bobby, Lewis, and Carl. I thought he'd say something about how to shoot a gun or gibe a guy good. Matt thought for a moment and said, "They started out with almost nothing, way poor. They still haven't got a lot. And they're happy. I mean, they're really happy."

Years ago, I rolled the dice. I think it turned out okay.

Matt and I have entered the wood behind Bobby's house. Matt has his two rabbits; I've killed one. It's cooler in the wood compared to the bare field. Even without leaves, the wood's arching branches of tall hickories, white oaks, and walnuts are a roof against the sun. The wood isn't primo rabbit territory. Its brush piles are made mostly of large logs that are more easily accessible to predators. Because of the tree canopy overhead, ground cover doesn't grow thick. In ten years, unless the tall trees are thinned and the woodpiles topped with branch cuttings, the trees will be even more dominant, the ground cover sparser, and the rabbits fewer. This morning, spiderweb architecture hangs in geometric patchwork from tree to tree, and the sticky threads cling to our hats and coats and waft behind us like silvery tails.

"Rowdy, are you done for the day?" I ask as the dog jumps playfully at my feet.

"You better hope not," Matt says. "Low man cleans."

"Rules change. Young man cleans. We need a picture of you with the three rabbits."

"Only two are mine," Matt says.

"So what? Who'll care fifty years from now?"

Matt angles his head and smiles. "I'm still not cleaning the third rabbit."

Matt and I hunt the wood without success. Across a pasture next to Bobby's house is a fence thick with blackberry briars, wild mint, and orchard grass. But it looks as if Alex might be right and it will rain soon, so Matt and I leave the fence for another day. We empty our guns, fill a water bucket, grab a gut bucket, and take up a spot in the wood behind Bobby's house near Alex's antique Coke machine, which he has filled with cheap Falls City beer. The machine is set on nickel-a-bottle but Alex always hands out the key so the men can take a free beer. I snap that picture of Matt, his gun on his shoulder, the three rabbits dangling by their back legs in his hand, Rowdy dancing at his side. Alex comes out of the house, gets a Falls City, and joins us.

"You know how to gut 'em?" he asks Matt.

"Yeah, I'll do 'em," Matt says.

"Well, they're your rabbits," Alex says.

"I know, I'll clean 'em." Matt lifts a dripping rabbit from the water bucket, takes the rabbit's head in his right hand, holds its body firmly at its chest in his left, twists as if he were opening a stubborn jar of pickles, yanks, and drops the severed head into the gut bucket.

"Careful not to lay the skinned rabbits in the dirt," Alex says.

"I'll be careful," Matt says.

Matt has turned over an aluminum garbage can to use as his cleaning table. He's taken off his hunting jacket, and his long underwear shirt gleams bleach-white in the sunlight that has just popped from behind the clouds and is squeezing through the leafless trees. The sky is clearing, and it looks as if Bobby was right: the rain didn't make it past Paducah. Alex hovers over Matt and leans down to check his handiwork in the way my wife used to hover over me at the kitchen sink when she didn't yet believe I was capable of giving Matt a baby's bath. Before long, Alex reaches down and holds open Matt's gutted rabbit so Matt can pick off the innards that have clung to the carcass like pieces of lint. Before long, as Matt slices out pellets buried under the rabbit's skin, Alex reaches into the water bucket, takes out a rabbit, and begins to clean.

Nate Smith's Dairy Farm

I dreamed the other night that I was cleaning a rabbit. It was skinned and gutted, its sinewy body red and glossy and lying across my hand when it jumped up, bounded to the ground, and ran off, headless and without feet, across the field. It was like watching a cartoon. Even as I dreamed the dream, I knew that, once again, my mind was mulling the morality of hunting. As Alex and Matt and I pull into Nate Smith's dairy farm, I'm thinking about that dream and the words of my father: "You shoot an animal, Butch, and it bleeds." We park in front of a tenant farmer's rough, tin-roofed cottage, where the trucks of Bobby and Carl are already parked. We see the men in a far field across a pasture of cow pies. The dogs have been howling, and just as we arrive at the trees where the men are posted, a rabbit darts from the forest. I fire and kill the rabbit.

"Good shot, Walt!" Matt hollers.

Bobby strolls over. "The dogs been runnin' that rabbit forever."

"Guess I came at the right time."

As ever, I savor the hunt—the laughing and joking, the camaraderie and skill. I love, as Matt said, the almost surreal experience of immersing myself in the aura of field and forest, sky and wind, cold or warmth, the crunch of leaves, sway of branches, shades of color, the scents, angles of light, play of distance, the scudding, billowing, streaking clouds, the variations on sky-blue. I think of the anthropologist Stuart Marks, one of the few scholars to have deeply studied the rituals of hunting in America, who says that hunting "appropriates parts of the 'natural' universe and makes them part of the 'human' world." That pretty much says it. The rabbit I just shot is soft and warm in my hand. I hold it at its belly, which is malleable like a kitten's belly. With just a light grasp, my fingers indent its body. Its fur feels like the soft lining of a leather glove.

Once, when we were hunting at Barren River Lake, I came upon a dead deer, a doe, lying on a bed of johnsongrass. She'd been shot in the stomach the day before. Deer season was a week past, and she was no doubt killed by a poacher who then couldn't find her in the woods. The deer lay on her side, her legs outstretched, reminding me of the deer you see pulling Santa's sleigh, deer in full lope. A deer is a beautiful creature. Its eyes are dark and clear and moist with long lashes. Deer, like humans, have tear ducts. No wonder we have the term "doe-eyed." For thousands of years, deer and rabbits have been appropriated in literature to symbolize purity and innocence. In legend, Christian saints were often escorted by deer. Saint Thomas More used the example of a live rabbit being thrown to dogs as evidence of human depravity. In *Walden,* Henry David Thoreau wrote: "The hare in its extremity cries like a child." Then came Thumper and Bambi. The dead doe certainly looked like the purest of creatures: lean, with thin, graceful legs, and a delicate neck that narrowed into a perfectly feminine head, mouth, and nose. It seemed as if I could have nudged her with my toe and she'd have bolted to her feet and bounded off.

This morning, the men and Matt and I go about making the natural universe part of our human world. We curse the stench of the cow pies in the pasture. We see the wonder of a pack of howling dogs barrel past a squatting rabbit hidden in the short grass and see the savvy rabbit scurry off into the woods and freedom. We come to a pond, and Bobby tells us we will never see a rabbit drinking water, because rabbits get their water from the plants they eat. Nobody argues with Bobby. In the forest, Alex finds saplings whose trunks weave around one another like braided cinnamon twists, and he says that country people used to make walking sticks out of those trunks. When Matt and I come to a fence, I take his gun and hold up the barbed wire for him to duck under. Once on the other side, Matt returns the favor. Alex and Lewis shoot at a rabbit at the same time, and Alex bags him. "You shot the dirt," Lewis says. Alex later whispers to me that Lewis shot that rabbit, although he never tells Lewis, who bitches all morning that Alex stole his rabbit. About halfway through the hunt, Bobby starts getting on Matt about not yet shooting a rabbit: "Matt, you gotta get off that egg." I accidentally grab a hot-wire livestock fence, drop it instantly, and shake off the electric sting that rockets up my arm. Everybody laughs. Around all this human ritual, we've done what we claim we came to do—killed rabbits, eight of them. I've killed two, Lewis the one that Alex pilfered, Goat two, Carl two, Bobby one.

I've got blood on my hands this morning, not figuratively but in fact. It has dried on the backs of my fingers, where it didn't rub off when I wiped my palms on my hunting pants. Blood defines my cuticles as if it had been drawn on with a fine-tipped marker. Rabbit blood isn't as thick as human blood, which is to rabbit blood what paint is to whitewash. My hands are red-washed in its traces. I think of that deer in the woods. I again think of my father's words. "You shoot an animal, Butch, and it bleeds."

The right or wrong of hunting has nagged at me from the beginning, and after a decade of hunting I finally set out to think it through. I agree with the sentiment of writer Edward Abbey: "Hunting is one the hardest things even to think about." As is my way, I began by reading up on the history of hunting and the raging debate over its morality. Every schoolchild learns that Homo sapiens were born hunters. The *Encyclopedia Americana* begins its hunting entry with this sentence: "Man has always hunted." Our prehuman ancestors hunted a million years ago. Some anthropologists believe that the teamwork hunting required may have helped wire human brains for cooperative enterprise, shaping the human sexual division of labor and the very nature of family structure. A Paleolithic man or woman engraved a shamanistic image of a speared and disemboweled bison on their cave wall in Lascaux. The Greek goddess Artemis was a huntress. It was her affection for her fellow hunter, Orion, that caused her jealous twin brother, Apollo, to have Orion killed. In her grief, Artemis hung her friend's likeness in the nightly sky for us to see even today. Closer to home, in Barren County, hunting dates back at least ten thousand years to the last ice age, as do cottontail rabbits. Native Americans later consecrated the county's land "bloody ground" in honor of the buffalo they slaughtered every year. In the nineteenth century, American city dwellers demanded so much game that commercial hunters annihilated entire species, most notoriously the passenger pigeon. It was sportsmen hunters—now so often decried as brutes by antihunters—who first demanded an end to such blue-sky slaughterhouses.

It wasn't the *history* of hunting that seemed to me most important, however, it was the *meaning* we had made of hunting. If you read only one book on the cultural significance of hunting, read *A View to a Death in the Morning* by anthropologist Matt Cartmill: "The importance of hunting lies in its symbolism, not its economics." In ancient Greek literature, hunting symbolized the just conquest of man over beast. In medieval European thought, hunting was a stand-in and training ground for war. To Romantics at the turn of the eighteenth century, hunting was a depraved human intervention in the natural beauty of nature. With Darwin's nineteenth-century survival of the fittest, hunting looked like nothing more than a piece of nature's brutal course. With the rise and fall of Nazism, hunting came to symbolize man's innate tendency toward violence, a view that Cartmill says strongly influenced the creators of the famous Walt Disney antihunting film *Bambi*.

The battle over the *meaning* of hunting still rages, with hunting opponents arguing that its practitioners must be somehow deranged, even sadistic. The best of the critics believe no sentient being should be put to death in field or slaughterhouse when humans no longer need flesh to survive. I respect the critics who eat no meat, poultry, fish, eggs, or cheese; who drink no milk, wear no leather or felt; who carefully read supermarket labels to be sure any item they buy is free of animal by-products. They are battling for a high-minded cause. Our culture exists on the exploitation of animals, and these people pay a huge daily price in effort and sacrifice.

It is the lazy hunting-haters who gall me. People like the woman at my first rabbit feast years ago, who said, "I can't believe you killed those little bunnies." People who partake in the routinized, industrial, daily bloodbath of animals but who think shooting a single rabbit is immoral. Every year, hunters kill 135 million rabbits, doves, squirrels, ducks, quail, pheasant, deer, geese, and elk. A mind-boggling slaughter? It's very little compared to the more than 800 million animals killed in slaughterhouses every year. We are a society awash in animal blood. Most people eat flesh as guiltlessly as they breathe air. So why do so many believe hunting is immoral?

Remember, it's not hunting; it's the hunter. Men don't hunt for sustenance anymore. We hunt for the anthropologists' reason— as a piece of human ritual. I hunt for the pleasure of forests and fields, companionship, for what my son can learn about lives foreign to his own. I hunt to experience the moments of heightened acuity that modern life seems to dull. I hunt to experience the story. Yet, as I returned to hunt year after year, I came to realize that hunting was more than a search for human meaning in place and experience. I was struck when I read the words of Montana nature writer M. R. James: "How can any man or woman, city born and bred, expect to know firsthand—to understand—that killing is a daily part of life for all of us? . . . There is no blood, urine, and fecal matter mingling on the polished aisles of grocery stores. There are no steaming piles of intestines, no sounds of hide being ripped away from muscle, no odor of death in the conditioned air. . . . If the emotional issue is one of life itself, I ask, does not the calf waiting in the feedlot surely value its existence as much as the deer standing in the forest shadows?"

I believe this on principle. It doesn't matter to a rabbit what kills him—fever, flukes, worms, weather, hawks, or me. The rabbit is dead. No mystical link exists between the rabbit's life and death and my motivation in killing him. The rabbit doesn't care. We care. Those who despise hunting seem to believe that killing and eating an animal, as opposed to eating an animal that has been killed for us, stirs in men some primal sadism. "There is a passion for hunting something deeply implanted in the human breast," Charles Dickens wrote. Those who despise hunters believe we can conquer that passion if we eat only animals that have been killed anonymously. Man's buried inhumanity then can be kept at bay because the beast has not been stirred, as if blood once felt warm and damp on our hands will make us crave more killing.

Only hunting—actually killing animals myself—taught me how wrong, how upside down, that perspective is. It's what the intellectuals would call counterintuitive. Killing an animal doesn't deaden the human conscience; it enlivens it. It jars it into being. It shocks the conscience awake like a bucket of cold water thrown in a sleeping man's face. Not the small conscience of venial sins but the big conscience of original sin—the sin of existence. Paradoxically, the inhumanity of killing an animal calls forth a man's buried humanity. I am a novice hunter, and shooting rabbits is hardly even hunting for men in the tradition of stalking bull elk in Norway, brindled gnu in Africa, or warthog on the Nile. Still, the sensations for the hunter must be universal. I remember once standing over a rabbit I had shot and seeing that it had no visible sign of a wound, that the rabbit looked as pure as its mythology. Then blood began to flow from just above the rabbit's hip in a rivulet that expanded and pooled in a quarter-sized, then a half-dollar-sized lake bounded by an oval bank of fur. I watched and thought that this flow was the last motion of life this animal would ever know. *And I had done that!* I told myself that slaughtering the rabbit was no different from the slaughter of a chicken I would guiltlessly buy at the Safeway. But, God, it *felt* different. And it continues to feel different, forever. Hunting isn't golf or tennis, which demand only technical mastery. Hunting isn't merely an exercise in male bonding, as so many believe. Hunting has moral gravitas. "Every good hunter," philosopher Ortega y Grasset wrote, "is uneasy in the depths of his conscience when faced with the death he is about to inflict on the enchanting animal. . . . It is the frightening mystery of blood."

That's why it's right that I should have dreams in which dead animals are resurrected in my hands, because killing doesn't feel good. Hunting contradicts my idea of my own decency. And having killed many animals doesn't make me feel less guilty for the last one I killed. The last animal killed only reminds me of what I've done, and what I'll go on doing—in either field or supermarket. I now realize why the moments just before, during, and after the killing compare to life's moments of grace. In the words of the hunter and poet Bruce Woods: "At such moments I am as pure a creature as I'll ever be, involved in an act of monumental seriousness." Remember William James on the instant of religious conversion: "The mysteries of life become lucid." Only after I began hunting was I hit with the shock that something deep inside me gets excited when the prey appears, when the dogs howl, and that maybe I'm not that different from those dogs, that I must work at being human. The poet James Dickey understood.

> And I pluck my longbow off the limb
> Where it shines with a musical light,
> And crouch within death, awaiting
> The beast in the water, in love
> With the palest and gentlest of children,
> Whom the years have turned deadly with knowledge:
> Who summons him forth, and now
> Pulls wide the great, thoughtful arrow.

For centuries, hunting has been a metaphor for the way we would like to imagine ourselves. I take the unromantic view that big fish eat little fish, that forests are always trying to colonize pastures, that a doe rabbit can bear forty-nine offspring a year because rabbits are the McDonald's restaurant of the wild. I believe all this goes on without human meaning, a machine in perpetual motion. As much as I admire anthropologist Cartmill's book, his conclusion reveals the confusion of a man who has never hunted: "The anti-hunter can still legitimately retort that enjoying the fruits of the kill is not the same thing as taking pleasure in killing itself." If Cartmill were a hunter, he would know better. It is people who enjoy the fruits of the kill without feeling the ominous responsibility of the killing who are morally delinquent. Is a family spread around the Thanksgiving dinner table, heads bowed in prayer before a golden-brown store-bought turkey, any less guilty than a hunter of taking part in a human ritual at the expense of a sentient being?

Even those who refuse to eat meat or wear leather, who are trying to live their beliefs, can't escape their place in nature's balance—or imbalance. Habitat destruction from development is far more devastating to wild animal populations than is hunting, but animal lovers still buy new homes and shop at malls. They pour insecticides on their lawns. They drive cars that kill countless wild animals a year. And what of the vegetarians who eat grains from croplands that sprawl as far as the eye can see and have wiped out boundless acres of animal habitat? It's a silent slaughter, and being blissfully ignorant of the carnage makes it no less ferocious.

I was at my dining room table eating a rabbit just the other day. While I was tearing a slice of thigh off the bone, I found myself thinking something I had never thought before: Which rabbit is this that I am eating? Is it the rabbit at the old Collins place that I had smashed in the head to kill? Is it the rabbit Matt killed in the blackberry patch beyond Bobby's barn? Is it the rabbit Alex held open on the upturned trash can so Matt could pick off the last bits of organ? Or is it the rabbit Alex had quietly cleaned despite his gruff assertion that Matt should clean his own rabbits?

I have never wondered any such thing about a bite of Thanksgiving turkey.

What has any of this to do with Alex, Bobby, Lewis, Carl, my son, myself, or modern manhood? Well, I wonder if it's only cultural nurture that ninety percent of America's fourteen million hunters are men. I wonder if the switch that I throw in my head allowing me to sleep with the tabby kitten curled next to me and still slice open the belly of a warm animal is an inherently male mechanism. I wonder why the words of my father have always reverberated so loudly in my mind: "You shoot an animal, Butch, and it bleeds." That matter-of-fact declaration, I imagine, chills many people to the bone. But I believe it's a piece of the essence of manhood, old and new, the manhood I learned from my father and that I see in Alex, Bobby, Lewis, and Carl. The noblest qualities of men have always been that they take responsibility for acting, for showing their love by doing and protecting, for keeping a cool head in tough times. Men are realists. And when a man hunts, he accepts the most realistic of burdens: that something—plants or animals or, often, both—must die for him to stay alive. When I feel guilty for killing a rabbit, it isn't weakness in me; it isn't my conscience telling me that hunting is wrong. I think of Alex, who has never liked the killing but who hunts anyway, and I have finally figured it out.

I'm not supposed to hunt without guilt.

I'm supposed to hunt *despite the guilt.*

If this confounds you, think of these lines from Barry Lopez's beautiful book *Arctic Dreams*: "No culture has yet solved the dilemma each has faced with the growth of conscious mind: how to live a moral and compassionate existence when one is fully aware of the blood, the horror inherent in all life, when one finds darkness not only in one's own culture but within oneself. If there is a stage at which an individual life becomes truly adult, it must be when one grasps the irony in its unfolding and accepts responsibility for a life lived in the midst of such paradox. . . . There are simply no answers to some of the great pressing questions. You continue to live them out, making your life a worthy expression of leaning into the light."

I'm glad my son, even if he never hunts again, has experienced that paradox. I'm not at all worried that hunting animals will make him cold and heartless, because I understand now that hunting animals nurtures the heart. I'm glad he has entered a world of allegedly brutish men and realized their humanity, that he has gotten some inkling that there is more to heaven and earth than is in his philosophy. I'm glad that he has learned what it means to hold life and death in his hands, to be mindfully alert, to watch the world near and far away at the same time. I'm glad he has recognized that what so many self-righteously view simply as a good-versus-evil debate is the place where real thinking must begin. I'm glad he has realized that appropriating Nate Smith's cow pies, barbed-wire fences, and rabbits for our affirmation is the inevitable way we go about making ourselves human, that we are, like rabbits, a footprint in this place.

And I'm glad I have realized all these things myself.

On my first Thanksgiving morning in Glasgow, I had set out to humor my father-in-law, to keep from looking like a city effete who imagined he was too good to get down with the menfolk. It was a minor social obligation. A decade later, my obligatory experiences were coming back to me with new meaning. Compared to the mysteries of life I discovered while hunting with the men, the matters that once obsessed me in Washington—achievement and stature, money and image—seemed awfully trivial. I thought about my Washington friends who had no hope of comprehending how little they understood about hunting, which they believed they understood completely. How little they understood about men like Alex, Bobby, Lewis, and Carl. I didn't want to convince them otherwise. I just wanted to remember that I myself had once thought that way, too. I wondered how many other of my beliefs, how many confident opinions I held about matters and people unknown to me, were equally shallow, arrogant, and wrong. Once again, my time with Alex, Bobby, Lewis, and Carl had made me humble.

Long ago, a woman at my table said to me, "I can't believe you killed those little bunnies."

I now know what I should have said in response.

"I can't believe you ate those little bunnies without killing one."

Picnic in
Bobby's Wood

Alex, Bobby, Lewis, and Carl are spread out in just the way I want to remember them. The morning hunt is done, and Alex has baked beans, turnip greens, pork, and venison cooking in the house. A few of Alex's old air force buddies are visiting from Louisville today, and Alex is glad the morning hunt gave up a dozen rabbits so the men don't have to go home making excuses. Alex's friends are lounging on the ground leaning back on their arms with their legs extended and crossed at the ankles or sitting on the low porch of Alex's country store with elbows planted on their thighs. Alex, Bobby, Lewis, and Carl are holding down the far end of the porch, Bobby sitting against the rough-hewn corner post that Alex picked from the pile of cedar logs where I, mindlessly running in place, shot my first rabbits. Bobby is turned a bit toward Lewis, who's sitting next to Carl, who's working the nub of a cigar. Behind the men, Alex is leaning against a wooden whiskey barrel. They're relaxed and smiling: the perfect image of Kentucky Gothic.

"I missed that rabbit worst than anything," Carl says of a shot he took this morning.

"We know," Alex says. "Everybody seen it. You missed twice."

"I didn't miss but once."

"Well, you said *twice* that you missed."

"That's different!"

"Boom!" Alex yells. "So much dust, I thought somebody was spinnin' his wheels."

Lewis comes to Carl's aid, mentions that Alex has finally gotten rid of his sorry dog, Red.

"Alex just wouldn't get rid a Red for the longest time," Lewis says.

"I had to give 'im a chance," says Alex.

"A chance?" hollers Carl. "Hell, we been tellin' ya to get rid a Red for three years!"

After the laughter, Bobby clears his throat with a cough. It's story time.

"Hey, Carl," he says, "pull that pipe out and turn it around." The men chuckle at Bobby's reference to a story he has told before. But Alex's old friends haven't heard the story, which is about a man who was told that he could straighten out his mule's crossed eyes if he slipped a pipe up the mule's butt and blew real hard. The man had a dumb friend who offered to help, and when it was the dumb friend's turn to blow, he pulled out the pipe, put it in the other way, and blew. "Why'd you change ends?" his friend asked incredulously. The dumb man smiled and said, "You didn't think I was gonna blow on that pipe after you had it in your mouth, did ya?" Everybody laughs hard, although Lewis laughs the hardest. One of Alex's friends ventures in and tells a funny story, then another. Lewis gets to his feet and starts pacing, hands stuffed into his pants pockets, shoulders slouched, mouth working in silent agitation. Lewis, looking bewildered that Bobby would let this go on for so long, glances at Bobby, furrows his brow.

"I tell ya what," Bobby finally says, "I knew these three jokers . . ."

Bobby then tells the story of three good friends. Sadly, one of them, Bubba, got killed in a fire and was charred beyond recognition. So his friends were called to the morgue to identify the body. "Nope, that's not Bubba," one of the friends said. "That man's only got one asshole—Bubba's got two assholes." The medical examiner, perplexed, asked how Bubba's friend knew that. "Well," the friend said, "when the three of us walk down the street, people always say,

'There goes old Bubba with them two assholes.'" There is an instant's hesitation—then everybody roars with laughter. Lewis roars the hardest, kicks the dirt, does a quick victory jig.

"Ol' Bobby's cookin!" he yells, downright proud.

I was working in my office at home when the call came. It was Ed Lambeth, an old journalism professor and friend from my days at the University of Missouri. Ed had been reading *The Chronicle of Higher Education*—not a publication on my regular reading list—and noticed that the University of Illinois was looking for a new journalism professor. "The ad sounds like it was written just for you," Ed said. "You interested in teaching?" I wasn't, or at least I hadn't really thought about it. But Ed's phone call did have a certain bookend synchronicity to it because twenty years earlier it had been an out-of-the-blue call from Ed about a job advertisement in *Editor & Publisher* that had sent me packing from the Midwest to the East.

"No," I said. "Thanks, but I'm happy here."

"Well," Ed said, gently persisting, "I'll send it on anyway."

That evening, I cooked pineapple chicken for dinner. I remember, because when I went to get a can of pineapples from the cabinet, we didn't have any, and I had to make a quick trip to the Safeway. After eating, the kids ran off and Keran and I sat talking. Her job was rough then. While I was working mostly at home and avoiding commuting and office politics, she had suffered through three corporate downsizings in a few years. She'd had three new bosses, each with his own quirky personality and management style. She'd had to fire her own friends. Then she waited to see if she was next. She wasn't. But Keran's work just didn't satisfy anymore. When we were first married, Keran used to read three or four books a week. By the time she was earning $75,000 a year, working fifty hours a week, commuting, raising two kids, and taking care of me, she was reading three or four books a year. I knew it was hard, but in Washington, living the way we did, there was no way she could ever stop working.

"You want to move to rural Illinois and retire?" I asked lightly as we cleaned the kitchen.

Keran's voice went brittle. "In a minute."

"What? Are you kidding?"

Keran stopped loading dishes and looked straight at me. "In *one* minute."

It all happened fast. In a few weeks, I had visited Illinois and been offered a professor's job. It was a radical change from out of nowhere. Once I started thinking on the idea, however, it seemed more and more right. Keran and I had grown up and gone to college in small Illinois towns. A lot of people from mountainous places can't live in central Illinois. In the winter, the gray dirt that unfolds in every direction makes them feel dissolute. In the summer, the fortress walls of corn evoke a kind of natural claustrophobia. But to us the landscape was comforting. We'd never quite adjusted to the mountains and trees of the East. We missed seeing the sunsets fanning over a flat, far horizon. When I had visited the University of Illinois campus in Champaign-Urbana, I also realized I missed something else—the scent of farmland at dusk.

I'm sure that some of the move's appeal grew from predictable middle-age reflection, the desire to get out of the rat race, enjoy life more. For me, though, those matters had been pondered through the lens of my time with Alex, Bobby, Lewis, and Carl, my time hunting, my time wrestling with the meaning of hunting and with the satisfaction I saw in the men's lives, with what I had come to see as missing in my own life by comparison. I had already changed myself as a result, tried to resist my craving for status and recognition, to get back to the joy of my youthful passion, to build a more organic life even in the culture of Washington. Wasn't going back to Illinois just one more step down that path? I don't imagine I'll ever understand my mix of motivations beyond a doubt but that's okay. I've always liked Oscar Wilde's quip: "Only the shallow know themselves."

This much was certain: when the time for a life-changing decision came, Alex, Bobby, Lewis, and Carl were in the front of my mind;
I wanted to write the story of my time with the men. I'd been thinking about the idea for a couple of years but knew that no book publisher was going to pay me a big enough advance to live in the manner
to which I had become accustomed in Washington, not for so odd
ball a book. With college for the kids approaching, I couldn't afford
to lose another year's income, as I had with *Crossings*. My job at the
Post was way too demanding to do a book on the side and still see
Matt and Kyle and Keran. But university teaching—thirty weeks of
work a year—would leave me five months a year to work on my own
projects. Once my mind got loose on the freedom of it, I had plenty
of other ideas, too. I wanted to do a college textbook titled *Intimate
Journalism,* a how-to collection of in-depth articles not on politicians
or celebrities but on ordinary people, folks just trying to make it
through the night. I wasn't modest in my ambition. I wanted the book
to influence a generation of aspiring young journalists to look closer
and longer and see the beauty around them. For some time, I had
also wanted to write about the furniture maker I knew whose workshop was only a few steps from his back door. Laboring craftsmen
were rarely given the respect I believed they deserved because brain-
work intellectuals seem to have so little understanding of the tacit
knowledge that's earned when head and hand work together. The
subject was far too arcane for the *Post,* but the editor of *This Old
House* magazine loved the idea and agreed to let me do a fourteen-
article series on the creativity of fine craftsmen. I recalled Ben Bradlee's
question put to me fifteen years earlier: "Do you write for the fun of
it?" And I could feel the old passion rising.

Finally, I thought about teaching. I remembered reading about
a half-century-long study of men who had graduated from Harvard
around the start of World War II. The men had answered question-
naires repeatedly over the decades. Those most satisfied with their
lives had been blindly ambitious in their youths but had mellowed

in middle age and begun to think of themselves as teachers to the young people around them. Oddly enough—that synchronicity again—one of the study's "happy-well" was Ben Bradlee. I took it as an omen. The last piece of the puzzle came from my friend Ed Lambeth. I told him that if I was going to teach young journalists, maybe I should aim to teach at either the University of Missouri or Northwestern University, by reputation the country's best journalism schools. It turned out that Missouri was out of the question because my graduate degree was from Missouri. To avoid in-breeding, the school rarely hired its own. Fortunately, my friend Ed, who had gone to the elite, expensive, private Northwestern University, also knew me well enough to make me remember the gift that I had once seen as a deprivation to overcome: "I don't think you'd like teaching all those rich kids. At a state school like Illinois, you'll be helping youngsters coming up like you did."

That was it. I decided I wanted to go.

Only one glitch could hold Keran and me in Washington—money. If we went to Illinois, we'd go from $165,000 a year in family income to $70,000. At first, the $95,000-a-year shortfall seemed insurmountable. Then we did the math. Instead of a $2,500-a-month mortgage on an elegant home, we could have a $700-a-month mortgage on a modest home. Instead of putting 60,000 miles a year on our cars, we'd put 10,000. In rural Illinois, our car insurance would be cut in half. Instead of spending thousands a year on pricey work clothes, we'd have almost no clothing costs at all. Plus no dry-cleaning bills, no eating out because we were too hurried to cook, no cleaning lady, no car phones. And I had learned something in the last decade. We could live without Sokol Blosser Pinot Noir, trips to the Caribbean, new convertibles, original artwork, and lush Oriental rugs. When we added it all up, we figured we could shave $50,000 a year off our expenses. Throw in taxes and some freelance income, and the $95,000 shortfall would be a clean wash. Years ago, I had stood in my yard at dusk, a glass of wine in my hand, and felt a rush of satisfaction for all the things I had acquired. Then I quickly worried about whether those acquisitions might someday be a trap that would force me to work at what I no longer enjoyed just to pay the tab. Since then, I had seen friends bury themselves in beautiful houses and private schools, resort-season vacations to the French countryside. I saw them begin to do their work for the money and not for the joy of it. I didn't think less of them. I just didn't want to be like them.

"We'll be a lot poorer," I told Keran.

"No, we won't," she said, and I knew what she meant.

I took the job in Illinois, left it all behind.

The storytelling dual between Bobby and Alex's old buddy from Louisville is over quickly. After Bobby's Bubba story, he tells the story of a woman who picked up a man in a bar because she saw he was wearing size-14 shoes. The next morning the man woke up to find fifty dollars on the bed table and figured he must have been pretty good in bed to have earned a payment, that is until he read the note the woman had left behind: "Go buy yourself a pair of shoes that fit." Bobby then tells the story of a man who walked into a bar carrying a club and leading an alligator on a leash. The man bragged that for a hundred dollars he'd let the alligator give him oral sex. Somebody took the bet and when the alligator's grip got a little too tight, the man clubbed his head to remind him of the need for delicacy. When the alligator finished, the man asked, "Now, any of you wanta try it?" From across the bar, a man sheepishly said, "I'd like to, but I don't know about getting hit on the head with that club."

Again and again, Lewis does his victory jig.

Alex's friend goes mute. He doesn't stand a chance, not on Bobby's home turf, which the man recognizes and takes with grace. He later shrugs and tells me, "These guys been friends forever." For the first time, I realize what my role really is among the men. I think of a friend from college whose parents had emigrated from Ireland. I would sometimes visit his house and over dinner with his parents, brothers, and sisters, my friend's father, in a beautiful Irish brogue, would tell stories about my friend. "Did Pete tell you about the time . . ." Then he'd be off on a story about Pete that may have gone back nearly to his infancy. I loved the stories, which were always mildly embarrassing for my friend, and so did his mother, brothers, and sisters, who always laughed as if they'd never before heard the stories. I knew even then that these stories weren't really for me. I was the excuse, the opportunity, for my friend's father to affirm the story that was his family. In Bobby's wood, I realize that I've been playing that role for Alex, Bobby, Lewis, and Carl for years. Under the guise of telling me stories about themselves, the men have been constantly affirming the story that is their family. I, like the men visiting from Louisville, am an excuse, an opportunity. Because the power isn't in the *memory* of the story; the power is in the *telling* of the story. The telling is what holds the moment, makes it immortal. I recall a line from Cormac McCarthy's novel *The Crossing:* "For this world also which seems to us a thing of stone and flower and blood is not a thing at all but is a tale."

Alex eventually hauls out his lunch and spreads it on the picnic table. It takes several trips to lug all the pans and bowls, hot sauces, barbecue sauces, plates, and silverware. The pork and venison are so tender that we tear them away with only our forks. Alex has seasoned the baked beans with an extra dose of brown sugar, and we all say they're the best baked beans we've ever eaten. The turnip greens, which are usually too bitter for my taste, have been slow-cooked to make them tender and seasoned with ham hocks. I take a second helping. Some men make sandwiches with the Sunbeam white bread, some use it to sop up the meat juice. I've laid in a good store of Rhinelander for us to wash it all down, and Alex's Coke machine is still giving away Falls City. It's not quite like that hour at the Everlasting Stream, but it approaches one of those slow-motion events when you can forget just about anything that ails you. The men, for instance, can forget Alex's annoying perfectionism, Bobby's claim to knowledge on just about everything, Lewis's tendency to get men arguing, Carl's insistence that he's the best hunter of the bunch. As Alex, Bobby, Lewis, and Carl banter and chew and laugh, I think of a time I once asked them what percentage of the best memories in their lives had to do with hunting. The men talked it over and decided that about a third of their best times ever came from hunting.

"That's a lot," I said.

The men glanced around at one another, shrugged.

"Yeah, it is," Carl finally said. "But I'd say it's about right, wouldn't you?"

Last Morning:
Old Collins Place

Billy Elmore has Bush-Hogged the old Collins place. The blackberry briars that once sliced lean gashes into the backs of my hands as I held my gun high to protect my face are buzz-cut. So are the timothy and honeysuckle, sumac and lamb's-quarters, goldenrod, foxtail, and poke. The men aren't sure what Billy plans to do with the land, maybe plant crops, maybe admire the landscape's gentle roll that the new manicure has revealed. It's Billy's land; Billy can do what he wants with it. But if he keeps it cut, the rabbits will be scarcer.

"Can't expect a man to leave his property for us to hunt," Carl says.

Things change. And much has changed since I moved to Illinois. Alex's wife—Keran's mother and my mother-in-law—died. Alex and Celeste were married forty-eight years. Alex may be rugged and thick-skinned with his friends, but he mourned his dead wife less self-consciously, more freely, than I have ever seen in a man. He did something I thought distasteful at first. He insisted that after the church service, Bobby, Lewis, Carl, Matt, and I help him carry Celeste's coffin into his living room, where it was opened for an evening's visitation. "That's the way they did it in the old days," Alex said. A hundred people ate potluck and mingled. Everybody told stories about Celeste: the beauty of her piano playing, the boot-camp way she ran the First Baptist choir, the tough way she took no guff from Alex, the tender way she handled my children. People talked about the dignified way she had accepted her illness without self-pity, saying,

"God didn't promise me a rose garden." People were laughing and sobbing, talking so intently that sometimes Celeste was lying along the far wall of the living room by herself. Alex would notice and go over, stand at her side, his head and his shoulders bent and weak, his white handkerchief held to his face with his left hand, his right hand resting gently on her coffin, and he would weep, without embarrassment. It was the most beautiful memorial I've ever seen.

This year, Matt didn't come hunt with us. He has that high school basketball game back home. Last summer, I finally bought Matt the hunting knife I had told myself to buy him years ago. I looked and looked and settled on a folding Buck knife with a cherry-wood grip that felt right in my hand. When I thought about what to have inscribed on its handle, I remembered a line from William James: "Prayer is religion in act." Embedded in that line is an idea that fit what Matt and the men and I had done together over the years, that captured what my father was trying to make me understand when he told me, "It's not what a man says but what he does that counts." I had Matt's knife engraved with these words: "From Dad to Matt: Life is Love in Act." I'll give it to him for Christmas. Matt is wiser than I was at his age. I believe he will understand.

Truth is, I worry that Matt will never get the chance to use his knife, that, as he makes his own way, he won't find time to hunt with us before the men are gone. Bobby's arthritis is worse this year. He couldn't lift his wrist yesterday, but he took some Aleve and he's well enough to hunt today. Carl is up to four Aleve a day for his arthritis, which is worst in his left shoulder. He figures he'll have to hunt one-handed if his shoulder keeps going, which, he says, would about even the odds for the rest of us. The men's hunting dogs are dying off. About six months ago Carl found Spud dead in his kennel. Then a couple months ago, Carl's favorite hunting dog, Bullet, got sick. Carl, always tight with a dollar, was so worried he did something that amazed his friends—he took Bullet to the vet at a cost of a hundred and twenty-four dollars. Two days later, Bullet was dead. Carl buried him on the farm near Coral Hill, took a sip of whiskey, and said words over his grave. Lewis's young dog Trouble, the one he had such high hopes for as the last hunting dog he'd ever need to own, ran off on a deer trail in the field one day and didn't come back. The men searched for days but never did find Trouble.

The rabbits are fewer this year. Carl thinks it's coyotes. Bobby thinks it's feral domestic cats. The wildlife naturalists think it's more likely from habitat lost to clear-all farming, malls, factories, and houses. Whatever the reasons, Carl figures rabbit hunting will die out in Barren County in the next twenty years. He was hunting not long ago and needed to stop in the woods away from civilization to take a whiz. He drove and drove and drove, and never did come to a place along the country road where a new house wasn't watching. He went home.

I'm thinking about all of this as we walk northwest across the old Collins place's newly cut field toward the wood with the village of groundhog holes, the natural spring, and the ruins of the old lime-stone springhouse that used to keep meat, milk, and butter cool year-round. It's sunny but chilly and we talk in clouds. I notice that the sun has melted the frost on the eastern side of the foliage at our feet but that an opaque glaze still covers its shaded side, an instant of demarcation that will pass in just a few minutes. Carl is annotating the barking of the dogs.

"That's Earl," he says. "Pay attention to Earl. He knows what he's doin'."

My new life in central Illinois—or *east* central Illinois, as the natives assiduously call it—is certainly different, and I like it. A traffic jam in Champaign-Urbana, sister towns with a total of a hundred thousand people, is six cars backed up at a stop light. Everything is a few steps outside my door. I live two miles from my office and take a fifteen-minute bus ride door-to-door. I think of a man in Washington who once said, "Show me a guy over thirty who rides the bus, and I'll show you a loser." I am really glad to be away from fools like that.

In my new town, instead of being surprised when clerks in stores are pleasant and helpful, I've come to expect it. People sit patiently in their cars at four-way stops waiting for the other guy to go first. The gym costs thirty dollars a month. Parking-meter fines are three bucks. If you don't pay up in a week, watch out—it jumps to six dollars. Our first week in town, we went to hear the great bluesman B.B. King, who was performing on the University of Illinois campus. Four thousand people attended. After the show, we were home in ten minutes.

Of course, a town with a university of nearly forty thousand students and faculty isn't Glasgow. There's a lot of educated people, Pulitzer Prize winners, a PBS television station, two NPR-affiliate stations, one broadcasting classical and the other public affairs. Several radio stations play jazz and blues throughout the week. A dozen times a year, the university's performing arts center presents the likes of Ravi Shankar, Michael Feinstein, Wynton Marsalis, Denyce Graves, Marvin Hamlisch, the London Symphony Orchestra. Keran and I leave home a half hour before curtain and still have time for a glass of wine in the foyer before the show.

Best of all, I can see Matt and Kyle and Keran off and on all day and night. A professor's schedule is fluid—a few hours a week in class, a few set office hours, a couple of committee meetings. I can work around everything else, making life and labor a single piece. Combine that with the ease of getting about town, and my life is as close to organic as I expect it will ever get. It was a little tougher adjusting to a $95,000-a-year cut in family income than Keran and I had optimistically anticipated. We knocked off quite a bit of savings before we remembered how to deny ourselves the wine and artwork and vacations. But we got into the rhythm of it. I think occasionally of that lawyer I knew who'd left Washington and $200,000 a year for Helena, Montana. He was right: life is better this way. At least for me. Or the me I've become.

Keran's happier, too. She spent two years noodling around the house and the yard, cooking elaborate meals, volunteering at Kyle's elementary school, shuttling the kids around to every imaginable activity without it being a horrific balancing act for her and me. We really don't need cell phones. The end of commuting has added two hours to our days. We have time to make love again with pleasant regularity. Keran went back to reading three or four books a week, from James Patterson to Amy Tan to Susan Sontag. She's working her way through the Sixty Greatest Novels Ever Written—the Brontës, Flaubert, Joyce, and the like. When Matt got his driver's license and could get himself around and help shuttle his sister, he freed up Keran to take a part-time job at the Urbana Free Library. She checks out books, helps people find things, comes home telling a million stories about the amazing array of oddballs who pass through the doors of a public library every day. It's a long way from running a multimillion-dollar line of insurance business, but that's fine with Keran. As far as she's concerned, we could've come here a long time ago.

The big-city life was always for me. Well, not so much the life, but the work and everything it embodied. In Washington and places like it, achievement is a religion, and work is that religion in act. In the culture of Washington, people are doers first. Family and friends, small pleasures, aren't ignored but they aren't the meaning of life. *I do therefore I am.* To matter, to make a difference, is evidence of existence. Achievement is affirmation—stature, self-respect, and, as a bonus, money. I don't want to demonize that culture. In an era when many people's jobs are deadeningly bureaucratized, work in the achievement culture can be joyous. I won't lie and tell you that leaving it behind for the heartland was all easy. I had withdrawal. A leopard doesn't change its spots. Fortunately, I turned out to love teaching. The documentary writer and Harvard professor Robert Coles told me just before I came to Illinois that decades of teaching had kept him young, and now I know why. College kids are fresh. Working with them is like reading along in a good book, confident that every unread next page will be a thrill. The kids are always emerging, and they remind me that I'm still a work in progress, too. I was them thirty years ago, and now I'm not. In thirty years more, who will I be?

It took me time to decompress, to adjust to the amble of Midwestern life. At first, all those people sitting at four-way stops waiting politely for one another to go drove me nuts. *Jesus! Somebody step on the gas!* Again and again, I would hurry a piece of mail down to the college office over the noon hour only to find the door locked— the office was closed so the secretaries could all go out to lunch together. *How inefficient! How bush league! Don't they know I'm a busy man!* At such times, I had to stop myself and say: *Wait a minute. What am I thinking? Life is better this way. More humane. People should be polite at stop signs. The secretaries should be able to eat lunch together. That's why I moved here. I'm the one who needs to change.* I began to think of these little annoyances as the charming eccentricities of my new community.

In my work, I did what I set out to do. I finished my book on the journalism of ordinary life, and it has become popular in college journalism classes. I wrote my stories on the creativity of fine craftsmen for *This Old House* magazine, and I learned that the creativity of the hand is every bit as blessed as the creativity of the head. And, finally, I told the story of my years of hunting with Alex, Bobby, Lewis, and Carl. Later, when the World Trade Center towers crumbled and so many Americans began to rethink what was important in their lives, I realized that I had already done that kind of thinking.

I am a fortunate man.

The downside? Oh, how I wish it weren't true, but I miss the modicum of fame that came with being a big-time *Washington Post* reporter. I go to parties now and nobody knows who I am, nobody has read anything I've written. Nobody wants to tell me their story hoping I might want to write it someday. Nobody wants to know what Bob Woodward is *really* like, or what I think of Jesse Jackson after spending a couple of months with him, or whatever became of that high school genius, that stock car racer, that gospel singer I wrote about a while back. I'm probably the only academic in America who thinks that being a full professor is a big step down from being a reporter. I know I could tell people that I *used* to be a staff writer for *The Washington Post.* But I'm either too sane or too proud to be that transparently needy. I see the contradiction: I *claim* that I want to work for the joy I felt working as a young man, to be motivated not by acclamation but by my own bearings. I'm doing that. Yet I still yearn for strangers to tell me I'm worthy and admired. The need is so deep I can't will it away. I suppose it's like sin. You just have to resist.

There's a saying: *Wherever you go, there you are.* Can't get away from yourself. That's true but not so true. You won't be a Baptist if you're raised in Kathmandu. You won't learn to set a crab pot on a ranch in Wyoming. You won't learn to smell the roses if you haven't got time to take a whiff. The circumstances of our lives matter, mark the boundaries and frame the possibilities. At least I believed that for myself. I had to get to where, in my better moments, I imagined I wanted to be and then cut a path to that place. My new life grew on me. The calls to keep tabs on who was up or down at the *Post,* to get the early gossip on Bill and Monica, to discover who had the inside track on the year's Pulitzers—those calls dwindled and disappeared. I talk now with a handful of old friends about work, sure, but mostly about children and spouses and lives. I've realized many of them envy my new life, and I admit to liking that a little bit.

I've changed and I've stayed the same. I took my Tallia suits and Ike Behar shirts and gave them to the Salvation Army. For work, I wear gray Slates from JC Penney, black Gap polo shirts, and tweedy jackets from S&K Famous Brands menswear. Different circumstances frame different possibilities. Today, I write for the fun of it again. It's the freedom I knew as a young man. I feel blessed. Yet some things I can't change. I still work long hours. I know people who say a man's work shouldn't be his life, that his family and his friends are what he leaves behind, his accomplishments. They say that nobody on his deathbed says, "I wish I'd spent more time at the office." Well, a while back, when I was flying on a plane that got buffeted with severe turbulence, it flashed through my mind that if the plane crashed, Keran and Matt and Kyle would be sad at my death and I felt bad for them. But this was my very next thought: *I wish I'd had time to finish that book on Alex, Bobby, Lewis, and Carl.* I'm sorry, but if the current President George Bush were to call me tomorrow and tell me I could spend the next eight years of my life following him through his presidency to write a book about it, I know I would consider it. I don't think I'd do it. But the offer would be like sin, and I'd be tempted.

Gotta face it: I'm just wired that way.

A long time ago, meeting Alex, Bobby, Lewis, and Carl made me begin to ask myself, *What is a life well lived?* It took me years to frame that simple question. I don't regret the choices I made in my life. For all my youthful blind ambition, I couldn't have dreamed my path. For reasons deep within me, I wanted to do work my children could be proud of. I accomplished that. Along the way, however, I bought into the notion that an accomplished life was one lived in stereophonic sound, one lived within an echo-chamber of public affirmation. An accomplished life was one that ended with an obituary in *The New York Times.* I lost track of the value and beauty of a small life. And I'd forgotten that, really, all our lives are small.

So what is a life well lived? Wish I knew exactly. But I think it has to do with contentment. I think that's the distilled meaning of my time with Alex, Bobby, Lewis, and Carl, the message of my father's life for me. Alex's gift to me wasn't a shotgun. It was a reminder that enthusiasm for living, the joy of it, no matter our circumstances, is pretty much the game. A man hopes to get to a place where time hunting with friends—or opening gifts on Christmas morning, watching a ball game on TV, walking the dog, planting spring flowers, eating a cherry, or, if you are lucky, doing your work—has the feel of that hour I spent years ago at the Everlasting Stream. Waking lucid moments when we experience life not only as a collection of facts but as pure sensation. A life mindful of precise particles of experience— moon and stars, dogs and weeds, wind and temperature, banter and idiom. A life mindful enough to notice the synchronicities that can make us reconsider our lives again and again. No matter where your obituary runs, a life well lived must mean that you sometimes *hear* the rabbit hit the ground with each bound.

Back at the old Collins place, as the men and I enter the wood surrounding the earthen bowl, a rabbit leaps from a pile of brush. Alex and I fire at once. In all my years of hunting, I've never before shot a rabbit in the earthen bowl. The rabbit falls dead and his momentum carries him behind an uprooted shagbark hickory tree that has been lying like a stone in the same spot for years. When Alex doesn't move to get the rabbit, I walk over and bag him.

"You shot second," Alex says.

"I waited for you to go get 'im and you didn't."

"How long'd you wait?"

"As long as you'd wait for Lewis."

"That's my rabbit," Alex insists, and he might be right. I keep it anyway.

Lewis isn't hunting with us this morning. We went by his garage, where we found him outside with a hog head right out of *Lord of the Flies.* He was making hog's head cheese. By the time Lewis splits the head into pieces with an axe, cuts out its eyes and ears, scrapes out its brains, boils off the scum, scoops out the bone, seasons the brew with salt, pepper, sage, and thyme, and then lets it cool until it's congealed and ready to be sliced—well, let's just say hog's head cheese is an all-day job, and Lewis couldn't go into the field with us this morning.

The men and I hunt the earthen bowl with no more luck, and I get out ahead and into a field of goldenrod, whose dry stalks make a gentle, rolling, *click-click-clicking* in the wind. The goldenrod all look the same to me, although I know better. Since I've been coming to the farm, I've learned that although the plant always flowers in bright yellow rays, in this little region of Kentucky alone, goldenrod comes in fourteen species—goldenrod with narrow flowering plumes, with flowers bursting atop a flurry of stems, with flowers riding on arched wings. There are so many varieties of goldenrod that to tell one from another, to see that narrow world wide, you must get down on your hands and knees and examine the flowers one petal at a time, stay in one place for an hour, a day, or a lifetime. In the goldenrod field with me is a single dog. It's Shorty. I know because his black-saddled back turns stark white at the middle of his ribs and stays white to his toes. Shorty howls and a rabbit bounds back toward the earthen bowl.

"Rabbit your way!" I holler.

No shots.

When I find myself being mindful of the world around me—not only the markings of a hunting dog, or the rays of goldenrod, or the frost on the underside of the morning's foliage but an unexpectedly hearty laugh from Matt or Kyle at a joke I have made, the way a shy student averts her eyes ever so slightly as she speaks to me, the way the lamplight makes the burls of the curly-maple table in my living room seem to roll and heave like ocean waves as I walk around it at night . . . At those times, I often think of my dad—*"Everything's beautiful if you look at it right,"* a sentence so rich that I'm still discovering its meaning forty years later. Not long ago, I asked Matt if when he killed and cleaned a rabbit, he felt as I did, humbled. If in the killing he sensed his own fragility in nature's big scheme. He looked at me blankly. "I don't know what you mean," he said. I hope it's a measure of my maturity that I didn't try to explain, didn't feel the need to *make* Matt understand, to give advice. Hunting is morality in act. Whether tomorrow or forty years from now, the meaning will someday come around to him as a man.

So many people these days believe that manhood is out of whack, that the rise of feminism and the entry of women into the work world have confused young men about their place, undermined men's traditional image of themselves as pillars of strength without giving them a satisfactory new image to replace the old. Men Matt's age have supposedly been forced to find their idea of themselves not in the examples of their fathers and grandfathers but in media-hyped images meant to sell products—sneakers, music, cars, coffee. I don't know whether these social critics are right or wrong. I do believe that for Matt, anyway, knowing Alex, Bobby, Lewis, and Carl has been a kind of inoculation against this feared modern malady.

The men are about as far from media creations as you can get. These days, the word "authentic" is cynically applied to everything from bad spaghetti sauce to fashionable blue jeans, but it's a tight fit on Alex, Bobby, Lewis, and Carl. They're pure like springwater—not bottled springwater but springwater dipped in a bucket at fifty-one degrees, summer or winter. The men didn't become friends because of career convenience, or because they shared a taste for coffee harvested on the slopes of the Mauna Loa volcano in Hawaii, or because their pleated-front khakis signaled that they inhabited like social strata. They became friends because of birth and geography, shared family and friends, and a love of hunting. They remained friends because of tolerance and forbearance and because their lives entwined. Alex, Bobby, Lewis, and Carl are not modern men. They aren't easy with their emotions. None of them will ever ask you to share your pain, and they will not share their pain with you. If you are dying of cancer, they'll give you a ride to the doctor as often as you need. But they'll never ask on the way if you are afraid to die. They'll not encourage you to unburden yourself. They'll never know what it's like to be in the delivery room when a child is born. Or the joy of lying all night on a couch with a child on their chests. Or the satisfaction of seeing their wives kick ass at the office. But even if Matt never hunts again, if all the habitat disappears and Matt never plays dog for his son and kicks the brush piles in the wood behind Bobby's house, I believe he has glimpsed in the remarkable richness of the men's lives—

across the boundaries of age, race, education, and social class—the universality of manhood. Maybe, by combining the new with the old, he will take these lessons: a man can cuddle his children, listen intently to the feelings of his wife, reveal his self-doubts to those who love him—and *still* be emotionally strong, strive to control his world, not whine but act. Maybe the mantra of Matt's generation can be: "What a man *does* matters but what he *says* matters, too."

I leave Shorty in the field of goldenrod and traipse ahead through a wood of tall oak and ash trees. Well into the forest, I find a fallen grave marker that I've never come across before. It lies amid the decaying leaves like a biblical tablet, moss growing on its gray face and sprigs of still green ivy stretching across its arched top. The marker's inscription reads:

JAMES M.

SON OF

WM. L. & ELIZABETH

COLLINS

BORN

May 7, 1861

DIED

October 18, 1868

It all seems so permanent and then it isn't. When my daughter was very young, she got in the habit of leaving her bed in the middle of the night and climbing into bed with Keran and me. This went on for years. We gently teased Kyle about it, facetiously complained that she took up too much room, rolled around kicking us with her feet and clubbing us with her arms. We eventually began to wonder if maybe we should insist that Kyle sleep in her own bed at night, send her back when she came, break her of the habit, make her grow up. Then one night, Kyle didn't climb into bed with us. And she never climbed into bed with us again. What seemed permanent was not so that fast, and I have missed her kicking feet and her clubbing arms ever since.

Native Americans lived in North America for twelve thousand years. A few hundred years after Europeans arrived, the Native American world was as good as gone. That fast. As a realist, why would I expect the world of Alex, Bobby, Lewis, and Carl to last? I think of the Inuits of Canada, the Maoris of New Zealand, the Aleuts of Alaska—indigenous peoples who are the last vestiges of ways of life that right-minded folks would like to protect against the modern onslaught. Yet people don't think of my friends that way. They're either quaint or retrograde. Either way, their world is doomed. I think of Ivan Turgenev's *Sketches from a Hunter's Album.* Turgenev stops time in rural Russia between 1847 and 1851 and marks it forever. In each story, his narrator heads out to hunt grouse, duck, partridge, or rabbit. But the stories aren't about hunting. They're about a cast of ordinary characters: Yermolay, who never feeds his hunting dog but lets him fend for himself in the wild; Vladimir, a freed serf who has taught himself to read and write and play music; Pyotr Petrovich Karataev, who says, "The past's a foreign country, you shouldn't go there." I don't believe that. The past is a memory, and the past has a memory.

JAMES M.

SON OF

WM. L. & ELIZABETH

COLLINS

BORN

May 7, 1861

DIED

October 18, 1868

I work my way across the oak and ash forest to the old Collins place's cedar wood. I can see from the many tracks in the dirt that deer inhabit the wood, which is too clear of undergrowth to offer rabbits much protection. The men have joined me and when a woodpecker knocks loudly, Bobby mentions that his old Aunt Kate used to flavor her dumplings with woodpecker meat. As we walk along, Bobby and Carl talk about how they've lived in Barren County so long that a lot of people they don't know personally seem to know them, call them by name on the street. I recall Bobby's joke about the dead man with two assholes and say, "That's because they know you're Bubba's friends," and the men laugh.

I haven't shot my gun for two hours when Earl scares up a rabbit. Carl and I head into the bordering field. No telling where Earl's rabbit is running. While I wait, I follow Carl's old advice and kick the thick growth along the wood's edge. A rabbit bolts from the foliage at my feet and into the forest. I raise my gun, follow the rabbit's path, seem to take forever, and fire. He falls dead. When I get to him, glistening blood is puddled on his side. When I pick him up, the warm blood pours over the back of my hand. I put the rabbit in my bag, wipe my hand on my pants, and take a few more steps through the foliage. Another rabbit bolts, this time bounding across Billy's newly cut field, which rises slightly in topography from where I'm standing and means I am shooting up at the rabbit's tail. I raise my gun, let him get out about twenty-five yards so my pellets will do the least damage to the meat. I know it's my imagination, but I *hear* the rabbit hit the ground. I fire, and the rabbit tumbles, heels over head. When I reach down, the rabbit suddenly kicks his hind legs violently and drubs my hand twice before I can pull away. I remember that a rabbit can kick and stun even a skunk with those powerful legs. I use the butt of my gun like a deadfall and club the rabbit's head. After I do, his left eye dangles from its socket. I take out the knife that I will give to Matt at Christmas, slice the eye free, and put the rabbit in my bag. Behind me, Carl fires and kills the rabbit Earl has been chasing.

"I'm ready to go clean rabbits," I tell Carl.

We all meet back at the trucks. Carl whistles for the dogs, and all except Earl are soon back in their cages. We wait a long time but, finally, make the short run back to Bobby's barn without Earl to clean our rabbits and jack our jaws. Over the years, I've read an awful lot about hunting, and one of the recurring themes is that hunting is for men a social ritual that imbues their lives with meaningful tradition in an era when tradition is hard to come by. Remember the first morning Matt hunted with us in Lawson Bottom and I tried to talk him out of eating the C&J Restaurant's heavy breakfast of fried eggs, ham, bacon, grits, biscuits, and gravy? Matt laughed and said, "Dad, the breakfast is part of the ritual." It has taken me a long time to realize the difference between the meaning of such ritual to outsiders like Matt and me, for whom the breakfast is an unforgettable aberration, and its meaning to Alex, Bobby, Lewis, and Carl. The men don't think of their breakfasts at the C&J, or The Hunters' Breakfasts, or cleaning rabbits behind Bobby's barn as ritual. That's the beauty of it. The men don't *try* to create ritual in the way that, say, Martha Stewart goes about teaching America to remember how to trim a Christmas tree in the old-fashioned way, as if doing so could somehow rekindle the old-fashioned values we've lost. That's when ritual becomes sentiment, a desperate shadow of ritual. The men don't plan the memorable moments in their lives; the moments happen. The men are like the rabbits they hunt. A rabbit will tear across a field and suddenly skirt left or right and back as naturally as water rolls and roils over the rocky bed of a shallow, fast-moving stream. The men live life. They don't watch themselves live life. When we get to the point of building rituals to help us remember to remember, we become voyeurs of our own lives. As modern people, we like to watch. The men don't have that problem. They are in attendance at their lives. They didn't eat breakfast at the C&J Restaurant in order to create a ritual. They ate at the C&J because they were hungry, and the C&J was on the way. It's called life.

As we clean our rabbits, Bobby tells us that a man must take eggs out of the nests of Guinea hens with a spoon or the human scent will scare the hens off their roosts. Alex says large pig's feet must be split between the toes for frying. Bobby tells a story about a man he knew who once came home drunk, guzzled a whole bowl of beet juice from the refrigerator, woke up vomiting in the middle of the night, and called the paramedics because he thought he was throwing up blood. Alex complains again that I stole his rabbit. Carl is unusually quiet.

"We gotta go get old Earl," he says. "A man lose Earl, he done lost his all."

So Carl and I climb into his truck and drive back to the old Collins place, past where we usually park at the sheds and up to the summit of a hill where we have a clear view of Billy's field and the forest that surrounds it like a horseshoe. We climb from the truck.

"Earl! Yo! Yo!" Carl hollers in his basso profundo.

I take out two Arturo Fuente Curly Head Deluxe Maduros and hand one to Carl.

"Yo! Yo! Yo! Come on, Earl!" Carl yells.

We light up, lean against the hood of Carl's truck, and wait in the sunshine. Carl says he won't have any more hunting dogs after Earl and Shorty. They should be dogs enough for the five or so years he figures he has left to hunt. Rowdy and the two pups she bore with Shorty and Lewis's couple of no-name pups should get them through. I tell Carl I doubt that I'll hunt after he and the men are done. Carl doesn't look surprised. I don't tell Carl that I worry that if I were to hunt without them, the hunting for me might qualify as the kind of murder some people claim all hunting is. It might qualify as murder because it would occur outside the time and place and web of humanity that give it meaning for me. If I can find that web again, I'll hunt, with Matt or his son, or genuine men friends. But I'll never hunt for the sake of hunting.

I think of a day last summer when I visited one of the men's old hunting buddies, Ed Lee, a man I always liked. These days, he's nearly housebound from a galaxy of maladies. That day, just chatting, I asked Ed Lee if he had a favorite memory from his lifetime of hunting. He didn't need to think for long. He smiled and sighed and looked away, out the window.

"There was this day in Lawson Bottom at the Everlasting Stream . . ."

Then he stopped talking. I could see he was fighting back tears.

"I know," I said softly. "I was there."

Ed Lee looked back at me and nodded. That was all we needed to say.

It saddens me that I and many men of my generation gave up this kind of kinship with men to climb the career ladder and to be better fathers and husbands. Even so, I know I'd do it over again more or less the same way. As I said, I'm just wired that way. But if I had a second act, I'd find more time to be with men. I'd use the phone, e-mail, plan trips together, make an effort. I could have managed that without doing injustice to Keran, the kids, or my work. I let it get away without knowing what I was losing. I hope Matt and men his age learn that lesson from the mistakes of their fathers. It's a little late now for me to recapture what I've lost, but since I moved to Illinois I've taken up golf, not so much to play the game but to spend time with my new men friends. If we play golf once a week for twenty years, maybe we'll become friends enough to share our memories without saying a word.

From the distant wood that houses the ruins of the old spring-house, Earl finally emerges and looks at Carl and me. His tail is down, and he's either repentant about going absent without leave or afraid Carl will smack him a good one. But Carl is just glad to see him.

"Come on, Earl!" Carl hollers with forgiveness in his voice.

Earl perks up, flags his tail, and barrels toward us across the sunny, buzz-cut field.

"Old Earl," Carl says. "He knows what he's doin'."

"He does," I say. "He sure does."

Author's Note
and Acknowledgments

The people portrayed in *The Everlasting Stream* are real. No one is fictional and none are composites of several people. All names are real. The book is a hybrid, comprising journalism, memoir, and essay. The action and dialogue in the book's scenes are by necessity compressed, but everything reported actually took place. No events, dialogue, or details are created for drama. The book's quotes and documentary details of weather, plants, animals, and geography are real and taken mostly from dozens of hours of audiotapes recorded during actual hunts, photographs, handwritten notes, U.S. Geological Survey maps, National Weather Service records, and field interviews with trained naturalists, although I have at times relied on my own recollections or the recollections of my subjects. I have altered quotes only for accuracy, brevity, and clarity. When I have done so, I have read the quotes to the speakers and received their approval.

Some quotes, dialogue, and scenes are recalled from memory and cannot be considered verbatim accounts. I have reported such material to my main subjects for confirmation and approval. When I have quoted significant historical figures, I have reported those comments as I remember them. When I have reported personal conversations with old friends or acquaintances, I have reported those conversations as I remember them. Quotes and events that occurred within ongoing scenes are written in the present tense. Quotes and events that occurred outside ongoing scenes but which are used within scenes are noted by use of the past tense. Without claiming that recollections are ever completely accurate, I have reported only memories and events that I actually remember or have reconstructed through reporting. In other words, *The Everlasting Stream* is not—consciously, at least—fictionalized.

To avoid slowing down my story, I have sometimes made references to the work of various authors without naming sources. Books, poems, and articles quoted or referenced but not identified in the text include: *Meditations on Hunting* by José Ortega y Gasset; *The Varieties of Religious Experience* by William James; *Synchronicity: An Acausal Connecting Principle* by C. G. Jung; *A Hunter's Heart: Honest Essays on Blood Sport* edited by David Petersen, and several essays in that collection—"Restoring the Older Knowledge" by Ted Kerasote, "Dealing with Death" by M. R. James, "The Hunting Problem" by Bruce Woods, "Blood Sport" by Edward Abbey, and "Deerskin" by Terry Tempest Williams; *Southern Hunting in Black and White* by Stuart A. Marks; *In Defense of Hunting* by James A. Swan; the poem "The Summons" by James Dickey, appearing in *Drowning With Others;* the poem "A Man Who Takes Time" by R. P. Dickey appearing in *Running Lucky;* the poem "Happiness" by Raymond Carver appearing in *All of Us: The Collected Poems;* and "The Prophet Faulkner" by Larry Levinger, appearing in *The Atlantic Monthly; The End of the Affair* by Graham Greene; and *Blood and Grits* by Harry Crews.

Books that were invaluable sources of factual detail include: *Wildflowers of Mammoth Cave National Park* by Randy Seymour; *Mammals of Kentucky* by Roger W. Barbour and Wayne H. Davis; *Trees and Shrubs of Kentucky* by Mary E. Wharton and Roger W. Barbour; *Weeds of Kentucky and Adjacent States* by Patricia Dalton Haragan; *The Kentucky Breeding Birds Atlas* by Brainard Palmer-Ball, Jr. Useful books on the practice and folklore of rabbit hunting were *Beagles vs Cottontails* and *I'd Rather Be Rabbit Hunting* by Dave Fisher and *The Cottontail Rabbit* by John Madson. An infinitely helpful resource was *The Rabbit Hunter* magazine. Helpful books on the history of hunting include: *The Story of American Hunting and Firearms* published by *Outdoor Life; American Game Shooting* by Paul A. Curtis; and *Small Game Hunting* by Francis E. Sell. I want to thank Duke University anthropologist Matt Cartmill for his help and Harvard University's Dr. Robert Coles for helping me reconstruct his quote that begins the book. For more than twenty years, the work of Dr. Coles has been both model and inspiration.

Helpful sources on the history of Barren County, Kentucky, include: *The Times of Long Ago* by Franklin Gorin; *The Discovery, Settlement and Present State of Kentucky* by John Filson; *Barren County Heritage: A Pictorial History of Barren County, Kentucky* edited by Cecil E. Goode and Woodford L. Gardner, Jr.; *Black Life in the Barrens* published by the Museum of the Barrens; *Wild Life in Kentucky* by Delbert Funkhouser; and *Geography of the Penny-royal* by Carl Ortwin Sauer. Useful books and articles on the biology and habitat of cottontail rabbits include: *The Relationship of Illinois Weather and Agriculture to the Eastern Cottontail Rabbit* by Stephen P. Havera; *Food Habits of the Cottontail Rabbit in Southern Illinois* by Edward Lawrence Corder, Jr.; *Environmental Factors Affecting the Habitat Preference of the Cottontail Rabbit* by Wayne H. Bruckner; *Cottontail Rabbits Habitat Requirements* published by the North Carolina Cooperative Extension Service; *Habitat Improvement Practices and Guidelines* by Thomas G. Barnes, Jeffery D. Sole, and John Phillips; *Rabbits* by Jeffery D. Sole; *Seasonal Changes in Abundance of Kentucky Cottontails* by William M. Giuliano, Charles L. Elliott, and Jeffery D. Sole. Helpful books on the history and issues of masculinity include: *American Manhood* by E. Anthony Rotundo; *Masculinity Reconstructed* by Dr. Ronald F. Levant with Gini Kopecky; and *Stiffed: The Betrayal of the American Man* by Susan Faludi.

Many people on the ground in Kentucky helped me in gathering information or in understanding the biology of rabbits and habitat. Thanks to Jim Hyatt, Jeffrey Sole, Chris Garland, Randy Seymour, Bill Lynch, Donald Depp, J. Douglas Hatchett, Charles Lapham, Chris Mason, James Nelson, Jimmy May, Wayne Taminga, Kay Harbison, Douglas Peden, and the workers at the National Weather Service in Bowling Green, Kentucky.

Thanks also to the workers on the reference desk of the Urbana Free Library and those in the University of Illinois College of Communications Library, especially its director Lisa Romero, for answering an infinite number of questions large and small. Thanks also to Bryan Dunne, a University of Illinois astronomy graduate student, Dr. Joseph Thulin, director of the University's Division of Animal Resources, and two of his veterinarian students, Mary Swanson and Jim Bollmeir. Thanks to the University of Illinois Department of Journalism and College of Communications for research assistance, and thanks to those invaluable researchers Grace Lee Uy, Courtney Greve, Andrea Melton, and Kesha Green.

For critiquing various versions of my book, I want to thank David Grogan, Mike Sager, Bob Reid, John Cotter, Norman Denzin, Steve Weinberg, Ray Elliott, Patsy Sims, Pete Earley, and Jay Lovinger. Their contributions are many. All flaws are mine alone.

Many friends and family of Alex, Bobby, Lewis, and Carl helped me. Thanks to Celeste Elliott, Charles Mansfield, Ed Lee Chambers, Chevalier Ann Ragland Chambers, Juanita Martin, C. J. Elliott, Louise Stockton, Reid Lawson, Milford Martin, Nate Smith, Billy Elmore, B.C. Witt, Gerald Harris, Don Barbour, Jesse Tyner, Harry Anderson, and Russell James. Thanks also to my parents, Leonard and Catherine Harrington. Thanks especially to my wife, Keran, my daughter, Kyle, and my son, Matt, who was a sport to let me write about him. I want to give special thanks to my agent at ICM, Sloan Harris, who worked hard to find a wonderful home for so odd a book. Thanks to Don Kennison, whose precise and thoughtful copy editing has made me appear far more literate than I am. And thanks to my fine editor, Morgan Entrekin, who saved the day for me.

Finally, thanks to Alex Elliott, Bobby Elliott, Lewis Stockton, and Carl Martin. After these guys came along, they broke the molds.

It was my privilege.